China's Spatial Economic Development

The spatial patterns of China's rapid economic transformation fundamentally challenge conventional geographies of urban and regional development. This book provides a theoretically informed case study of the local character of regional change in China's lower Yangzi delta, as well as a new conceptual framework for understanding China's unique form of economic modernization.

The development of 'market socialism' in China has contributed to a spatial economic transformation characterized by an apparent capacity to rapidly industrialize without transferring large numbers of people into big cities. The author offers an explanation of the emergence of these relatively productive non-urban regions, an area where conventional theories of development, industrialization and urbanization have proved inadequate. China's distinctive experience is also held up as a unique source of reflection on the critical dimensions of regional change in an increasingly volatile global economic environment.

China's Spatial Economic Development contributes both a new theoretical framework and a wealth of original research material to the study of rural transformation and urban transition in China. It will, therefore, be of vital interest to Asian studies scholars, geographers and economists working on the transitional economies.

Andrew M. Marton is Reader in Chinese Geography in the Institute of Contemporary Chinese Studies at the University of Nottingham. He has contributed articles to numerous journals, including *Asian Geographer* and *Pacific Affairs*, and to the recent edited volumes *Rural–Urban Transition and Development in China*, and *Hong Kong in China*.

Routledge Studies on China in Transition
Series Editor: David S. G. Goodman

1 The Democratisation of China
Baogang He

2 Beyond Beijing
Dali Yang

3 China's Enterprise Reform
Changing state/society relations after Mao
You Ji

4 Industrial Change in China
Economic restructuring and conflicting interests
Kate Hannan

5 The Entrepreneurial State in China
Real estate and commerce departments in reform era Tianjin
Jane Duckett

6 Tourism and Modernity in China
Tim Oakes

7 Cities in Post Mao China
Recipes for Economic Development in the Reform Era
Jae Ho Chung

8 China's Spatial Economic Development
Restless Landscapes in the Lower Yangzi Delta
Andrew M. Marton

9 Regional Development in China
States, Globalization and Inequality
Yehua Dennis Wei

China's Spatial Economic Development

Restless landscapes in the Lower Yangzi Delta

Andrew M. Marton

LONDON AND NEW YORK

First published 2000 by Routledge
2 Park Square, Milton Park, Abingdon, Oxon OX14 4RN

Simultaneously published in the USA and Canada
by Routledge
605 Third Avenue, New York, NY 10017

Routledge is an imprint of the Taylor & Francis Group, an informa business

Typeset in Sabon by
Florence Production Ltd, Stoodleigh, Devon

British Library Cataloguing in Publication Data
A catalogue record for this book is available from the British Library

Library of Congress Cataloging in Publication Data
Marton, Andrew M. (Andrew Mark), 1960–
    China's spatial economic development : restless landscapes in the
    lower Yangzi Delta by Andrew M. Marton.
        p. cm.
    Includes bibliographical references and index.
        1. Regional planning—China—Yangtze River Delta. 2. City planning
    — China—Yangtze River Delta. 3. Economic development—China—
    Yangtze River Delta. 4. Marxian economics—China—Yangtze River Delta.
    5. Urban economics—China—Yangtze River Delta. 6. Yangtze River Delta
    (China)—Social conditions. 7. Yangtze River Delta (China)—Economic
    conditions. 8. Yangtze River Delta (China)—Economic policy. I. Title.
    HT395.C552 Y365 2000
    338.951'2—dc21   00–030826

ISBN 13: 978-0-415-22779-7 (hbk)

To the memory of Joseph, Robert and Ian

Contents

Plates   x
Figures   xi
Maps   xii
Tables   xiii
Preface   xv
Romanization   xviii
Abbreviations   xix
Penglang   xxi

1. Introduction   1
   Rationale, scope and objectives 1
   The lower Yangzi delta region and Kunshan 3
   Redefining a new critical regional geography 9
   Development theory in crisis: beyond the impasse 14
   Issues and methodology 18
   Organization of the book 20

2. Regional development and industrialization:
   towards mega-urbanization   25
   Confronting the post-modern void in China: taking
      diversity seriously 26
   Linkages and the transactional revolution 28
   A new geography of production: making space for place 30
   Cities, towns and rural transformation: the Chinese
      development debate 35
   Rural and urban in China's regional development:
      seeking a middle ground 42
   Mega-urbanization in the lower Yangzi delta: enterprise
      location and the reconstitution of local space 45

3 The lower Yangzi delta: historical geography and
contemporary patterns of change   57
The lower Yangzi delta from the Late Imperial period 58
Pre-reform political economy 63
Reforms and transformation in the rural economy 66
Spatial economic patterns in the lower Yangzi delta 78
At the edge of Shanghai: Kunshan to the fore 86

4 Transforming the Kunshan countryside: structure of
local government and relationship to enterprises   97
Bifurcation of the functions of local government 98
Spatial proliferation of enterprises 111
Formalizing local institutional structures in a partially
   reformed command economy 115
Socialist new rural area with Chinese characteristics 124

5 Restless landscapes: the local character of spatial
change   131
Transportation 131
Dianshanhu Town 141
Tongxin Village 146
Specialized development zones 150

6 Linkages and the location of non-agricultural
production   160
Investment in local development 160
Ownership, land and labour 165
Enterprise procurement, marketing and management 168
Transactional environment 176

7 Mega-urbanization in the lower Yangzi delta:
theoretical and policy challenges and responses   180
Negotiating and managing the regional transformation:
   institutional parameters and rural agglomeration 181
Theoretical implications: urban transition or regional
   resilience? 187
Planning and management agenda: Chinese solutions
   for Chinese problems 193

Appendix 1: Notes on Chinese statistical sources   202
Appendix 2: Structure of Chinese administrative divisions   206
Glossary of Chinese terms   210
Bibliography   214
Index   231

Plates

1.1 Crop production in the lower Yangzi delta   6
1.2 Rural industrialization in the lower Yangzi delta   6
3.1 Household sideline production   69
3.2 Office farmers   69
4.1 Rural enterprises   112
4.2 Surgical glove factory   112
4.3 Restless landscapes   116
4.4 Agricultural land protection zone   116
5.1 Town road   134
5.2 Village road   134
5.3 Main canal   140
5.4 Small canal   140
5.5 Fields of canola   148
5.6 Fields of factories   148

Figures

2.1 Rural industrialization and the development of rural
    urbanization   43
2.2 Post-reform rural transformation and mega-urbanization
    in China's lower Yangzi delta   46
4.1 Sectoral distribution of enterprises, employees and output:
    Kunshan   114
6.1 Procurement methods of enterprise inputs in Kunshan   169
6.2 Distribution channels for sales of enterprise production
    in Kunshan   170
6.3 Source distribution of the procurement of enterprise inputs
    in Kunshan   171
6.4 Distribution of markets for enterprise production in
    Kunshan.   172
7.1 Rural agglomeration and mega-urbanization in the lower
    Yangzi delta   188

Maps

1.1 East China, the lower Yangzi delta and Kunshan, 1998   4
3.1 Prefectures, counties and cities: Jiangsu and Shanghai, 1998   59
3.2 Agricultural output value per *mu* of arable land: Jiangsu
and Shanghai, 1995   71
3.3 Population density: Jiangsu and Shanghai, 1998   73
3.4 Non-agricultural employment as a proportion of the rural
labour force: Jiangsu and Shanghai, 1998   76
3.5 Rural per-capita net income: Jiangsu and Shanghai, 1998   79
3.6 Rural industrial output: Jiangsu and Shanghai, 1997   81
3.7 Gross value of industrial output: Jiangsu and Shanghai,
1998   82
3.8 Industrial output per-capita increase, 1985–1991:
Jiangsu and Shanghai   84
4.1 Kunshan: administrative divisions, 1998   99
5.1 Kunshan transportation: roads and railway, 1997   133
5.2 Kunshan transportation: canals and waterways, 1997   139
5.3 Location of rural enterprises: Dianshanhu Town,
Kunshan, 1996   143
5.4 Special development zones: Kunshan, 1997   152
6.1 Kunshan: location of enterprises surveyed   166

Tables

1.1 The lower Yangzi delta in China, 1997   7
3.1 Total agricultural output and sectoral distribution: Jiangsu,
     1978–1998 (selected years)   68
3.2 Total value of output, sectoral distribution and the
     number of industrial enterprises: rural Jiangsu, 1978–1998
     (selected years)   74
3.3 Total labour force and sectoral distribution: rural Jiangsu,
     1978–1998 (selected years)   75
3.4 Total value of output and sectoral distribution: Kunshan
     and China, 1980–1992 (selected years)   87
3.5 Gross domestic product and sectoral distribution: Kunshan
     and China, 1988–1998 (selected years)   88
4.1 Structure and development of community administration
     in Kunshan, 1978–1997   101
4.2 Town level public finances in Kunshan   107
5.1 Transportation in Kunshan: passenger and freight volumes,
     1980–1998 (selected years)   135
5.2 Town and village industry and agriculture: Dianshanhu
     Town, Kunshan, 1989–1996.   142
6.1 Residential savings and investment in fixed assets in
     Kunshan, 1980–1998 (selected years)   162
6.2 Distribution of markets by product category and
     distribution of product categories by market: Kunshan   173

Preface

This book emerged from a nagging sense that the remarkable and frequently traumatic changes in China over the past two decades have not been adequately captured in the plethora of macro-studies of this transition. Having had the opportunity to travel to every region of China over the past sixteen years, it became clear that such macro-perspectives simply could not accommodate and explain the deep diversity and variable impact of recent restructuring in the spatial economic landscape. Moreover, like most outsiders, I entered the field with an array of conventional analytical and conceptual tools to answer, what seemed at the time, to be fairly simple questions. These were quickly and rudely confronted by profoundly complex and unconventional phenomena. Rather than cling to the sometimes spectacularly irrelevant conceptualizations relating to urban and regional development and spatial change, I began the search for meaningful alternatives. This book sketches the contours of that search, highlighting the essence of a particular place along the way. Others will judge the outcome. If nothing else, I will have betrayed my utter fascination, both professional and personal, with that entity called China. Inevitably, indeed, necessarily, this has been an exploration one can never undertake alone.

I wish to express my deepest gratitude to Professor Terry McGee, for his patience and encouragement and for providing me with the opportunity to fulfil my dream of living and working in China. In the streets of several Asian cities and Empress lounges around the Pacific, from his lectern, and during Sunday afternoon 'dissertation strategy meetings' in the 'seminar room' on Dunbar Street, his counsel and intellectual support have been inestimable. I have also benefited from the guidance and expertise of Dr David Edgington, who undertook meticulous editing of earlier drafts which added to the clarity and readability of the manuscript; Professor Graham Johnson, who introduced a sceptic to the many delights of Guangdong cuisine; and Dr Robert North, with whom I frequently compared notes about a restructuring China in the context of the wider socialist world in transition. I must also record a special note of thanks to Dr Claude Comtois in the Department of Geography at the University of Montreal, for his camaraderie and support. His vigorous probing of my early speculations, mostly while mutually engaged in intensive fieldwork in China, challenged me to refine and focus my enquiries.

These investigations were facilitated by research collaborators, colleagues, and friends in China to whom I express my profound appreciation. To my teacher and mentor, Liu Junde, Professor of Geography at East China Normal University in Shanghai and Director of the Research Centre for Administrative Divisions of China, I am especially grateful. Professor Liu embodies all of the finest qualities of a truly remarkable scholar and gentleman. His wisdom and energy in the field (his students call him the 'fieldwork tiger'), combined with a subtle unpretentious manner, opened China to me in a way that revealed the essence of her underlying qualities and complexities. The greatest first-hand assistance in the field was provided by two friends and confidants, Zhang Ming and Wu Wei. Research collaborators and fieldworkers extraordinaire, they endured with immense intellectual and intestinal fortitude and good humour my persistent prying and determination to get at the whole story. I also wish to express my deep gratitude to certain individuals in the Civil Affairs Bureau in Kunshan who shall remain nameless. Two in particular, who love to fish in the streams and lakes of Kunshan, frequently reminded me of their philosophy regarding the size of the fish they caught ...

A special debt is owed to Jeanne Yang who transformed the original written manuscript into beautiful type, and Catherine Griffiths who turned the maps and charts in my head into illustrations in the text. I also wish to acknowledge J. F. Proulx, wherever he may be, for preparing earlier versions of some of the maps. He was part of a small coterie of like-minded graduate students who afforded the stimulating environment so vital to my intellectual development. Among them, Charles Greenberg, must be singled out for special mention. From the foot of glaciers in the coast mountains of British Columbia, to the klongs and golf courses of Bangkok, the back alleys of Ho Chi Minh City and the rural backwaters of southwest India, he has provided the most enduring scholarly sustenance and friendship.

The research for this book would not have been possible without the generosity of a number of organizations. A doctoral fellowship from the Social Sciences and Humanities Research Council of Canada, a Young Canadian Researchers' Award from the International Development Research Centre, Ottawa and a Research Scholarship from the Canadian International Development Agency funded the fieldwork in China. A Canada/China Scholar Exchange Fellowship, jointly from the Canadian Department of Foreign Affairs and International Trade and the Chinese State Education Commission, furnished two return airfares to Shanghai and two years of critically important official status in China as a Senior Advanced Student. East China Normal University provided office space, access to other university facilities, and a monthly stipend. The East Asian

Institute at the National University of Singapore was my scholarly home during the preparation of the final manuscript. Final revisions were prepared just as I began my new appointment in the Institute of Contemporary Chinese Studies at the University of Nottingham. I wish to record my sincere gratitude to all of these organizations.

The sustained intensity of the work necessary to successfully complete the research and writing of this book has also placed enormous demands upon my family. These demands were especially onerous as they coincided with the birth of our twin daughters, Vanessa and Suzanne. Now six, they have never quite understood why *baba* always had to go back to work after supper and on weekends, although they have remained largely cooperative throughout. Their cheerfulness and exuberant curiosity are a constant source of delight and spiritual nourishment.

Finally, and far above all else, I wish to acknowledge the prodigious forbearance and patience exhibited by my wife, Wei, whose love and understanding eased my endeavours in the research and writing of this book. Not only has she toiled tirelessly behind the scenes, helping with the fieldwork in China and clarifying my clumsy translations, she has simultaneously undertaken most of the parenting of our children, as well as the academic and research demands of her own graduate degree.

Yet through all this, the experience has been thoroughly and entirely enjoyable and fulfilling. This is deeply reassuring, since the publication of this book signals not the end of a prolonged and arduous project, but rather the beginning of a much longer and profoundly more important journey.

Andrew Marton
Nottingham
December 1999

Romanization

The People's Republic of China uses the *pinyin* system of romanization. Therefore, with only very minor and infrequent exceptions, I have used *pinyin* throughout this book. As a result, certain Chinese names, perhaps better known by their older more conventional spellings, have been slightly altered. Thus, Mao Tse-tung becomes Mao Zedong, Nanking and Peking become Nanjing and Beijing respectively, and Yangtze becomes Yangzi.

The name 'Yangzi' traditionally referred only to the lower reaches of the great river beginning near the city of Nanjing and running downstream to the sea. Although this name is now rarely used by the Chinese, for the sake of convenience and familiarity I will refer to the river as the Yangzi. The more common Chinese name for the Yangzi is *Changjiang* – literally Long River.

In Chinese, surnames are written first (usually one character) followed by the given name (usually two characters). Chinese names which appear in the text or footnotes will also adhere to this style. I have cited books and articles which included older forms of romanization by their exact title. However, when quoting from translations, texts, or articles, I have taken the liberty of substituting *pinyin* for the original romanization in which some words may have appeared.

Abbreviations

AAAG	*Annals of the Association of American Geographers*
CSGH	*Chengshi guihua (City Planning)*
CCP	*Chinese Communist Party*
DLKX	*Dili kexue (Scientia Geographica Sinica)*
DLYJ	*Dili yanjiu (Geographical Research)*
ECNU	East China Normal University (Shanghai)
ECC	Economic Cooperation Commission
GVAO	Gross value of agricultural output
GVAIO	Gross value of agricultural and industrial output
GVIO	Gross value of industrial output
HDDTNJ	*Huadong diqu tongji nianjian (East China Area Statistical Yearbook)*
IJURR	*International Journal of Urban and Regional Research*
JSJJTT	*Jiangsu jingji tantao (Jiangsu Economic Inquiry)*
JSNJ	*Jiangsu nianjian (Jiangsu Almanac)*
JSSSXJ	*Jiangsu sheng shixian jingji (Jiangsu Province City and County Economy)*
JSSXJJ	*Jiangsu shixian jingji (Jiangsu City and County Economy)*
JSSSN	*Jiangsu sishinian 1949–1989 (Jiangsu Forty Years 1949–1989)*
JSTJNJ	*Jiangsu tongji nianjian (Jiangsu Statistical Yearbook)*
JSXZQN	*Jiangsu xiangzhen qiye nianjian (Jiangsu Rural Enterprise Almanac)*
JJDL	*Jingji dili (Economic Geography)*
KSJJXX	*Kunshan jingji xinxi (Kunshan Economic Information)*
KSTJNJ	*Kunshan tongji nianjian (Kunshan Statistical Yearbook)*
KSSDMT	*Kunshanshi diming tu (Kunshan Municipality Place Names Map)*
KSXZ	*Kunshan xianzhi (Kunshan County Gazetteer)*
OECD	Organization for Economic Cooperation and Development
PLA	People's Liberation Army
PIHG	*Progress in Human Geography*
RMB	Renminbi (Unit of currency in China)

SJQTZH	*Shanghai jiaoqu tongji ziliao huibian 1990 (Shanghai Suburban Statistical Information Compilation 1990)*
SHJJ	*Shanghai jingji 1949–1982 (Shanghai Economy 1949–1982)*
SHJGQD	*Shanghai shi jiaoqu gongye qiye daquan (Complete listing of Shanghai's suburban industrial enterprises)*
SHNJ	*Shanghai nianjian (Shanghai Almanac)*
SSB	State Statistics Bureau
SZJTTC	*Suzhou jiaotong tuce (Suzhou Transportation Atlas)*
SZNJ	*Suzhou nianjian (Suzhou Almanac)*
SZSDT	*Suzhou shi ditu (Suzhou Map)*
SZSJTT	*Suzhou shi jiaotong tu (Suzhou Transportation Map)*
SZTJNJ	*Suzhou tongji nianjian (Suzhou Statistical Yearbook)*
TIBG	*Transactions of the Institute of British Geographers*
WXTJNJ	*Wuxi tongji nianjian (Wuxi Statistical Yearbook)*
ZFNJTG	*Zhongguo fenxian nongcun jingji tongji gaiyao (China County Rural Economic Statistical Summary)*
ZGNCJJ	*Zhongguo nongcun jingji (China's Rural Economy)*
ZGNCTN	*Zhongguo nongcun tongji nian jian (China Rural Statistical Yearbook)*
ZGTJNJ	*Zhongguo tongji nianjian (China Statistical Yearbook)*
ZGXZHC	*Zhongguo xingzhengqu huajiance (A Brief Summary of China's Administrative Regions)*
ZZZZ	*Zhouzhuang zhenzhi (Zhouzhuang Town Gazetteer)*

Penglang

*Penglang is a small lower Yangzi delta town in the southeastern fringe
of Jiangsu Province. Located near the historic city of Suzhou and at the
edge of the great metropolis of Shanghai, the town and its twenty-four
villages were simultaneously in the midst of these large conurbations while
somehow not quite a part of them. The expanse of bright yellow canola
and luxuriant green wheat crops were frequently interrupted by small
settlements, many with factories nearby or sometimes alone among the
fields. In the distance, an old man in faded blue tunic and trousers tending
a gaggle of goslings, stumbles off a dirt track as two fastidiously attired
young women swoosh by on scooters. Down the main road a throng has
gathered to watch two drivers, in the vicinity of two overturned trucks,
loudly arguing among a shambles of spilt running shoes and bamboo
shoots. At one end of the scene a man pushing a large black bicycle,
hopelessly overloaded with hundreds of compact discs to which were
lashed several fresh bamboo shoots and a new pair of running shoes,
weaves recklessly through the distracted crowd. There were many such
prominent and paradoxical elements of the countryside here which did
not conform to the sharp boundaries between city and rural so clearly
indicated on the map.*

*Touched by these ambiguities, I retreated later that evening with a
colleague, as I always did after arriving in a new field site, into the lanes
and back alleys of Penglang's old-town. Though I had never before been
there, the ambience was familiar to me. Wandering from the government
offices and the new two lane bridge over the main canal which established the administrative and economic centre of Penglang, it took about
an hour to find what I was looking for. Clinging to the end of a row of
whitewashed two-storey buildings, beneath the slanted tile roofs black-
ened by the shading of coal dust and the smoky air that always hung
over such towns in the still of the early evening, was the New Joy
Noodle and Wonton Shop. Proprietor Jiang, in scruffy white T-shirt and
boxer shorts which belied his heavy gold chains, new watch, and rings,
beckoned to us from the now deserted establishment. Through the door
to the back was the cooperatively owned hatchery that he managed*

and which supplied this shop and others as far away as Shanghai and Zhejiang.

Several hours later, satiated with bowls of noodles and salubrious tea-boiled goose foetuses, and relaxed from the libations, Mr Jiang proclaimed that if anyone could understand what was happening between his shop and the primary school some 400 metres or so to the south, they could understand China. That is: down the narrow cobbled lane, past the lodgings of his neighbours and the tiny store that sold us the beer – bottled at a brewery a few kilometres down the road; across the stone bridge that arched over the pitch black water of the canal, filled with barges laden with construction materials, cabbages, and large ceramic jars of pickled vegetables – a famous local speciality food; past the gates of the garment factory and around behind the chemical plant, still audibly wheezing even at this late hour; along the path next to the new house with colour television blaring from the second floor veranda, with two shiny motorcycles parked in front, and a white picket fence enclosing a rose garden that faced fields of ripening winter wheat extending across the delta to a village some distance away; to the now quiet four-storey primary school with the silver-grey dome of its astrophysical observatory perched incongruously on the roof.

Embedded in those 400 metres was the epitome of all the social, cultural, political, and economic character of the region, and all the human and physical geographies which defined this particular place. A place signifying the tantalizing prospects for change and its enormous problems and complexities, yet also a place that has somehow compelled loyalty and in many ways defied change. Surrounded and absorbed by the subject of my enquiries, I became conscious of an underlying tension that I would need to confront more directly during the remainder of the fieldwork. It was a tension, when resolved, that cautioned against a spatial and cultural voyeurism in my approach and attitude towards the investigations, in favour of something profoundly more sensitive and exquisite in its experience and flavour.

Later, as we groped along the labyrinthine alleyways of old Penglang on our way back to the guest-house, arms extended sideways touching the walls through the darkness, and eyes cast skyward to follow the ribbon of stars between the curled roof-tops, I knew Mr Jiang's simple, but deeply perceptive words about that place, indeed about China, would stay with me for a long time.

June 26, 1992

1 Introduction

Rationale, scope and objectives

This book is about understanding the processes of development in places like Penglang as part of the wider transformation occurring across the region and throughout China. The degree to which modern China has been transformed and the way in which this transformation has been expressed are at once fascinating, encouraging, baffling, and bothersome. Since 'Liberation' in 1949, the development of a centrally controlled economy with shifting policies towards industry and agriculture, and cities and countryside, has been arduous and at times painful. By the late 1970s, however, a fundamental reorientation of the strategies for development in China began to emerge. The major turning point was the institution of reform experiments in the countryside authorized by resolutions promulgated at the Third Plenary Session of the Eleventh Central Committee of the Chinese Communist Party (CCP) in December 1978. These reforms had, by the early 1980s, culminated in the household production responsibility system in agriculture and other policies which gave a more prominent and flexible role to the development of non-agricultural activities in the countryside. Other macro-economic and industrial reforms were generally characterized by the gradual abandoning of the command economy structures and parallel efforts embedded in the 'open door' policy designed to encourage the input of foreign capital, technology, and expertise. Notwithstanding very short-lived attempts to roll back economic reforms and recentralize the economy, the now widely accepted goal of transition to a 'socialist market economy with Chinese characteristics' was officially proclaimed in 1992.[1]

The inherent ideological ambiguities and contradictions of such proclamations were captured in bizarre theoretical concoctions which rationalized elements of the reforms which did not neatly conform to socialist orthodoxy.[2] But there are other reasons why development in China deserves attention. The sheer magnitude, rapidity, and spatial extent of changes which have affected one-fifth of humankind simply cannot be ignored. Furthermore, contemporary 'socialist transition' in China has differed from the reforms implemented in Eastern Europe in the 1960s which merely tinkered with the existing system to rationalize and improve the command economy structures.[3] It has also differed from the 'big bang' reforms implemented in the 1990s in the former Soviet Union which aimed to accomplish a quick transformation to a market economy. The more gradual, sometimes halting approach to economic reforms in China, on the other hand, should be viewed more as a pragmatic attempt to avoid the trauma and large costs of a sudden transformation, rather than as ambivalence about the objectives of the reform measures.

Perhaps the most important reason for paying attention to the socialist transition in China is the truly intriguing and unique patterns and processes of growth and development which have emerged during the reform period. Chief among these, was the apparent capacity to rapidly industrialize without transferring large numbers of people into big cities. One of the most striking elements of this transition has been the phenomenal growth and spatial proliferation of industries in the Chinese countryside. Through a combination of circumstances, sometimes deliberate, but often not, China has fallen upon a means of dealing with the worst problems of massive uncontrolled migration to large cities. That is not to say that cities in China were not undergoing tremendous stress, nor do I wish to suggest that they were unimportant in the development process. However, with perhaps 850 to 890 million people residing outside urban agglomerations, the patterns and processes of development in the Chinese countryside were clearly extremely important. The opening up of markets and the increasing autonomy of enterprises with reforms, also entailed an erosion of the divisions between rural and urban, reflected in the emergence of particular administrative and institutional responses. The old unitary hierarchy of command relations, which relied upon distinct administrative and economic boundaries between rural and urban, has yielded to modes of interaction which more vigorously utilized a diverse array of manipulation, concessions, coercion, and partnerships. Changes in the structure of ownership also meant that increasingly independent economic actors in a restructuring space-economy were negotiating and managing their own mutually beneficial interactions and interrelationships.

What were the spatial consequences of this transition in China and how, if at all, did they resemble the patterns and processes suggested by the conventional expectations? The scope of this study is framed by two assertions. First, that development of market socialism in China has contributed to spatial economic restructuring most clearly demonstrated by the rapid industrialization of particular areas of the countryside. This book will assess the transformation in the countryside of the lower *Changjiang* (Yangzi River) delta region since 1978. It will focus in particular upon the growth and spatial proliferation of industrial activities in areas hitherto considered 'rural'. The dramatic changes seen in the lower Yangzi delta, as with other similarly transforming regions in China, were imbued with a host of ideas about industrial prosperity and urban life as well as a body of political and socio-economic values which have confronted the integrity of the modern socialist system. Viewed from afar, as they most often were, such changes seemed 'wondrous'.[4] Up close, as this study will show, the story was 'messier and more complicated'.[5] The patterns and processes of development in the lower Yangzi delta, in fact, conformed to few of the conventional expectations.

This brings us to the second assertion that the conventional wisdom of existing theories of development, industrialization, and urbanization does not adequately explain the emergence of these relatively productive regions. What were the characteristics of spatial economic transformation in the lower Yangzi delta which made it different from the outcomes predicted in models based upon advanced, mostly Western, market economies? The objectives of this book are to identify the key patterns of this transformation and to determine the crucial processes and mechanisms which drive local and regional development in the delta. Two further objectives include an exploration of the theoretical implications of this transformation and the resulting challenges for planning and policy formation.

To address these objectives the research undertaken for this book was contingent upon two fundamental assumptions. First, modernization in China is profoundly more variegated and complex than is commonly appreciated. Second, the trajectories and contours of this variation and complexity are revealed within deeply Chinese circumstances and conditions. In other words, development in China was more a product of Chineseness than of anything else. My hunch was that there were latent patterns and trends *sine qua non*, built into Chinese socio-economic and institutional sub-structures, which were emerging as more prominent under the reforms. Our first evidence of this is revealed in an introduction to the particular circumstances of regional development and spatial economic transformation in China's lower Yangzi delta.

The lower Yangzi delta region and Kunshan

This study will focus on an area of the lower Yangzi delta defined initially to include the eight prefectural regions of Suzhou, Wuxi, Changzhou, Zhenjiang, Nanjing, Yangzhou, Taizhou, and Nantong adjacent to the Yangzi River in southern Jiangsu, and the Shanghai Municipal region.[6] Map 1.1 illustrates the nine major cities and forty-five county level administrative units that comprise the lower Yangzi delta region, and the position of Jiangsu Province and Shanghai in East China. Some studies include all of Jiangsu, Anhui, and Zhejiang Provinces in addition to Shanghai as part of the lower Yangzi delta, while others focus on southern Jiangsu, Shanghai and northeast coastal Zhejiang.[7] The particular areal focus of this study is somewhat narrower for two reasons. Cursory examination of the statistical evidence, and extensive field observations, suggest that the spatial similarities and contiguity of the regional transformation between southern Jiangsu and Shanghai were much stronger than that between Shanghai and northeast Zhejiang. A number of geographical and historical circumstances

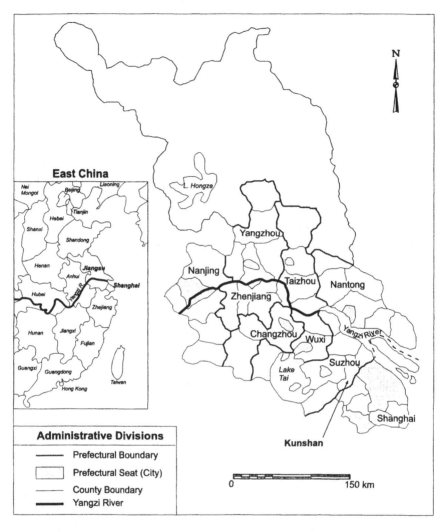

Map 1.1 East China, the lower Yangzi delta and Kunshan, 1998.
Sources: Adapted from: *SHNJ 1998*, p. 41, Map appendix; *ZGXZHC 1997*, pp. 27–29.

elaborated upon in subsequent chapters help to explain this phenomenon. The other reason was a more arbitrary methodological decision to exclude any of the region of Zhejiang Province to avoid the burden of having to consult a third largely separate set of statistical sources. Acknowledging that many of the specific findings of this study almost certainly also apply to the region of Zhejiang Province to the south of Shanghai, it is the southern Jiangsu region of the lower Yangzi delta wherein the spatial economic transformation was most dramatically demonstrated.

The clearest indication of this transformation arose when passing through the delta's countryside. Infused into the scenes of agricultural production among the dense clusters of rural settlements were a variety of non-agricultural activities. Plates 1.1 and 1.2 provide a glimpse of the spectacular results of crop production in the lower Yangzi delta and just one example of the way tens of thousands of industrial enterprises have insinuated themselves into the agricultural landscape.

The development of industry in rural communities such as villages and small towns I will now label rural industrialization.[8] This is to be distinguished from processes of industrial decentralization from large urban centres to secondary cities or into the countryside.[9] The term rural is defined initially as areas that were administratively classified below the county level including towns (*zhen*), townships (*xiang*), and villages (*cun*). County level administrative seats, usually large towns (*xianshu zhen*) or small cities (*xian cheng*) were excluded. Rural industry will refer to most enterprises owned and operated at or below the level of towns, townships, and villages. Most state-run 'rural' enterprises owned and operated at or above the county-level were in fact located in county-level seats or areas they administered, and should not be considered rural. Similarly, most other county-level enterprises were also located in county cities.[10] Agriculture refers to the five standard Chinese statistical categories of cultivation, animal husbandry, household sidelines, fisheries including aqua-culture, and forestry.[11] Thus, for the lower Yangzi delta, rural non-agricultural activities will refer to industry, construction, transportation, commerce and other tertiary level services located in rural areas. Many of these designations here defined become rather more complicated when issues of ownership and spatial administrative classifications are further elaborated. The resulting complexities will be discussed throughout this book as they arise.

Some of the reasons which justify a focused and sustained examination of recent changes in the lower Yangzi delta are highlighted in Table 1.1. The table positions the 54,645 square kilometres of the delta in a national context as the most important economic region in China.[12] Nearly fifty-two million people – 4.19 per cent of the national total – live here, on only 0.57 per cent of China's territory, making the delta one of the most densely populated contiguous concentrations of people in Asia. It generated 11.11 per cent of China's gross domestic product in 1997, and 4.66 per cent of total agricultural output.[13] However, the delta's most significant contributions to the national economy were in terms of industrial production. Nearly 14 per cent of China's industrial output was concentrated here in 1997. The relative importance to China of industrial output in the lower Yangzi delta was almost four times its population and twenty-nine times its area. Even more noteworthy was that 52.2 per cent of industrial output in the delta was generated by rural enterprises, accounting for well over one-fifth of the nation's total rural industrial output (see

Plate 1.1 Crop production in the lower Yangzi delta. Canola fields near Tongxin Village, Kunshan.

Plate 1.2 Rural industrialization in the lower Yangzi delta. Transplanting rice seedlings near a large textiles enterprise in Shipai Town, Kunshan.

Table 1.1 The lower Yangzi delta in China, 1997

Area (km²)	54,645
Share of national area (%)	0.57
Population (millions)	51.75
Share of national population (%)	4.19
Average population density (people/km²)	947
Gross domestic product (GDP) (billion RMB[a])	831.05
Share of national GDP (%)	11.11
Gross value of agricultural output (GVAO) (billion RMB[a])	114.65
Share of national GVAO (%)	4.66
Gross value of industrial output (GVIO) (billion RMB[a])	1,563.86
Share of national GVIO (%)	13.75
Rural GVIO (billion RMB[a])	815.49
Share of national GVIO (%)	22.61
1981–1997 Average annual growth in GVAO[b] (%)	7.6
1981–1997 Average annual growth in GVIO[b] (%)	20.6
1981–1997 Average annual growth in rural GVIO[b] (%)	29.3

Notes
a $US 1 = RMB 8.3 (midpoint in 1997).
b Figures here are for Jiangsu Province.

Sources: Calculated from: *HDDTNJ 1996*, pp. 105–117; *JSTJNJ 1998*, pp. 28–29, 335–373; *SHTJNJ 1998*, pp. 8, 180; *ZGNCTN 1998*, p. 297; *ZGTJNJ 1998*, pp. 8, 20–23.

Table 1.1). The 1981–1997 average annual growth rates in agricultural output (7.6 per cent), industrial output (20.6 per cent), and rural industrial output (29.3 per cent) shown at the bottom of Table 1.1 were also substantial. These latter figures refer to all of Jiangsu Province excluding Shanghai, and should be considered the minimum average values for the region of the lower Yangzi delta within southern Jiangsu (*Sunan*).[14] The growth rates in Shanghai over the same period were 4.9 per cent for agriculture and 11.1 per cent for industry, while for China the growth rates in agriculture and industry were 6.8 per cent and 15.6 per cent respectively.[15] The relative prominence of these values for output and growth of rural industry in the lower Yangzi delta provides the initial empirical evidence and rationale for an in-depth study of spatial economic restructuring in this region.

The finer elements of this restructuring will be explored in a detailed case study of Kunshan, a county level city (*xianji shi*) located in southern Jiangsu Province adjacent to the Shanghai Municipal region (see Map 1.1). The centre of Kunshan is located 55 kilometres from downtown Shanghai and 36 kilometres from the city of Suzhou. Comprised of twenty towns and 463 villages, Kunshan covers an area of 865 square kilometres, 54.2 per cent of which was arable land in 1998, with another 22.3 per cent containing lakes, rivers, and canals.[16] At the end of 1998 the population was 587,509.[17] The average annual growth rate of industrial output in Kunshan between 1979 and 1996 was 32.7 per cent.[18]

There were several reasons why Kunshan was selected for the most intensive analysis undertaken in this study. In addition to the conspicuousness and rapid pace of its spatial economic change, Kunshan's physical and administrative position in the delta were appropriate for an evaluation of a range of potential forces which might have influenced the patterns and processes of this change. When I initially entered the field specifically to conduct the research for this study, I envisaged an analysis that would focus on the linkages between rural areas in Kunshan and nearby urban centres such as the cities of Suzhou and Shanghai. I considered it important in this context to select an area that was not administratively subordinate to a large city. This ruled out areas such as Wu County around Suzhou City or Wuxi County around Wuxi City and all of Shanghai's suburban counties.[19] Kunshan's administrative status was essentially equal to that of the city of Suzhou.[20] Kunshan was between and adjacent to two large urban centres, but also administratively distinct and more independent than other areas lower in the administrative hierarchy.

It also seemed reasonable to expect that proximity to China's largest urban industrial complex would provide ample analytical fodder. It turns out, for reasons which will become clear later in this book, that external forces from Shanghai and elsewhere did not influence local development in places like Kunshan in the ways and to the degree initially anticipated. Thus, Kunshan's location at the edge of Shanghai and near Suzhou City would preclude distance from urban areas as a variable in rural restructuring. It might have been easier, for example, to demonstrate that the influence of large cities was less important in an equally well developed area further away from Shanghai. Kunshan was also topographically fairly uniform and, as well as straddling major regional and national transportation corridors, had its own well developed internal transportation network.

For all these reasons, Kunshan provides a quintessential example of the local character of regional change. Like the unique confluence of bio-geoclimatic circumstances which allow the exquisite *qionghua* flower to blossom between 20 April and 10 May only in Kunshan, it is necessary to understand specific local processes and mechanisms, as they intersect and articulate with exogenous forces in particular ways over space to produce patterns of regional development in the lower Yangzi delta.[21]

Lastly and in more practical terms, Kunshan was an area that I could easily penetrate from my research home in Shanghai. It was also accessible in terms of contacts and networks of informants arranged through colleagues and friends in Shanghai. I am also convinced that I was able to establish a deeper rapport and trust with my hosts in Kunshan since I could converse, at least to a limited degree, in the local dialect.

What then, are the key questions which must be answered in order to understand regional development in the lower Yangzi delta? In the context of economic reforms and a particular focus on industrial development in the countryside, satisfactory elaboration of the multidimensional nature of spatial economic restructuring in the delta will need to consider a number of complex interrelated issues. How do the wider forces of economic reform interact with particular local circumstances to condition local and regional outcomes? What is the scope of influence of community based individuals or agencies to significantly determine such outcomes? What are the relationships between these economic and political actors at the local, regional, national and international levels? How do local actors reproduce, reconstitute or reject the wider forces of change? What are the relationships among individuals and agencies operating at the local level?

Answering these questions will require an analysis of the regional transformation from a local perspective since understanding the complexities and interactions at this level is crucial to realistic analysis of the wider patterns of change in the lower Yangzi delta. However, as will be demonstrated, localities must also be treated holistically by seriously considering the role of space and place in such questions, and not merely juxtaposed against some conveniently abstracted spatial construct. In practical terms these questions are addressed through investigations in the lower Yangzi delta along five overlapping modes of analysis. The first will survey the geographical and historical pre-conditions and circumstances of contemporary change. The second will elaborate upon the spatial patterns of economic restructuring. The third will explore the structural parameters of interactions and interrelationships among individuals and agencies. The fourth will examine the demographic dimensions of population and labour movements. The fifth will concentrate on the specific morphology of industrialization in the delta.

The subsequent theoretical and empirical explorations undertaken in this study are framed by three fundamental questions: (1) What is the nature of the spatial economic restructuring that has occurred in the lower Yangzi delta region since the beginning of reforms in 1978?; (2) What are the key underlying processes and mechanisms which determine the character of this spatial economic restructuring?; and (3) What are the theoretical implications of this restructuring in the delta for conceptualizing the forces which drive regional development in China? It turns out that an adequate grasp of the essence of spatial economic restructuring in China will require setting aside most of the conventional theoretical and methodological assumptions.

Redefining a new critical regional geography

Bai wen buru yi jian (It is better to see once than to hear a hundred times).

Chinese Proverb

Geography based on books is mediocre. With maps one can do a little better. But the only way to do it well is in the field.

Paul Vidal de La Blache[22]

Chinese landscapes of transformation and the representation of place

Pondering the mood of this study I could not help recalling the famous painting *Qingming Shanghe Tu* (Qingming Festival by the River).[23] Painted sometime between 1111 and 1126 by the virtually unknown court artist Zhang Zeduan, the 5.25 metre long horizontal hand-scroll depicts scenes in and near the Northern Song capital of Bianliang (or Bianjing – modern Kaifeng in Henan Province). One of the great masterpieces of landscape painting, it captured the transition from countryside and farmyards to the busy streets of a traditional Chinese city. The poignancy and relevance of the painting for this study lie in its two main features. The first is the exquisite detail and accuracy of the landscapes captured in the original, and how the tone of the composition is informed by a delicate realism and a magnificent sense of space and perspective. The second is the relative inconsistencies, inaccuracies, and artistic attributes of the dozens of later copies, and the nature of the subsequent debates about their authenticity, which have emerged in the nine centuries since the original.[24] Taken together, these features highlight important issues about the transformation of landscapes and place in China and the ways in which this transformation is experienced, understood, interpreted, and represented.

Perusal of the scroll itself reveals from right to left three mutually interdependent landscapes each flowing gracefully into the next. It begins in the flat countryside and gives a clear view of the distant trees and a group of nearly deserted farm buildings. Families and other groups are seen coming towards the viewer and proceeding in a quickening pace towards the city, while others are reluctantly leaving. Perusing further, great barges moored along the river come into view in the foreground with a few street activities and shops behind and to the right. This section climaxes where one of the barges tracks into the oncoming current to pass under Rainbow Bridge and into town. Leaving the river, the scene then follows a street as it crosses a moat outside the city walls and enters the capital through one of its imperious gates. The busy vibrancy of the city streets then reach a peak in this section before gradually tapering-off towards the end of the painting.

Throughout its length, the scroll is replete with meticulous detail, revealing keen powers of observation and a deep familiarity with the scenes portrayed. The painter knew the atmosphere of the hustle and bustle of street activities, the configurations of flowing water and the navigation of barges, the subtleties of architecture and construction and how to render them and the ambience of the countryside. Rather than merely depicting the many types of individuals and activities, moreover, the painter was secure enough to characterize them – sometimes humorous, often excited – but always truthfully. The painting embodies a vivid sense of space and various perspectives, by suggesting at every point a continuation beyond or inside that which is actually portrayed. Zhang Zeduan's style and technique were deeply linked to the specificity and character of the subject. In his knowing and loving representation of countryside, people and the built environment, objects and their character and form coincide.

The honesty of the painting's full and accurate description also revealed a thorough indifference to the conventional artistic formalities. There were, of course, other examples of such realism among the established elite through Chinese history. Excited by the dramatic landscapes of Mount Hua, the fourteenth century doctor Wang Lu felt unable to convey his true experiences filtered through the traditional stylistic norms.[25] Rather, his paintings, poetry and travel writings reacted directly to the particular forms and characteristics of the landscapes which had so moved him, fundamentally questioning the accepted narratives. Similarly, the great traveller Xu Xiake conveyed with unmediated vision, meticulous detail, and concise style his experiences of a direct encounter with the landscape. His prose captured a strong sense of the reality of travel in seventeenth century China, revealing insights into the nature of the environment and places as a 'fascinating texture of interacting phenomena'.[26] Zhang Zeduan's *Qingming Shanghe Tu*, however, seems to have emerged as the supreme instance of a unique and gentle realism in Chinese landscape painting.[27]

The work was frequently copied, but the integrity and veracity of the original scroll were never duplicated. Seen from a distance these copies retained the basic layout of countryside, river scenes, and city-scape. Upon closer examination the subtleties and clarity of arrangement in the original are lost. While there are dozens of examples, the most obvious contrast is with the barges depicted in the original which lie according to the current.[28] In several copies, the barges are moored with their bows converging on Rainbow Bridge with the sterns of some facing upstream, an impossible situation in the presence of a current. Such copies were apparently based only on literary references to the original, written records of the capital, or in rare cases, access to the original scroll itself. Later painters of *Qingming Shanghe Tu*, as was common with historical chroniclers and subsequent commentators in China, clearly had a greater desire to render works of aesthetic and erudite merit than to produce an accurate representation of the subject. The tendency to manipulate key elements and to crowd the painting resulted in elegant visual images, organically implausible and difficult to read in terms of continuity, space and form. The techniques and style employed by Zhang Zeduan, characterized primarily by ingenious changes in perspective to suggest unseen activities within as well as continuing further space beyond the scenes depicted, are in sharp contrast to the later versions. Yet it is the relative attributes of these copies which also serves to emphasize that what was true in the elaboration of the original composition – its consummate detail and subtle transitions – was also true of the complex landscapes it so uniquely and eloquently portrayed.

Regional geography: as method and as theory

I have indulged in this reverie on *Qingming Shanghe Tu* as a metaphor for the two underlying perspectives of this study which are linked to my assumptions about the complexity of the transformation that has occurred in China and the 'Chineseness' of its inherent processes and mechanisms. The first and more explicit aspect of the metaphor has to do with the nature of how investigations into complex socio-spatial phenomena are undertaken. Here I wish to stress a major goal of the 'new' regional geography in examining how the specificity of place is at once preserved and modified within the wider patterns of regional change.[29] Such change may emerge from within the region, penetrate from outside it, or more likely, arise through some combination of and articulation between the two. The latter phenomenon is generally perceived in spatial terms as the local–global dialectic.[30] Whatever the case, the approach advocated here necessarily focuses on the linkages between the circumstances and characteristics of locality and place, and the processes through which the social and economic relations of production are established and modified within regions.[31] This approach may be operationalized by creating a set of analytical categories to 'interrogate historical geographical situations' to provide 'empirical substance'.[32] In terms of this study, this implies specific methods of analysis which include the selection and detailed exploration of particular inter-actions and interrelationships over space, the resulting structures of economic production, and the historical, cultural and political circum-stances in which they were embedded. Furthermore, the results of these explorations will suggest configurations and connotations 'consistent with the questions and regional setting under consideration'.[33]

More will be said about the finer theoretical methodological implica-tions in the next chapter. For now, I merely wish to emphasize that it is the landscapes and places themselves, as they were for Zhang Zeduan, Wang Lu and Xu Xiake, that should always be the subject of our first and most direct attention. This approach is not preoccupied, at least not initially, with the etiquette and social critique of those unable or unwilling to conduct meaningful fieldwork. It is impossible really, to fully under-stand spatial economic transformation in China, unless you have actually been there to *feel* it. Prolonged field investigations, and the physical and intellectual discipline they compel, are essential for the larger project of refining our theoretical understanding of these Chinese landscapes of transformation. They are, moreover, fundamental to what we do as geographers.

The second aspect of the metaphor I wish to infer from *Qingming Shanghe Tu* has to do with the conceptualization of space and place. Like the new critical regional geography alluded to above, Zhang Zeduan has moved well beyond mere description and representation of the landscapes. He has also touched upon the essence of their underlying character with a style, technique and set of perspectives which evoke the functional dynamics and mutual interactions among the constituent elements. By synthesizing his keen observations of the finest details of these elements and their wider spatial context, Zhang Zeduan has highlighted the relationships which at once produced and linked different landscapes. The original portrayal of *Qingming Shanghe Tu* fundamentally captured more than the mere sum of its parts, giving it the presence of a masterpiece and distinguishing it from all subsequent copies.

Thus, the new critical regional geography I wish to invoke here, collapses methodology and the conceptualization of spatial differentiation and change, into a theoretical framework concerned with the particular intersection of relations (social, economic, cultural, political and historical) as they were manifested in and as they constituted place. It is the linkages and interrelationships of such dynamism over space which are important here. However, I do not wish to conflate place with the local, although as Tuan has argued, '[i]n experience, the meaning of space often merges with that of place'.[34] The notion of place I am invoking here includes more than just the sense of a local setting that is derived solely from the connections which individuals and institutions attach to it, as it is most often defined.[35] Clarifying some of the other terms which will appear throughout this book will reveal some of the underlying elements of this approach. The term locale is seen as the physical setting across and through which interactions and interrelationships occur over time.[36] Unlike the conventional definition of locale, however, I will not limit such encounters only to the social. The term region will refer to spatial segments, at various scales and frequently ill-defined, which incorporate some 'formal, functional or perceptual significance'.[37] While conventionally perceived as bounded in some way, I am less concerned at this point with defining a particular region than with establishing a conceptual focus on the critical interactions and interrelationships which it encompasses. Thus, the relevance of these terms for this study is how they draw attention to local circumstances and the need to contextualize the wider patterns of spatial economic change as they are embedded within such processes. Rather than treating the region as a convenient neutral backdrop for spatial change, there needs to be a greater commitment to probing the dynamics of the processes of regional formation as they articulate with those changes.[38] Ultimately, I wish to argue that understanding spatial economic restructuring in China requires conceptualizing the underlying processes and mechanisms in the context of the local geographical and historical circumstances which shape and reflect the character of the region. This assertion seems to be straightforward. However the essence of this argument has important implications for the way in which processes of spatial economic development in China are conceptualized, interrogated and represented. The rather fractious theoretical debates about development serve as the point of entry into the conceptual and analytical deliberations of this study.

Development theory in crisis: beyond the impasse

Whether or not one acknowledges a crisis in development theory, fragmentation of the debate presents at once challenges and opportunities for the construction of new approaches to understanding regional development in China. From one side press criticisms that the discourse is a sophisticated whitewash of perspectives which rationalize Western dominance. From another side are realizations that Marxist inspired theories flirt with irrelevance as they appear incapable of dealing with real world complexity.[39] Much debate has also erupted regarding the relationship between development theory and praxis.[40] Each of these issues will be elaborated upon briefly with reference to China along with proposals for overcoming the 'impasse' if, indeed, there is one.[41]

Critics of Marxist and neo-Marxist theories (dependency, articulation of the modes of production, world systems, etc.) highlight at least four dimensions of this work that are said to have caused its stagnation.[42] The first refers to the teleology rooted in structural Marxism in which capital is defined in terms of laws that produce fixed outcomes. This results in a 'disorientation' founded in the notion that underdeveloped countries are necessary under capitalism rather than attempting to explain the underlying processes. The second dimension refers to a generalized economistic determinism in which the cultural, social, and political complex is seen as a consequence of national and global economic systems.[43] This interpretation effectively usurps the study of how historical and geographical factors can, first of all, act independently and second, how they might influence (or largely determine in some cases) patterns of development. A third dimension refers to the paradox that Marxist-influenced development theory has been especially weak in building an understanding of the socialist third world.[44] This is particularly disturbing in light of the dominant role of the state and its constituent institutional structures in countries like China.[45] The fourth dimension of the critique refers to the propensity of Marxist perspectives to overlook relevant issues leading to highly polemical confrontations with what Booth calls 'mainstream literature'.[46] One example that will be discussed in more detail in Chapter 2 is the paucity of theorization regarding processes of industrialization especially in contexts where the state plays a particularly central role such as China.

Among the numerous commentaries summarizing the critiques of Marxist inspired development theories are suggestions that new approaches are required to illuminate the complex circuits of interdependency of political, social and cultural factors in the third world in a rapidly evolving global economy.[47] In a superb review of these new approaches, Corbridge characterized them under the rubric of a more sensitive post-Marxism.[48] While relying on certain commitments of classical Marxism (a materialist ontology, causal analysis and a focus on inequalities that emphasize contradictions in the processes of accumulation), post-Marxism departs from the original by rejecting epistemologically privileged exclusivism, the necessities of economistic determinism, functionalist accounts of agency and power, and dualisms that ignore the diversity of both capitalism and socialism.[49]

Post-Marxist development theories accommodate certain uniquely geographical insights into the broad tasks of understanding the role of institutional structures and of time and space which begin to address these concerns. Investigations of socialist development strategies that reveal territorial, economic and political possibilities and contradictions are an example of the former. Understanding development patterns in China, for example, requires an examination of state-led or inspired organizations, their constitution and powers and their capacity to mobilize and transfer resources.[50] Moreover, such studies must seriously consider social, cultural and institutional parameters, and the geo-politics of territorial and sectoral administration to uncover the basis of any transformation. Post-Marxist theories are also sensitive to the circumstances of capital accumulation over space and time and pay attention to the composition and changing dynamics of an evolving world system. More importantly they recognize the complex interplay of the local, meso- and macro-scales in the joint production of place in what Corbridge calls the 'spatiality of the development process'.[51]

Against this post-Marxist backdrop is a small literature on development in the socialist third world.[52] Urban and regional development in the socialist third world has been generally characterized by an ideological commitment to egalitarianism and a slower rate of urban growth accompanied by a reduction in the degree of urban primacy. Forbes and Thrift note that such 'polarization reversal' is the intended result of ideological convictions and/or the unintended outcome of more fundamental state interests.[53] While models that seek to explain these phenomena in the context of a transition to socialism have been useful for revolutionary and post-liberation periods they are not adequate for understanding the socio-spatial implications of recent reforms in countries like China.[54]

Currently, such partially reformed command economies are allowing, even encouraging, market forces to play an increasingly important role as the focus of urban and regional development shifts from self-reliance, spatial equality and economic egalitarianism towards openness, economic efficiency and entrepreneurialism. This raises fundamental questions about what will happen to city and countryside, and interregional relationships and disparities. In the context of China there are a number of issues which add to the underlying complexity of these recent reforms. The Chinese government has, for example, always been deeply concerned about the implications of uncontrolled mass migration into large cities.[55] Moreover, since industrial space in these large cities is dominated by a largely immobile state sector, this has implications for the location of new non-state industry and the emerging patterns of land-use. The key point is that economic transformation, characterized in China by rapid industrialization without a commensurate transfer of large numbers of people into big cities, is unfolding as part of a set of spatial processes. While this is not unique to socialist developing countries, it is more explicit there because of the declared commitment of Marxist–Leninist regimes to the social use of space that serves mass rather than just elite interests.[56] The primacy of these ideological and political aspects to the organization and function of space forces deeper consideration of these realms.[57]

It is necessary therefore, to go beyond the traditional economic domain of regional planning to examine Chinese social and political (institutional) structures and how they are organized in space.[58] Such an approach potentially enables us to see how spatial economic patterns are related to historically grounded variations in national and local socio-political structures as they articulate with a post-cold war global economy. It provides an opportunity to challenge the preoccupation in recent urban and regional development literature with advanced and peripheral capitalist societies and the Eurocentrism which imbues such studies.[59] The intersection of political economy and sensitivity and understanding of place-specific factors in development will begin to address the hegemony and parochialism of Western inspired theory, in spite of the disdain by some for the 'heavy breathing over locality and a reconstructed regional geography'.[60]

This approach will also point the way towards a development praxis which will avoid policies based on dogmatic, unilinear and universalistic views. The present challenge then is the construction of non-reductionist, non-teleological 'post-impasse' development theory which balances abstract conceptualizations, which do not result in relevant development praxis, and empirical research.[61] Here I begin to identify elements of a 'middle ground' which conceptually (and literally as will be demonstrated later) seeks to build a new framework for understanding and explaining the rapid spatial economic transformation in regions like China's lower Yangzi delta. Ultimately, it will provide a theoretical basis for challenging present urban and regional planning policies and for proposing meaningful alternatives.

Recent discussions of development practice highlight the links between theoretical research and real experiences and circumstances at the local level.[62] '[H]igher-level work must grow out of and be based upon participatory research at lower levels . . .' with the objective of producing theory that has some meaning in practice and can be 'genuinely developmental'.[63] The issue of scale becomes important here because such an approach must ensure that both micro- and macro-levels are explicitly related. The methodological implications are clear. According to Edwards

> the crucial thing is always to build from the 'bottom upwards' ... to ensure that people's real experiences and concerns provide the raw material for higher-level analysis and synthesis. Any higher-level research which fails to do this may misinterpret what is actually happening and will therefore fail to inform development policy and practice at higher levels in a responsible way.[64]

However, a research focus on the linkages between micro- and macro-levels in which neither global nor local studies are privileged will not in itself point the way through the current crisis in development theory. It is also necessary to dispense with certain commonly assumed dyadic relations: global forces define the parameters of local or regional development; large cities drive rural transformation; small-scale indigenous factors are subordinate to larger scale exogenous forces. Theoretical emphasis on the macro-scale forces at the expense of the particular obfuscates understanding and the explanatory power of development research. While it is perhaps true that site specific studies have overlooked the importance of wider economic and political influences, development theory has, in general, concentrated on the macro-forces which are most often conceptualized as predominant in shaping local or regional characteristics. On the contrary, we must always examine wider forces and trends 'through the eyes of those who experience and act in them, for it is their perceptions and actions which give meaning to these forces'.[65]

Moreover, while acknowledging the role of macro-forces, such an approach can also accommodate aspects of development and spatial transformation in China that are in all the most important ways, locally inspired and propelled. This work

> avoids any false opposition or one-way determinism between the global and the local – but rather insists on studying both the specificities of particular places and the broader forces which shape and are shaped by particular local circumstances and histories.[66]

Corbridge does however, caution against an approach to development research which confines itself in theory and practice to the local without accommodating the facts of globalization.[67] The relevance of the new critical regional geography discussed above now becomes increasingly clear in this theoretical context. Some will argue, however, that generalizing from the particular can never provide grand theory, notwithstanding the proclivities of post-modernism, of which more in the next chapter.

Issues and methodology

My first entry into the region of the lower Yangzi delta occurred in May and June of 1983. After spending time in and around Nanjing and Yangzhou I travelled the length of the delta to the city of Shanghai. My initial views of China's largest metropolis were thus framed by experiences in places like Suzhou and the countryside of Kunshan. Like the landscapes portrayed in *Qingming Shanghe Tu*, the resulting impressions remained vivid and would set the tone for all my subsequent encounters with the region. Including a dozen research sojourns to China between 1989 and 1999, I spent a total of more than two and a half years in the region conducting the fieldwork for this study. The large number of visits over a long period of time, their duration, and the close personal and professional contacts they engendered provided me with unprecedented access to the region and to crucial sources of information through key informants and research collaborators.

This study is thus based upon a variety of data collected over a long period of time from a range of sources at several scales of analysis. First-hand sources included information collected from extended field observations, nearly 200 interviews with a variety of village-, town- and county-level informants, and a survey questionnaire of rural enterprises. Observations were documented through hundreds of slides and a detailed photo-journal, dozens of sketches and extensive notes written in the field. I visited every prefectural level administrative unit in *Sunan* in addition to all of northeast Zhejiang Province. I also spent time in every urban and county level administrative unit in Wuxi, Suzhou and Shanghai, and managed to visit all twenty towns and several dozen villages in Kunshan, as well as other towns and villages throughout the delta. Many of the resulting observations are specifically referred to throughout the book.

The interviews were largely unstructured and open ended, although they tended to follow a consistent format in terms of protocol, the questions asked and opportunities for follow-up and elaboration. Interviews averaged two hours in length, ranging from as short as an hour in some cases to all day affairs in others. There were three key informants in Kunshan with whom I had repeated exchanges over the duration of the fieldwork. In keeping with the spirit of this research, the interviews focused on studying the strategies and networks of these local actors within their wider economic and political contexts. Several officials were, of course, wary at the start about divulging too much, providing little more than the ubiquitous 'brief introduction'. I was usually able to penetrate the issues further by asking leading questions which revealed that I already knew at least part of the whole story. Most eventually provided detailed insights which, taken together, helped to create a fuller account of the relevant issues. Throughout the book I make reference to specific comments and views. To protect the anonymity of my informants, I will refer merely to 'interview notes' in the notes.

A further set of primary data was collected via a questionnaire admin-istered in Kunshan during June and July 1992 with follow-up work in May and June 1993. The eight-page survey was developed in close consul-tation with my Chinese research collaborators and officials in the Economic Research Centre in Kunshan. The objective was to elicit a range of infor-mation from rural enterprises across several towns in Kunshan. In addition to basic information about size, ownership, labour force and production, the questionnaire focused on the details of procurement and marketing activities of 104 enterprises and a variety of issues regarding their location. I will make no claims regarding the *statistical* significance or otherwise of the findings from this survey. The respondents were not entirely ran-domly selected, for example. I am confident, however, that when con-sidered in the context of findings from other sources, the results of this questionnaire can reasonably be viewed as representative. Basic owner-ship and output data from the enterprises surveyed, for example, were consistent with published county-level statistics.

In addition to these first hand data, a large number of secondary Chinese statistical and documentary sources were also consulted. Statistical sources were largely of the official published yearbook variety. I was also able to locate several supplementary statistical materials in the latest gazetteers, sometimes in local newspapers, but most often in limited circulation internal (*nei bu*) statistical bulletins and other documents. Though rarely seen by most researchers, I was able to obtain comprehensive statistics at the village level, for example. However, one must exercise great caution when utilizing such Chinese statistical sources. Issues related to the utiliza-tion of such statistics were of sufficient concern to be included in a separate appendix (see Appendix 1). Data were also gathered from a wide array of secondary documentary sources. These included local, regional and national newspapers and magazines, local gazetteers, maps and atlases, widely circulated government documents, and other materials provided by informants such as investment brochures and published regulations, and information from local commercial and labour fairs. Also collected were dozens of Chinese language books and academic articles published in scholarly journals, along with several more obscure research monographs.

The breadth and depth of these data permitted frequent cross-checks and triangulation. Specific figures provided by informants in interviews, for example, were substantiated by utilizing published sources or other informants. The same also applied to the detailed accounts and viewpoints about local developments provided by interviewees. Obviously, most officials spoke from the perspective of their own organizations. However, the versions of issues and events revealed by informants were confirmed and reiterated by other accounts, and were consistent with the larger and rather complex story of local and regional transformation that began to emerge. Findings from the survey questionnaire were similarly corrobo-rated with evidence gathered during field visits and interviews conducted at dozens of enterprises in Kunshan. Thus, while no single element of these data was sufficient on its own to accept or reject particular findings, taken together they provided coherent and consistent evidence to support the overall conclusions and conceptual reformulations.

Organization of the book

This book is organized in response to the theoretical and empirical inquiries necessary to address the three central questions introduced above. It begins in Chapter 2 with a critical review of the relevant literature along the three broad theoretical discussions of regional development, the geography of production, and urbanization. Elements of each debate relevant for understanding spatial economic restructuring in the lower Yangzi delta and China will be highlighted. In the context of crucial insights reviewed in the indigenous Chinese scholarship along the same themes, Chapter 2 culminates by proposing a new conceptual framework which seeks to capture the critical elements and the underlying processes and mechanisms which determine spatial economic restructuring in China's lower Yangzi delta.

Chapter 3 focuses on illustrating the historical and geographical patterns of structural transformation across Jiangsu Province and Shanghai. The chapter elaborates upon the particular features of these patterns not adequately explained by the conventional wisdom. It concludes by introducing some of the circumstances of spatial economic restructuring in Kunshan. Chapters 4 to 6 examine the detailed characteristics of the transformation in Kunshan. Chapter 4 will explore the relationships between local government administration, the development of rural industrial enterprises, and the nature of the institutional structures which have emerged to manage local economic activity in Kunshan. Chapter 5 reviews the findings from four detailed case studies on transportation, Dianshanhu Town, Tongxin Village, and the nature of the special development zones located in Kunshan. The objectives of this chapter are to assess particular local patterns of change to reveal some of the complex processes and mechanisms which drive local development. Chapter 6 will focus specifically on the morphology of rural industrial growth and the spatial proliferation of enterprises in the Kunshan countryside. This chapter will highlight the linkages between specific processes and mechanisms identified in the preceding analysis and the location of rural industrial enterprises.

The concluding chapter will explore the theoretical implications of spatial economic transformation in the lower Yangzi delta and how they are relevant for understanding regional restructuring across China. Several specific clarifications are incorporated into the new conceptual framework introduced in Chapter 2. The final section of Chapter 7 concludes the book by proposing a planning and management agenda for the lower Yangzi delta that is sensitive to the local level realities of regional change.

Notes

1. See for example: Naughton, B. (1995) *Growing out of the Plan: Chinese Economic Reform, 1978–1993.* Cambridge: Cambridge University Press.
2. Perhaps the best example was the 'primary stages of socialism' arguments which emerged to justify certain particularly capitalist-like aspects of the reforms. See: Lieberthal, K. (1995) *Governing China: From Revolution Through Reform.* New York: Norton.
3. The discussion here is based on Naughton, B. (1995) op. cit., pp. 3–24.
4. Theroux, P. (1993) Going to see the dragon. *Harper's Magazine* (October), 34.
5. Ibid.
6. For a detailed explanation of the hierachy of administrative units in this area see Appendix 2.
7. Chreod Ltd. (1996) The Yangtze delta megalopolis. *International Conference on Towards a Sustainable Future,* Qinghua University, Beijing, 26 April; Zhou, Y. X. (1991) The metropolitan interlocking region in China: A preliminary hypothesis. In N. Ginsberg, B. Koppel and T. G. McGee (Eds.) *The Extended Metropolis: Settlement Transition in Asia.* Honolulu: University of Hawaii Press.
8. Small towns are comprised primarily of townships (*xiang*) and market towns (*jizhen*) that are settlements economically and socially integrated with the surrounding rural areas. Also see Appendix 2. The term 'community' will in some cases also refer more generally to the county level unit.
9. Sigurdson, J. (1977) *Rural Industrialization in China.* Cambridge: Council on East Asian Studies, Harvard University.
10. The confusion arises because of the way statistics are compiled in China. Spatial designations in the context of industrial statistics, for example, incorporate notions of ownership as well as location. For a good discussion see: Ho, S. P. S. (1994) *Rural China in Transition: Non-Agricultural Development in Rural Jiangsu, 1978–1990.* Oxford: Clarendon, pp. 6–7.
11. Prior to 1993 official statistics reported agricultural sidelines as a separate category. Since then such activities have been grouped largely within cultivation and some smaller elements into forestry. Meanwhile, commercial industrial activities undertaken by rural households as sideline production are still reported as a separate category.
12. I have not calculated similar 1997 figures for other regions in China such as the Pearl River (*Zhujiang*) delta in Guangdong in the south, the Shenyang–Dalian corridor in Liaoning, or the area around Beijing, Tianjin, and Tangshan. However, data presented in Zhou, Y. X. (1991) op. cit., p. 106, and more recently in Chreod Ltd. (1996) op. cit., p. 9, very clearly establish the lower Yangzi delta as China's dominant economic region.
13. For a definition of gross domestic product see Appendix 1.
14. The term *Sunan* will be used hereafter to refer to the part of the lower Yangzi delta defined earlier within southern Jiangsu and excluding Shanghai.
15. Calculated from: *SHTJNJ 1998,* p. 9; *ZGTJNJ 1997,* pp. 26–27; *ZGTJNJ 1998,* pp. 22–23. Growth rates for rural industrial output for Shanghai could not be accurately determined since the relevant data were not provided in constant values. However, it was possible to estimate the average growth in rural industrial output between 1981–1997 for China at about 20 per cent based on growth in the collective sector. See: *ZGTJNJ 1998,* p. 433.
16. Calculated from: *SZTJNJ 1995,* p. 15; *SZTJNJ 1999,* pp. 14, 80. Several sources, including the local statistical yearbooks, persist in reporting an area for Kunshan of 921.3 square kilometres. See Appendix 2 for a further elaboration of this issue.

17. *SZTJNJ 1999*, p. 48.
18. Calculated from: *JSSSN 1949–1989*, pp. 317–318, 393–394; *KSTJNJ* (Several Years), Preface (*passim*).
19. These two counties have since been elevated to county-level cities. In the case of Wuxi County its name was also changed to Xishan. This is discussed in more detail in the conclusion. Also, see Appendix 2.
20. See Appendix 2.
21. Interview notes. This delicate white blossom is often regarded by officials in Kunshan as the premier symbol of local development. Local officials also claimed that horticulturists in the famous Shanghai Botanical Gardens, barely 50 kilometres to the east and despite repeated efforts, were unable to cultivate a similarly exquisite blossom. Also see: *KSXJ* (1990), unpaginated preface.
22. Cited in: Butimer, A. (1995) Review of 'Vidal de La Blache: 1845–1918. Un Génie de la Geographie'. *AAAG* 85 (2), p. 406.
23. *Qingming* refers to the spring festival of remembrance of ancestors. At the time of the painting, tens of thousands of people from all walks of life converged on the capital and the banks of the Bian River. The original is probably in the Palace Museum in Beijing, although some believe it may be housed in the National Museum in Taipei.
24. Cohn, W. (1950) *Chinese Painting*. London: Phaidon, p. 75; Dong, Z. B. (1961) *Qingming Shanghe Tu* (*Qingming Festival by the River*). Taipei: National Taiwan University; Giles, H. A. (1918) *History of Chinese Pictorial Art*. London: Bernard, p. 168; Liu, Y. L. (1969) *Qingming Shanghe Tu zhi zonghe yanjiu* (*Qingming Festival by the River Comprehensive Research*). Taipei: Haitian; Loehr, M. (1980) *The Great Painters of China*. New York: Harper Row, pp. 163–167; Whitfield, R. (1965) *Chang Tse-tuan's 'Ch'ing-Ming Shang-He T'u'*. Unpublished Ph.D. dissertation: Princeton University.
25. Liscombe, K. M. (1993) *Learning from Mount Hua: A Chinese Physician's Illustrated Travel Record and Painting Theory*. Cambridge: Cambridge University Press.
26. Strassberg, R. E. (1994) *Inscribed Landscapes: Travel Writing from Imperial China*. Berkeley: University of California Press, p. 319. See also: Li, C. (1974) *The Travel Diaries of Hsu Hsia-K'o*. Hong Kong: Chinese University of Hong Kong.
27. Loehr, M. (1980) op. cit., p. 165.
28. Whitfield, R. (1965) op. cit.
29. Archer, K. (1993) Regions as social organisms: The Lamarckian characteristics of Vidal de la Blache's regional geography. *AAAG* 83 (3); Gilbert, A. (1988) The new regional geography in English and French-speaking countries. *PIHG* 12 (2).
30. McGee, T. G. (1995b) Geography and development: Crisis commitment and renewal. *Cahiers de géographie du Québec* 39 (108), p. 527. For reasons which will become clear below, I will not engage the burgeoning discourse on globalization.
31. Gilbert, A. (1988) op. cit., p. 210.
32. Pudup, M. B. (1988) Arguments within regional geography. *PIHG* 12 (3), p. 383.
33. Ibid.
34 Tuan, Y. F. (1977) *Space and Place*. London: Arnold; see also Taylor, P. J. (1999) Places, spaces and Macy's: Place–space tensions in the political geography of modernities. *PIHG* 23 (1), pp. 9–13.
35. Murphy, A. B. (1991) Regions as social constructs: The gap between theory and practice. *PIHG* 15 (1), p. 22.
36. After: Gilbert, A. (1988) op. cit., p. 212; and Murphy, A. B. (1991) ibid.

37. Murphy, A. B. (1991) ibid.
38. I will not engage any further than I already have the burgeoning literature about regions, locality and place, and the new regional geography. For a tiny sample of the most recent contributions, in addition to those already cited, see: Allen, J., Massey, D. and Cochrane, A. (1998) *Rethinking the Region.* London: Routledge; Bird, J., *et al.* (Eds.) (1993) *Mapping the Futures: Local Cultures, Global Change.* London: Routledge; Entrikin, J. N. (1994) Place and region. *PIHG* 18 (2); Massey, D. (1994) *Space, Place and Gender.* Cambridge: Polity; Massey, D. (1999) Space-time, 'science' and the relationship between physical geography and human geography. *TIBG* 24 (3); Thrift, N. (1993) For a new regional geography 3. *PIHG* 17 (1).
39. Peet, R. (1994) Review of 'Beyond the impasse: New directions in development theory'. *AAAG* 84 (2), p. 339. Peet does refer to one study which undermines this claim, p. 340.
40. Edwards, M. (1993) How relevant is development studies? In F. J. Schuurman (Ed.) *Beyond the Impasse: New Directions in Development Theory.* London: Zed.
41. Schuurman, F. J. (Ed.) (1993a) *Beyond the Impasse: New Directions in Development Theory.* London: Zed.
42. Booth, D. (1985) Marxism and development sociology: Interpreting the impasse. *World Development* 13 (7); Corbridge, S. (1986) *Capitalist World Development: A Critique of Radical Development Geography.* London: Macmillan.
43. Booth, D. (1993) Development research: From impasse to new agenda. In Schuurman, F. J. (Ed.) op. cit.
44. See especially: Forbes, D. and Thrift, N. (Eds.) (1987) *The Socialist Third World: Urban Development and Regional Planning.* Oxford: Blackwell; Post, K. and Wright, P. (1989) *Socialism and Underdevelopment.* London: Routledge.
45. Vandergeest, P. and Buttel, F. (1988) Marx, Weber and development sociology. *World Development* 16 (6).
46. Booth, D. (1985) op. cit., p. 762. Also cited in Schuurman, F. J. (1993b) Introduction: Development theory in the 1990s. In F. J. Schuurman (Ed.) op. cit., p. 13.
47. Toye, J. (1993) *Dilemmas of Development: Reflections on the Counter-revolution in Development Economics.* Oxford: Blackwell.
48. Corbridge, S. (1989) Marxism, post-Marxism, and the geography of development. In R. Peet and N. Thrift (Eds.) *New Models in Geography: The Political-economy Perspective.* London: Unwin.
49. Ibid. pp. 238–245.
50. Corbridge, S. (1991) Third world development. *PIHG* 15 (3).
51. Corbridge, S. (1989) op. cit., p. 247.
52. Corbridge, S. (1991) op. cit.; Forbes, D. and Thrift, N. (Eds.) (1987) op. cit.; Sidaway, J. D. and Simon, D. (1990) Spatial policies and uneven development in the Marxist–Leninist states of the third world. In D. Simon (Ed.) *Third World Regional Development: A Reappraisal.* London: Paul Chapman.
53. Forbes, D. and Thrift, N. (Eds.) (1987) op. cit., p. 6. See also Sidaway, J. D. and Simon, D. (1990) op. cit., p. 30.
54. One example is the model of urbanization advanced by Murray, P. and Szelenyi, I. (1984) The city in transition to socialism. *IJURR* 8 (1).
55. For excellent reviews of the traditional means of controlling and managing population mobility and recent changes see: Chan, K. W. (1994a) *Cities with Invisible Walls: Reinterpreting Urbanization in Post-1949 China.* Hong Kong: Oxford University Press; Kirkby, R. J. R. (1985) *Urbanization in China: Town*

and Country in a Developing Economy 1949–2000 AD. London: Routledge. Very recently, however, economic liberalization has led to increasing mobility of the population by dissolving long-standing social relations. This has in turn weakened the state's ability to micro-manage Chinese society.

56. Sidaway, J. D. and Simon, D. (1990) op. cit., p. 33.

57. Ibid., p. 32.

58. For now, I deliberately conflate 'political' and 'institutional'. Notwithstanding the voluminous literature that debates the nature of 'civil society' in China, political will refer to the nature of power and control particularly in terms of the relations across and through territorial and sectoral administrative structures. These structural relationships are largely institutionalized (formally and informally) and, as will be demonstrated later, have profound implications for the nature of economic (and social) relations of production. Unless otherwise stated, however, these terms will not refer to cultural and social institutions.

59. McGee, T. G. (1991b) Presidential address: Eurocentrism in geography – The case of Asian urbanization. *The Canadian Geographer 35* (4); Sidaway, J. D. and Simon, D. (1990) op. cit., p. 32; Seater, D. (1989) Peripheral capitalism and the regional problematic. In R. Peet & N. Thrift (Eds.) op. cit., p. 267; Watts, M. J. (1989) The agrarian question in Africa: Debating the crisis. *PIHG* 13 (1), p. 32.

60. Watts, M. J. (1989) op. cit., p. 32.

61. Schuurman, F. J. (1993b) op. cit., pp. 16, 32.

62. Booth, D. (1993) op. cit.; Edwards, M. (1993) op. cit.

63. An example of how this might be undertaken is advanced in Edwards, M. (1989) The irrelevance of development studies. *Third World Quarterly* 11 (1).

64. Edwards, M. (1993) op. cit., p. 83.

65. Ibid., p. 84.

66. Booth, D. (1993) op. cit., p. 55.

67. Corbridge, S. (1993) Marxisms, modernities, and moralities: Development praxis and the claims of distant strangers. *Environment and Planning D: Society and Space* 11, p. 467.

2   Regional development and industrialization: towards mega-urbanization

This chapter will review and synthesize elements from the often disparate debates on development, the geography of production, and urbanization relevant for the construction of a new conceptual framework for understanding spatial economic transformation in China's lower Yangzi delta. The need for targeted deliberations along these three sets of theories of spatial change arises as a result of the particular conceptual and empirical realities of the patterns and processes of change in China's largest and most rapidly transforming economic region. First, to understand the nature of regional transformation in the delta, it is necessary to carefully and systematically consider the role of local forces. Several recent commentaries have highlighted the way in which theories of development must reposition concern for locality, considered variously in terms of culture, history, or the socio-economic and political circumstances of place, within the broader context of regional development.[1] Thus, as development is increasingly seen as a localized phenomenon, this augers for a commensurate shift in the intellectual and analytical focus of inquiry.[2] Second, industrial growth, rural industrialization in particular, and the specific location of industries in the Chinese countryside is the rubric which frames the theoretical discussions and the detailed empirical investigations of this study. A critical review of the theories of the geography of production, therefore, also informs our analysis of the precise spatial economic characteristics of places in the lower Yangzi delta.[3] Third, examining theories of urbanization in the context of China's regional development and industrialization also highlights the role of exogenous forces, including external economies, the dynamics of agglomeration, and the role of large cities, particularly in terms of the purported transition or otherwise to conventional urban forms.

This focused elaboration on specific components from at least three substantive theoretical debates should be interpreted neither as inconsistency nor as conceptual indecisiveness. Instead, invoking a plurality of theoretical perspectives explicitly recognizes, and is a deliberate response to, the complex multiplicity of factors which determine the patterns and processes of spatial economic transformation in the lower Yangzi delta.[4]

Thus, this chapter begins with the apparent crisis in development theory, the need to accommodate diversity, and a discussion of linkages and the transactional revolution. This leads into an exploration of a new geography of production which confronts the spectacular irrelevance of much of the current discourse and is followed by a critical examination of conventional notions of urban and rural in the context of the Chinese development debate. Taken together, analysis of these debates highlights components of a middle ground which balances local circumstances with the broad theories of location and the production of industrial space, the local and the global, and theory and practice. This reorientation begins with the need for a profound understanding of the place where change occurs. The chapter concludes by proposing the concept of mega-urbanization to explain the circumstances of local industrial development as part of the regional transformation occurring across the entire lower Yangzi delta.

Confronting the post-modern void in China: taking diversity seriously

Is there a crisis in development theory? There are some who challenge the notion of a crisis and the impasse framework which informs much of the resulting critique, particularly of Marxist and neo-Marxist theories. Peet, in a stinging review of an edited volume of impasse/post-impasse studies claims that what has really happened in development research is a 'growing disagreement mainly between modern and postmodern social theorists'.[5] Underlying this debate is the notion that development studies have suffered in the absence of introspective self-criticism which involves rethinking issues of intervention, knowledge, discursive practice and power.[6]

Linked to the widespread disillusionment with the modernist project, this Foucauldian critique challenges the Enlightenment notion of truth, linking it to the power and ambitions of Western inspired developmental discourse and practice.[7] Furthermore, the post-modern mistrust of so-called 'totalizing' ways of theorizing is reflected in the quest for historically and geographically produced singularities, across which meanings are unstable, and the repudiation of modernization as the foundation for truth. The intersection of such perspectives has inevitably resulted in an anti-developmentalism (post-developmentalism) calling for the rejection of concepts of development altogether.[8] Elements of a critical deconstructionist post-modernism which attempt to redefine the terms of engagement are perhaps appropriate for those (individuals and agencies) who enter the arena of development burdened with the conventional wisdom of the Enlightenment in all its forms. However, the post-modernist preoccupation with discursive practice provides only infrequent glimpses of what might lie ahead for development theory under this leitmotif. Ill-defined notions of post-developmentalism that visualize possible paths into some yet unknown domain, simply will not do.

While attempting to incorporate certain of the insights of post-modernism without surrendering to its 'nihilistic excesses', Corbridge with his post-Marxism and Edwards who links development theory and praxis, go some way towards providing a viable theoretical alternative. Meanwhile, in a different vein, Peet offers a reconstituted Marxism with the flowering of a new critical political economy focusing upon transforming social relations, expressed in the politics of class, gender, interregional alliances, and local social movements, to 'make "science" serve the interests of the oppressed', 'empower', or 'put the last first'.[9] Noble and arguably necessary objectives indeed, but a perspective whose explanatory power and options for policy are limited by its universalism.

Development studies must, rather, confront the post-modern void by striving to be systematic about diversity and locale without falling into glorified empiricism. Small-scale studies can suggest wider trends in regional development which affect social and institutional structures in similar ways while the precise morphology of local growth or decline may vary. The reorientation proposed here then, begins with a profound understanding of the place where change occurs – the arena of development and all its geographies. Among the conceptual gymnastics and often tortuous prose of the 'neo-resurgent-post-impasse-ist-isms' are elements that will constitute part of a new theoretical and analytical framework for understanding the spatial economic transformation of the lower Yangzi delta and provide the basis for establishing meaningful policy priorities.

It is possible to trace three overlapping emphases in the geography of development literature. The first is the focus of orthodox studies on macro-level issues as the predominant parameters of national and subnational patterns of change. The second is the unabashed focus of traditional regional geography upon deeply empirical locality studies, and experienced development practitioners who condone such work as the basis for theoretical generalizations. More recently, under the rubric of more sensitive post-Marxist, neo-liberal, critical political economy, or post-modern theories, the focus has shifted to include examination of how macro-scale forces articulate with place-specific, generally small-scale local circumstances.

This third phase has enhanced our sensitivity to historically and geographically grounded variation in national and subnational development characteristics. Moreover, many have pointed towards a theoretical framework that links the various analytical levels as a means of highlighting the roles of all relevant actors.[10] This framework usually takes endogenous place-specific circumstances as agents that condition the local articulation of external or exogenous forces. This is an improvement on the conventional view that local characteristics of development are considered to be internally generated, self-sustaining, and independent.[11] However, endogenous forces are seen as important only in terms of their 'interplay' with exogenous forces and how this leads to regional variation. Or put another way, local characteristics play a role only in channelling the articulation of external forces. While recognizing the importance of local factors, macro-scale forces still serve as the dominant theoretical point of reference. This fact is most explicit in the work of Brown who refers to the 'imprint of development' on to the landscape as largely driven by external forces and that the impact of local factors 'which might produce self-sustaining, internally generated, autonomous growth is, by comparison, negligible'.[12]

If, as this study proposes, patterns of regional development in China are largely determined and driven by local forces, then a simple blending of analytical scales which retains its emphasis on global, exogenous or city-linked factors is inadequate. I am proposing here that in order to explain the transformation occurring in the lower Yangzi delta it is necessary to move further still towards a theoretical framework which accounts for the greater importance of local factors.[13] The shift in emphasis suggested here is a subtle, but important one. It moves beyond the confines of established epistemologies to embrace an approach that considers the totality of local circumstances of development relative to, but not defined by, exogenous forces. Thus, while '[g]eneralization remains the objective ... it needs to emanate from, rather than be imposed on, the locale being studied'.[14]

My intention is not to dismiss any of the existing theoretical frameworks, which are able to account for particular elements of regional change, but to introduce a further perspective which can explain persistent patterns that do not fit the conventional expectations. While relational patterns associated with these conventional expectations may be observed, especially notions of core-periphery (urban–rural) and urban industrial agglomeration, characteristics of the transformation occurring in the lower Yangzi delta suggest, on the other hand, the need for analysis that reveals much more about the underlying processes driving regional development. This calls for a sense of place that transcends conventional measures of relationships by recognizing that their meaning varies in different contexts, urging a research protocol that questions these relationships rather than accepting them at face value.[15] As part of this reorientation it is necessary to reexamine the nature of linkages between 'rural' and 'urban' (core-periphery relations).[16]

Linkages and the transactional revolution

In spite of the voluminous geographical literature on rural–urban migration, much less has been published on the wider interactions and linkages between rural and urban in developing countries.[17] Instead most research concentrated on analyses of rural and urban development as separate issues.[18] However, publication of Michael Lipton's famous book *Why Poor People Stay Poor* in 1977 initiated a debate surrounding the assertion of urban bias which began to focus research on issues of rural–urban linkages.[19] Subsequent work by Rondinelli and Stohr and Taylor among others, which makes reference to the position adopted by Lipton or his opponents, has provided a range of theoretical standpoints from which to view rural–urban interaction.[20]

While the ensuing debate revolved around rural–urban linkages relatively few of the detailed analyses of town and country relationships shed light on important theoretical and policy questions.[21] Within specific regional historical circumstances for example, theoretical clarification is needed to highlight the precise form and impact of the processes and mechanisms of rural–urban interactions. Moreover, regional and national policy and planning strategies (which implicitly involve settlement systems) often proceed as if it is quite clear as to the nature of the circumstances under which rural–urban linkages will influence the development process.[22] Even more fundamental, however, is the need to carefully reconsider the theoretical significance of the implied rural–urban divide.

Challenging town and country as distinct spatial and conceptual categories highlights several important issues. By reducing complex socioeconomic relations over space to a simple dichotomy, the rural–urban divide is elevated to the level of a major explanatory variable. The resulting squabbles usually revolve around definitions of urban and rural characteristics which attempt to demarcate the two categories. The rationale for examining rural–urban relations does not lie in seeking some 'new found general explanandum', but rather in the fact that the rural–urban dimension is an important component of the wider spatial economic transformation.[23] Yet there remains a nagging sense that this approach begins with the assumption that processes of regional transformation extend *from* the city *into* the countryside.[24] This study will, on the other hand, emphasize a view from the fringe that is less willing to assume that this transformation results primarily from the urban penetration and encapsulation of the countryside into new social and economic circuits largely controlled by or through large cities.[25]

While geographers have set out in clear terms the main categories of interactions between rural and urban, focusing on the identification and measurement of linkages and flows is often difficult, and in any case, addresses only part of a very complex picture. It is necessary to adopt an approach which relies less on the distinction between rural and urban, focusing instead upon the conditions which create such interactions and the circumstances within which they exist. The notion of a 'transactional environment' is introduced here to capture this broader perspective. 'Transactional' refers to the now standard framework of interactions and interrelationships initially proposed by Preston and elaborated upon by Rondinelli and Unwin: migration; flows of goods, services, energy and technological and social information; financial transfers and the transfer of capital in other forms; and other transactional activities.[26] 'Environment' refers to overlapping structural, organizational, and social relationships and interdependencies including: political and administrative imperatives and hierarchies; legal and regulatory frameworks; patterns of jurisdiction, decision-making and power; socio-economic exigencies and opportunities, and all their various transactional networks. Taken together these elements comprise a transactional environment, the analysis of which can provide insights into the mechanisms and processes that underlie regional change.

Based on the theoretical discussions so far, and preliminary glimpses of the spatial economic transformation in China's lower Yangzi delta, it is now possible to more clearly highlight three interrelated themes which delineate the research agenda for this study: deeper analysis of the role of locality; elaboration and analysis of institutional parameters; and careful consideration of the geography of production.

A new geography of production: making space for place

Although 'locality' can refer to areas clearly urban or rural in the conventional sense, the term is used here to include processes and mechanisms occurring in areas conceptually (functionally and spatially) between the two. For some elements it refers to village or township levels, for others it includes county level or regional-scale (lower Yangzi delta) circumstances. Conventional geographical analyses of regional restructuring and the concomitant patterns of settlement transition soon confront two characteristics of the lower Yangzi delta: the fact that highly productive agricultural areas also contain significant non-agricultural production activities; and 'rural hinterlands' that are equally important as providers of goods and services to central places, as well as markets for the goods and services from those central places. Theoretical and policy endeavours which place a high priority on urban dispersal, decentralization or deconcentration, usually investigated and implemented from urban centres, either overlook or underemphasize articulation with local elements of territorially based development. The objective here is to provide an analytical and theoretical middle-ground which legitimizes locale.

One set of arguments in the development debate revolves around how processes of urbanization or rural change liberate, constrain, or otherwise influence each other. What has unfolded along another path is a set of arguments that 'transcend' rural–urban relations – most notably class and politics.[27] Here I must echo criticisms from Corbridge who correctly points out that construction of a simple political economy with a reductionist concept of politics that concentrates on issues of class (urban, rural, or otherwise), cannot readily explicate complex individual or institutional political and organizational allegiances.[28] Instead, I wish to shift the focus to an examination of the structure and function of local and regional institutional frameworks. The objective is to develop at once more refined and more dynamic ways of thinking about organizational forms and functions which will enable us to discern the patterns of socio-political and economic relationships as they impact upon regional change. This suggests a theoretical framework that emphasizes analysis of process as part of the effort to trace mutually conditioning interactions between state and society in the Chinese space economy. Furthermore, it points towards a methodology by which the finest details of institutional structure, roles, and capacities are repeatedly juxtaposed with larger patterns and trends.[29]

Analysis of the functional dynamics of institutional parameters, and the transactional relations and social networks that create and drive circulation, needs to be merged with an examination of territorial practices, including enterprise strategies, to understand local and regional level industrial development. The proliferation of industrial activity in the lower Yangzi delta, insinuating itself as it has into all corners of the rural landscape, can be explained neither by abstract generalizations nor by mere empiricist micro-level descriptions. Issues of industrialization, and industrial location, provide a forum for building an analytical framework for understanding the geography of economic development, and the structures, processes, and mechanisms, shaped in part by their geography, which underlie such development.[30] While geographers have traditionally focused on the economic dimensions of spatial relations, the virtue of considering issues of industrial location in the context of development theory is that it broadens the emphasis on productive activities to encompass processes by which industrial production is established and modified in regions.

However, as Storper and Walker have shown, issues of industrial location have not figured prominently in theories of economic development.[31] Reasons for this can be traced through the critiques of traditional location theory and its roots in neoclassical economics, the radical reorientation in theories of uneven development and the enormous literature on empirical and locality studies that largely eschewed theory altogether. The original critiques focused on firm-centred, ahistorical theories which assumed tendencies towards economic equilibrium and treated space as an adjunct to economic relationships.[32] Radical alternatives involved exploration of structural forces and processes that sought connections between society and space to explain the large-scale patterns and geographies of uneven development.[33] Lastly, Smith has highlighted how the specifics of restructuring have induced detailed empirical studies of particular sectors and industries (especially high-tech), and analyses of individual localities 'conceived in the belief that much of the earlier theory involved little knowledge of grassroots changes [and attempted] to generate a place-specific empirical matrix of social, economic, cultural, and political change'.[34]

The inability of specific local experiences to inform general theory spawned the search for a middle level industrial geography that could provide a bridge between the two. The first significant contribution came from Doreen Massey who proposed a new theory of location based on the notion of spatial divisions of labour and which focused on organizational structure and the peculiarities of place.[35] Massey's recognition of the uniqueness of place, and how this emerges in relation to the formation of spatial structures of production, accommodates variation in the way in which economic activity incorporates and contributes to geographical inequality. The layering of successive 'rounds of investment' over a multitude of spatial structures is combined with the pre-existing nature of places each of which entails differing relations within the space economy. This necessarily requires consideration of cultural, political, and ideological 'strata' (with all their local specificities) in addition to layers of economic history. A geological metaphor is most often invoked to schematize Massey's analysis.[36] This popular, if misleading, representation conceals the key insights of her work: that localities do not merely reflect external processes, but in fact absorb, translate, and reproduce national and global impulses towards restructuring in different ways. 'The uniqueness of place and the constantly evolving and shifting systems of interdependence are two sides of the same coin.'[37]

Massey's approach has been criticized by many who claim she failed to bridge theoretical and empirical investigations of spatial economic restructuring.[38] While sensitive to the complexity and detail of specific industries and places, this greater concern with locational difference is most often preceded in practice by a jettisoning of theoretical frameworks that would allow greater comprehension of geographical restructuring.[39] I am less disposed to this critique than to the fact that Massey does not adequately address the way in which local circumstances articulate with the local and regional space economy. It is one thing to recognize the importance and uniqueness of place in the geography of production; however, Massey's approach, deeply rooted in what Gregory calls 'the totalizing discourse of a thoroughly modern Marxism', continues to subordinate local circumstances to the impulse of external forces of change.[40]

While Massey's work provides the foundation for a new critical regional geography others have instead focused on perspectives of capitalist production and economic theory to inform industrial location and processes of industrial development over space. This view is most clearly represented in the work of Scott, Storper and Walker, and various combinations thereof. This so-called 'new industrial geography' aimed not only to explain specific patterns and processes of industrial change, but also to explore how capitalist production is structured by space in addition to how capital constructs space.[41] What makes it new is theorization of the mediating processes of the organization of industrial production seen most often as a consequence of the technical and social divisions of labour in industry.[42] Walker builds on these notions by proposing a unified approach to industrial location that simultaneously considers such issues as enterprise location, economies of agglomeration, systems of cities and towns and analysis of linkages, and which treats geography as integral to the matter of organization.[43]

The essence of these arguments can be distilled down to a set of theoretical tools involving three interconnected dimensions of industrialization and regional development: their underlying institutional parameters; the mechanisms and processes of their evolution; and their geographical foundations and territorial specificity.[44] This framework accepts that political, economic and social processes are largely determined by the ways in which they are embedded in place and social relations. Much of this work, however, willingly adopts social theory at the expense of economic theory.[45] Walker, in his (premature) eulogy for the geography of enterprise for example, emphasizes an approach to 'geographical industrialization' derived from analysis of the social relations of production.[46] While justifiably critical of concepts such as cumulative causation and the new international division of labour that do not fully account for the disequilibrating forces unleashed by capitalist industrialization, Walker has glossed over important insights to be accrued from an analysis of the enterprise dimension.

I am not arguing for a separate geography of enterprise. What is needed, however, is recognition of the role enterprises play in the processes which determine how complex production systems are organized over time and space.[47] Enterprise location and organization in the lower Yangzi delta occurs within a dense web of administrative power and influence tied to particular places and articulated through complex networks of institutional and transactional relationships. Furthermore, as I will contend later, rather than emerging as a result of new or evolving social relations of production over time and space, the proliferation of industrial development in the delta is largely the result of a recapturing of former transactional networks – the shapes (morphology) are new, but the patterns have existed in one form or another since at least the late imperial period.

Geography contributes usefully to concepts in social theory by considering seriously the way in which space and place intersect with industrialization and social life. This seems quite reasonable if we accept an industrial politics of place 'in which real actions in real places produce history' and, as claimed earlier, the global is a product of the particular.[48] Problems arise with this new industrial geography, however, when the analysis is applied to overlapping issues of urbanization, agglomeration economies, the city and regional development. I do, of course, accept the view that the city, in terms of its agglomeration economies, emerges as a productive context in its own right, but Walker, among others, takes this further. Capitalist organization is constituted in and through spatial relations and cannot exist without cities. Thus, since industrialization is fundamentally linked to capitalism, industrialization without cities is 'ridiculous'.[49] Scott is even more explicit when he claims that industrialization and urbanization are inextricably linked.[50] The line in the sand is clearly drawn!

These authors, and others discussed below who work specifically on China, suggest that 'urban areas are the heart and soul of regional economic development'.[51] They all lay claim to the central role of external economies and agglomeration in the formation of industrial complexes within cities and across regions. While this may be appropriate for Pred's early nineteenth-century New York, Cronon's early twentieth-century Chicago, Scott's late twentieth-century Los Angeles, or Massey's restructuring British Midlands, all 'incubated in the heat and light of capitalist transition', even Walker concedes such a synthesized analysis cannot capture the 'often quite unexpected manner by which actual organizational ensembles evolve'.[52] Touché! Allusions to 'conjectural circumstances' pervade the voluminous geography of production literature and point up a lack of theoretical certitude about what makes regional development happen.[53]

The authors briefly reviewed here argue effectively for a theory of industrial location and regional change that can cope with the expansion, instability and disparities that characterize the geography of capitalist industrialization. Especially valid is the emphasis upon the imbrication of spatial relations and place in the fabric of the industrialization process in which general forces and locational specifics are mutually considered. The conceptual framework breaks down, however, and is unable to provide the necessary analytical insights, in the explicit assumption that the broader large-scale general forces fundamentally underlie specific local outcomes. Since national and global forces are most clearly articulated within and through large cities then, according to the internal logic of these theories, large cities are the necessarily dominant nodes driving regional transformation. Applied to China, this approach links regional economic restructuring inextricably to large cities by arguing, among other things, that rural industrial development is incapable of taking place independently or of being self-generated.[54]

Intersecting with this logic is another dimension of these theoretical investigations concerning the dispersal and vertical disintegration of production embodied in the post-Fordist, flexible accumulation literature. In a delightfully pompous rhetorical exchange Lovering criticizes Scott's theory of flexible accumulation as deterministic and economistic because it neglects particular local contingencies of industrial restructuring. Scott replies that Lovering's emphasis on the multidimensional complexity of production organization is indeterminate since it provides no meaningful analytical specifications.[55] Reference to this debate is useful in highlighting the inability of theories of industrial organization and location to adequately conceptualize the transactional environment. Conventional views of the transactional structure of a production system which focus on transaction costs tend to ignore the local institutional context and the detailed character of enterprises.[56] Furthermore, as Phelps has demonstrated, the transactional activities of industrial enterprises are as important as their production activities.[57] In a superb study of subcontracting linkages in Guangdong's Pearl River delta, C. K. Leung refers specifically to the need for a comprehensive examination of the transactional environment.[58] Leung's work is relevant to this study because of the way he combines analysis of micro-scale decision patterns of enterprises, their institutional and transactional contexts and place-specific socio-cultural, political, economic and historical peculiarities to explain the patterns and processes of regional economic development.

The conventional political economic approach, explicitly grounded in Marxism, adopts the view that regional change is the result of a set of necessary social relations of production. What makes the regional geography proposed in this study different is that it accepts not only that these relations are constructed over space, but that they are also largely determined by, and embedded within the unique intersection of circumstances which constitute place. This is most clearly demonstrated in the spatial proliferation of industrial activity in the lower Yangzi delta. The now widely accepted view that places have specific local characteristics that influence industrial location, however, does not fully explain the spatial economic transformation observed in the delta. Why, for example, was there not the same intensity of industrial activity around Nanjing as there was near other large cities in the delta (see Chapter 3)? Moreover, it is striking that the lower Yangzi delta can largely retain its prominence in a national context as the nation's premier agricultural producer region, while at the same time successfully industrializing. It would seem there are aspects of the transactional environment not fully captured in the conventional explanations of the dynamics of regional industrial expansion.

Cities, towns and rural transformation: the Chinese development debate

As part of the effort to theorize regional change in China it is essential that some attempt be made to review the perceptions and insights of indigenous scholarship. I will not endeavour here, however, to provide a detailed description of the historical patterns of urban and regional development in China. Nor will I attempt to summarize the ideological and policy priorities that have influenced patterns and processes in the Chinese space economy. Excellent reviews of these issues, and of the evolution of the associated scholarship, both inside and outside China, have already been published.[59] Rather, the objective here is to highlight certain elements from the Chinese literature that move us towards a theoretical framework for understanding spatial economic transformation in the lower Yangzi delta. These elements will be traced through a review of the large-city versus small-town debate, studies of the relationship between agriculture and industrial growth, research on rural industrialization and more general theories of urban and regional development. While discussion of these issues is readily accessible in widely circulated national and regional geographical journals and books, much important scholarship is available only as special reports or papers prepared for meetings or government bureaux, with limited often internal (*neibu*) or restricted circulation.

It is important to note at the outset that Chinese urbanization and regional development theories and practice, at least until the late 1970s, were fundamentally linked to the shifting politics and ideologies of the planned economy. That is not to say there was no debate, but it could only occur within a clearly delineated set of parameters most often characterized by the apparent theme of a pro-rural anti-urbanism and geo-strategic imperatives. Economic geographers concentrated on producing detailed regional resource inventories and politically safe territorial planning and management schemes serving centrally determined economic planning priorities. By the early 1980s, there was a significant theoretical revival under way as geographers faced the planning and policy challenges of newly introduced economic reforms. Several writers identified the need for a revitalized regional geography as the foundation for conceptualizing the spatial economic restructuring that had been unleashed in the late 1970s and was in full swing by the mid-1980s.[60] However, this scholarship did not really take on any theoretical significance until the emergence of the large-city versus small-towns in regional development debate which, for the first time, focused attention on the underlying dynamics of geographical processes of development.

Reduced to its simplest form the debate examined whether growth strategies should promote development of rural townships and small cities or allow the growth and development of large cities and metropolitan areas. On one side of the issue were proponents of small cities, towns, and even villages which they believe had been undersupported, thus failing to develop rationally into a larger hierarchy of settlements.[61] As with many such issues in China the essence of the approach was captured in a new slogan: 'Strictly control the development of large cities, rationally develop medium-sized cities, and vigorously promote the development of small cities and towns' (*yange kongzhi dachengshi, heli fazhan zhongdeng chengshi, jiji jianshe xiaochengzhen*).[62] In practice, it was believed, small towns could be developed much less expensively serving as nodes of regional industrial development. By the mid-1980s this notion of a Chinese road to regional development, distinguished by its small town bias, was being increasingly challenged by outspoken supporters of large city and metropolitan growth strategies.[63] While being careful not to dismiss the continuing ideological suspicion of large urban areas this new perspective chose to highlight the inevitability and advantages of metropolitan growth. Cities would be allowed to grow based on investments that proponents believed would improve economies of scale and increase industrial efficiency.[64] Implicit in this strategy was the increased mobility of labour and migration of rural people into large and medium sized cities. Coinciding with this perspective was the renewal of satellite-city policies to relieve population pressure and industrial concentration in core urban districts, and the notion of 'key-point cities' (*zhongdian chengshi*) which aimed to systematize preferential access to resources and to increase autonomy in urban decision making.[65]

Many geographers reacted to the official emphasis on small towns by invoking a crude stages theory of regional economic development.[66] The key economic characteristics of the majority of small towns in China in the early 1980s were seen as unambiguously agricultural, placing them at the lowest stage of development. The underlying weakness of the economic base would, therefore, preclude any efforts to promote local industrial development. The line of argument continued by claiming that urbanization and national economic development were inextricably linked.[67] The regional development envisaged would first see a greater concentration of population and industrial activity in large urban centres. New forms of 'dispersed urbanization' proposed by the small town lobby, often linked by critics to the slavish duplication of the policies of advanced capitalist countries, would mean skipping a necessary stage of development and were regarded as financially unviable. Moreover, investment in urban-style infrastructure in the myriad of smaller settlements would constrain the capital accumulation necessary for improving productivity in large and medium sized cities. While this work was highly critical of the official emphasis on smaller communities it fell short of openly advocating expansion of urban populations and failed to provide alternatives to the problems of surplus rural labour.

Evidence from regional economic restructuring and the conceptual hostility of the pro-urban advocates did, however, stimulate deepening theoretical interest in the processes of urbanization and regional industrial development moving beyond the slogans and platitudes extolling the virtues of small towns. By the late 1980s Chinese academics and bureaucrats were openly reappraising the impact of post-1949 policies towards urbanization and economic development. Investment in urban infrastructure had generally been considered as unproductive and came to lag seriously behind industrial development. The advantages of scale economies were quickly counteracted by severe structural inefficiencies which emerged in what one study called premature diseconomies of scale.[68] Some have also highlighted how decades of artificially separating rural and urban, administratively, socially and economically led to a disjunction between processes of regional development and urban based industrial structures. This (en)forced dualism defied the 'organic connection' between city and countryside and contributed to an industrialization 'divorced' from urbanization characterized in particular by a large number of rural townships that were able to compete effectively with large cities in terms of infrastructure.[69]

In a similar view, urban geographers in particular have demonstrated how the concentration on production without seriously considering issues of consumption has led to an underdeveloped tertiary sector.[70] Since links between industrial production and markets were largely determined artificially under the planned economy, the emergence of an urban based tertiary sector, still in its infancy and unable to adequately cope with the demands of recent reforms, left room for small cities and towns to develop their own organizations and structures. In the context of an underdeveloped hierarchy of settlements this fact is expressed, especially in more developed regions, by the proliferation of community based industrial organizations and local economic development zones that constitute part of a locally developed production complex. Weaknesses in the regional industrial structure were also identified that pointed to the artificial separation between industry and primary activities in agriculture and the production of raw materials, and the limited capacity to utilize labour efficiently.[71] Urbanization was said to lag behind growth of industry as the rate of transfer of agricultural labour and population into non-agricultural employment and urban settlements was lower than the rate of growth of non-agricultural output value.[72] While the big-city versus small-town debate elicited much rhetoric and extreme positions it did point up a further set of theoretical considerations worth highlighting. A great deal of literature examined the relationship between agriculture and industry and there was a new emphasis on the study of industrial location and the geography of enterprise.

Much has been written by Chinese scholars that considers the underlying connections between the agricultural sector and industrial development. Some have focused on the declining proportion of gross domestic product from agriculture as a means of tracing empirically the nation's overall economic development.[73] This work is often linked to the perceived idiosyncrasies of urban industrial development. Others have instead examined the evolving relationship between accumulation in agriculture and regional industrial investment.[74] This relationship is most often articulated as a set of five phases along a continuum:

1 'Agriculture supports industry' (*yinong bu gong*);
2 'Agriculture and industry nourish each other' (*nonggong hubu*);
3 'A shift to industry nourishing agriculture' (*gongyi fanbu*);
4 'Industry supports agriculture' (*yigong bu nong*); and
5 'Industry builds agriculture' (*yigong jian nong*).

Once again a complex set of interactions is captured in rhyming slogans. While still based on a set of empirically determined indices this work improves on what went before by attempting to conceptualize the role of capital accumulation and structural shifts in the sectoral distribution of labour. It also makes frequent reference to how such issues are related to specific local circumstances of ownership and management of enterprises and the economic development imperatives of community governments.[75]

In a parallel body of literature, geographers have examined how agricultural restructuring has affected patterns and processes in the regional space economy focusing particularly on the dramatic expansion of township and village industries. The relationship between agriculture and this sort of rural industrialization has been theorized in the context of at least four interrelated elements. First, gains in productivity brought about by diversification and commercialization of the agricultural economy have raised rural incomes and savings that have been exploited for local industrial investment.[76] Second, this coincided with the release of surplus agricultural labourers who, motivated by reforms to increase productivity to maximize personal gain, were available for off-farm employment.[77] Third, these elements in turn stimulated pent-up demand in the countryside for more manufactured goods, not only to supply the increasingly productive agricultural sector, but also increased local demand for consumer products.[78] Fourth, and the most important element conceptualized in my view, was the way in which agricultural restructuring revitalized the marketing and commercial functions of small towns.[79] Discussion of these elements is relevant for this study because of the way in which agriculture is fundamentally linked to industrial expansion and the development of villages and small towns. Historically too, the prosperity of agriculture in some regions, and the relatively high population densities it supported, was seen to foster the creation of numerous agricultural sidelines and off-farm activities which absorbed surplus labour and capital. This propensity for engaging in such activities led to a new social division of labour which underlies the prosperity of small towns and processes of rural industrialization.[80]

The significance of space and place in such conceptualizations is more obvious and less contrived than in the corpus of literature on advanced capitalist economies. In important ways the Chinese scholarship on these issues tended to exhibit greater sensitivity to the dynamics of local geographical circumstances when theorizing spatial economic transformation. The literature on the relationship between agricultural restructuring and industrial development has, for example, stimulated a reorientation towards more comprehensive studies of the regional space economy including, but not limited to, the transactional environment, institutional organizations and deep concerns about the deleterious impact on the rural landscape.[81] This reorientation is a response to the conventional separation of concepts of industrial location and the geography of production from the broader regional development and planning literature.

Industrial location scholarship in China has mirrored trends seen in Western theories, but continues to retain a largely quantitative focus.[82] In addition, several lengthy studies have appeared recently that catalogue in some detail development and reforms of China's industry.[83] In related work, Yang utilizes a modified theory of location to link issues of regional development and spatial economic change, moving beyond the classical factors of location approach of earlier studies.[84] Transformations and variations in regional industrial structure were being examined within a theoretical framework that formally considered space and place as they determined patterns in the spatial divisions of labour and the emergence of socio-economic organizations.[85] This latter focus on what I referred to earlier as institutional parameters, is particularly relevant since it is becoming an increasingly important element in theories of industrial location and models of regional economic development in China.[86]

The territorial structure of particular industrial sectors and the classification of industrial regions has also attracted much attention in the Chinese literature. Emphasis is most often placed upon understanding how industrial 'allocation' combines with the building of regional urban systems to provide a rational scale, structure and spatial pattern of development.[87] Similarly, much work has been done on special industrial parks and what the Chinese call 'special economic and technological development zones' (*jingji jishu kaifaqu*).[88] In most cases, quantitative models of industrial systems were constructed using variables of locational grouping, optimum size, and indices of inter-firm cooperation.[89] Still, this work highlights a growing recognition of how more detailed studies of the geography of enterprise can reveal important facets of spatial economic restructuring.[92] Fei, in two important papers, shows how little attention has been given to the way in which economic and administrative reforms have fundamentally changed enterprise behaviour, their 'spatial evolution' and implications for industrial location and regional economic development.[91] Ultimately, he suggests how understanding 'micro-mechanisms' and processes that determine enterprise location and growth provide insights into the evolution of 'macro-regional economic systems'.[92] Even old-school geographers, while still clinging to conventional notions of agglomeration and external economies, recognize that China's evolving industrial complexes are emerging 'organically' as the product of a multiplicity of small-scale local circumstances.[93] In terms of development praxis others identify the need to carefully consider local 'typicality' (*leixingxing*) – all the characteristics that determine internal mechanisms of change.[94]

This perspective is evident in discussions of the processes and mechanisms that underlie rural industrial development and the numerous models that have been constructed, based on particular local circumstances, to explain variations in rural change.[95] Furthermore, as we saw earlier, official policy pronouncements are embodied in catchy slogans: 'leave the land, but not the countryside' (*litu bulixiang*); and 'enter the factory, but not the city' (*jinchang bujincheng*). Fortunately, conceptual work on the rural transformation is more sophisticated. Most studies refer to certain ideological and historical preconditions for rural industrial development. While there have been many traumatic vacillations in policies affecting the countryside, the importance of rural non-agricultural activities, fostering demand for local production, and reducing rural–urban differences have remained relatively unchanged.[96] This is consistent with historical circumstances, especially in the more advanced agricultural regions, that underlie the emergence of rural industrial enterprises. Along with increased administrative autonomy are issues of ownership and the broadening mandate of community level governments to provide local social infrastructure and opportunities for employment. With the release of a 'great inner force' then, rural industrial development was neither unusual nor unexpected in the Chinese context.[97]

Theoretical work on rural industrialization has also provided an alternative perspective on the role of urban areas on regional development. Extended periods of highly productive agriculture and the intensity of the local transactional environment, have been at least as important in influencing the rural transformation as big cities.[98] Thus, despite the forced separation of rural and urban in China's planned economy, the intensity of development in the lower Yangzi delta has remained relatively high. Rural industry here is said to have extended the spatial division of labour within the countryside while at the same time linking rural areas to the wider division of labour.[99] The most important insight, however, is the way in which the development of rural industry has served as a catalyst for changes in the structure of local economic organizations and management.[100] Yet this theoretical perspective, which is useful in emphasizing the importance of local circumstances, is contradicted by numerous studies which directly linked the rural transformation to the proximity of big cities. Such research usually referred to evidence of urban–rural industrial linkages in the context of elegant regression analyses which established the direction and importance of the influence of large urban areas.[101]

Other work by Gu *et al.* who refer to the evolution of the 'urban fringe' in the context of the 'Chinese megalopolis' or from Zhou with his 'metropolitan interlocking regions', also links issues of regional development to processes of urbanization.[102] Thus, spatial economic patterns, and the mechanisms and evolution of regional development are conceptualized in terms of urban expansion or decentralization, converged urban systems, urban fringes and corridors or the extended metropolis.[103] While some have linked this urban theoretical bias to a retreat from the universal platitudes of egalitarian spatial planning in a partially reformed command economy context, I am more inclined to relate it to a kind of pragmatic orthodoxy deeply rooted in pre-reform methods for determining policy and planning priorities.[104] This is consistent with the view of some Chinese scholars who tend to emphasize macroeconomic regulation of regional economic growth with all the implications for control and management of large cities.[105]

The general pro-urban/pro-rural conceptual divide in Chinese theories of development has been challenged by scholars and bureaucrats who are seeking a middle-level framework that aims for better economic integration in the settlement hierarchy.[106] When such ideas were first broached in the mid-1980s big cities were taken as the 'nucleus' (*hexin*), medium sized cities as the 'link' (*niudai*) and rural small towns as the 'cell' (*xibao*).[107] As Kirkby pointed out, however, 'the actual mechanisms and divisions of economic and political responsibility necessary to the workings of such a system are left unstated'.[108] Conceptually speaking though, there have been some excellent studies over the last few years that have fleshed out notions of a theoretical middle ground and which hint at a path through the apparent impasse. These are introduced and developed in the next section.

Rural and urban in China's regional development: seeking a middle ground

The need for a new theoretical middle ground is underscored by the inability of current policy and planning strategies to respond effectively to a rapidly evolving space economy. Lin *et al.* refer to the dramatic impact of development in highly productive agricultural regions, while Miao highlights the problems of coordinating urban and rural industries.[109] Others have focused on the 'fusion' between town and country and issues of urbanization in economic development that illustrate how conventional theoretical frameworks cannot account for certain elements of regional change.[110] The mechanisms and processes which underlie this change have been viewed in terms of a 'rural urbanization' (*xiangcun chengshihua* or sometimes *nongcun chengzhenhua*) that attempts to accommodate characteristics not commonly identified in the conventional models.[111] Chief among these are the ownership and management structures of rural enterprises, and the community level motivation and means for establishing such enterprises. These features are also linked to the geographical and historical circumstances of local development.

Moreover, rather than emphasizing the role of big cities, this work tends to examine the importance of linkages between the countryside and cities and towns from a rural perspective. Some have even speculated that it is the intensity of the rural transformation that has in fact stimulated many of the urban state-run industrial reforms.[112] At the core of this perspective is recognition of a regional countryside and town system exhibiting a 'unified', 'integrated', or 'organic' spatial economic development.[113] Empirical evidence from the lower Yangzi delta discussed in the following chapters suggests it is neither clearly rural nor urban in character and it is certainly not urban initiated and driven. Several Chinese scholars and bureaucrats have conceptualized the processes of this spatial economic restructuring in the term *chengxiang yitihua* – literally translated as 'city-countryside integration'.[114] However, the deeper meaning implies an organic whole – a kind of ecosystem approach (or rural–urban symbiosis) in which there is a transformation of the countryside through the opening up and linking of smaller cities and towns to the surrounding regions.

Although *chengxiang yitihua* is sometimes associated with the specificities of rural–urban economic and or commercial linkages, I invoke its underlying meaning as a platform for building a theoretical middle ground. Interestingly, few Chinese studies have attempted to merge the processes conceptualized with the array of empirical findings that have identified key socio-spatial features of China's rural transformation. One notable exception was an internally published report from the Department of Geography at Nanjing Normal University.[115] The authors developed a schematic to indicate the relationship between several key features in the development of rural urbanization in the lower Yangzi delta (see Figure 2.1). Ignoring for the moment that the model overlooks certain elements such as the reproduction of capital and institutional parameters, it also

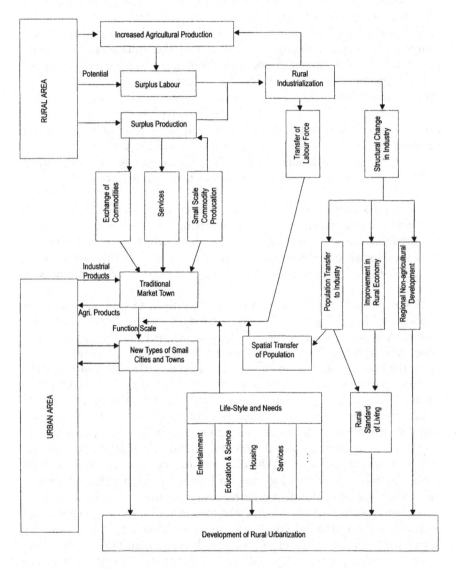

Figure 2.1 Rural industrialization and the development of rural urbanization.
Source: Human Geography Research Office, 1990, p. 59.

fails to elaborate upon the geographical processes which underlie the features illustrated. While the urban–rural distinction is once again emphasized the conceptual and morphological character of rural urbanization remains unclear. The model does, however, give some sense of how the features shown relate to each other and provides a useful preliminary framework for understanding regional development in the delta.

While many of the dimensions of this development are set in regional or national urban centres or even abroad, many local phenomena have an impact at these larger scales. Furthermore, understanding the complexity of the interactions between the local and extra-local is crucial to realistic analysis. Only by examining the structure of this transactional environment and its institutional framework from a local perspective can we begin to challenge the inexorability of the transition to conventional urban forms and the (imminent) demise of rural organization. This approach is largely inspired by the work of Koppel who highlights the processes of rural transformation to provide an analytical alternative to the prevailing rural–urban dichotomies.[116] Thus, interrelationships and linkages in a restructuring space economy are recognized as having an independent reality and are perceived neither as derivations nor reflections, but

> as representative and indicative of independent social [and spatial] facts – taking form, evolving, and varying for reasons attributable to urbanization and rural development; [and which take into account] other social, economic, and political processes ... that are idiosyncratic to the linkages in specific cultural and historical circumstances.[117]

McGee provides empirical and conceptual depth to this perspective by explicating the emergence of 'new regions of extended urban activity' surrounding large cities in Asia.[118] As with Koppel this viewpoint is less concerned with the distinction between rural and urban, focusing instead upon the transactional environment as it affects settlement and the emergence of particular regions of economic activity. Referred to as 'extended metropolitan regions' or 'mega-urban regions', they usually incorporate large urban cores with well developed transportation links, peri-urban zones surrounding cities which are within a daily commute, and densely populated rural areas of mixed agricultural and non-agricultural activities called *desakota* regions.[119] These latter regions are characterized by processes that include rapid growth in labour intensive industry, services and other non-agricultural activities, and an intense highly transactive environment especially in terms of the movement of people, commodities and information. The resulting patterns of development that distinguish urban from rural are, therefore, more difficult to delineate.

The middle ground proposed here consists of several overlapping elements. The first begins by rejecting the conceptual baggage associated with conventional notions of urban and rural. Mounting evidence of the existence of socio-economic patterns and processes which are, conceptually and spatially, between the two forces reconsideration of such notions. The second refers to the need for a middle level geography of production that balances broader theories of location and the production of industrial space with local experiences and circumstances. This can be achieved by considering the activities of industrial enterprises in their institutional and transactive contexts. The third requires closer examination of local level forces in relation to, but not ancillary to, global and national exogenous (usually urban centred) influences. I will unabashedly privilege the local in this part of the analysis to counter the prevailing focus on large scale issues and theoretical frameworks which have usurped much of the intellectual inquiry. The fourth element aims for a middle ground between theory and praxis which can provide a framework for meaningful analysis and a basis for planning and policy strategies for the management of China's mega-urban regions.

Mega-urbanization in the lower Yangzi delta: enterprise location and the reconstitution of local space

Three main assertions arise from the preceding theoretical analysis. First, the patterns and underlying processes and mechanisms of regional development in the lower Yangzi delta are fundamentally linked to intensely localized characteristics and circumstances within the wider Chinese space economy. Second, industrialization and the morphology of spatial economic restructuring in the delta are best understood and explained in terms of the complex interactions and interrelationships which constitute the transactional environment. Third, external economies, the dynamics of agglomeration, and the role of large cities and other exogenous forces, while important, are apparently less significant in determining the precise character of local and regional transformation in the delta than are endogenous forces.

Understanding spatial economic transformation in the delta requires transcending the conventional wisdom of urban and regional development and the *de jure* organizational frameworks which institutionalize such concepts. While cities are commonly viewed as the nexus of growth and linkages to the outside world, regional development in the lower Yangzi delta appears to be more complex than merely in terms of its purported dependence upon urban centred external forces. The critical parameters and the vitality of regional development in the delta were in fact centred within the multitude of localities, making large cities relatively less important. Moreover, while the primacy of agricultural activities (especially in terms of basic food production) has not diminished, new roles in industrial production and other non-agricultural activities have emerged that create new locally specific opportunities for accumulation making rural areas the foci for socio-economic and institutional transformation.

Elements of this rural transformation are illustrated in Figure 2.2 which incorporates the three main assertions described above into an alternative conceptual framework characterized as mega-urbanization. The objective here is to capture the complex interactions and interrelationships between

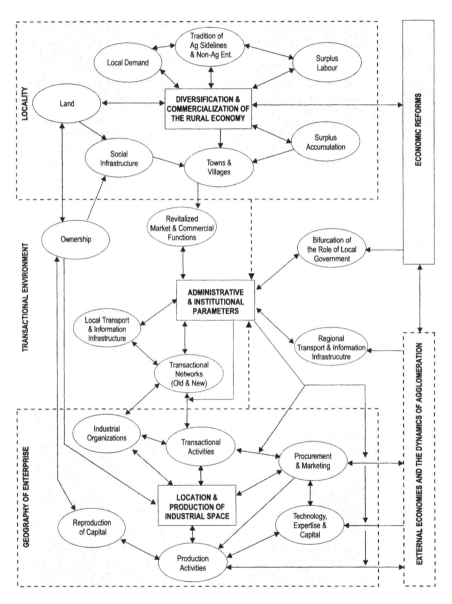

Figure 2.2 Post-reform rural transformation and mega-urbanization in China's lower Yangzi delta.

Note Ag = Agricultural

economic development and the form, nature, and organization of production in the lower Yangzi delta.

The framework is situated on a meso-scale level of abstraction between concrete local factors affecting the location of enterprises and the production of industrial space, including locality and the transactional environment, and macro-scale economic reforms, external economies and the dynamics of agglomeration. Clearly, however, I have chosen to emphasize small-scale micro-factors and their administrative and institutional parameters, which largely determine the character of the rural transformation. While the diagram is divided into five main components for discussion and explanation, it is important to consider this conceptual framework in its entirety. At its core, embedded within the transactional environment, are the fundamental elements which link locality and the geography of enterprise. Thus, the key features of diversification and commercialization of highly productive agriculture and the location of industrial enterprises are linked by locally determined administrative and institutional parameters, and via revitalized local marketing and commercial functions and various transactional networks. These are mediated through towns and villages and the transactional activities of enterprises. This set of central processes (organized vertically in the centre of the model) link the historical and socio-cultural circumstances of locality to the production activities of contemporary industrial enterprises.

In the top part of the diagram the transformation of agriculture, stimulated by the economic reforms introduced in Chapter 1 and which are discussed in more detail in subsequent chapters, has led to the emergence of other local factors in the context of the place in which change occurs. These are manifest in and influenced by space, especially through issues of ownership (as part of the transactional environment) and the control of land, which are fundamentally linked to the location and production of industrial space. This brings us to the lower part of the diagram. While production activities are partly responsible for the reproduction of capital, community level governments who own and manage enterprises largely through township and village collectives, are also able to influence the monetary practices of local banks, economic entities and individuals for the benefit of local production activities, and local transport, information and social infrastructure. Procurement and marketing, access to technology, expertise and capital, and production activities, while also linked to external economies partly as a result of 'open door' economic reforms, are profoundly mediated by locally determined administrative and institutional parameters.[120] The same is also true of externally inspired regional infrastructural development. The potential impact of local production activities upon the wider space economy and the emergence of industrial organizations, such as the large number of designated industrial areas and special economic and technological development zones are also taken into account.

The transactional environment is mediated through a number of formal and informal administrative and institutional parameters. These are linked to bifurcation of the role of local governments both as community administrators and as owners and managers of non-agricultural enterprises. Although this bifurcation has deep historical and contemporary roots, it is primarily the disengagement of the central government from local administration, that occurred with economic reforms, that has sharply enhanced the dual role of local governments. Within the transactional environment, processes of representation embedded in various administrative and institutional structures allow for the local mobilization of indigenous and external means of production. These locally determined representations manipulate the transactional network, sometimes creating new ones, in order to maximize community-based production opportunities. In the absence of a meaningful legal and regulatory framework localities are free to exploit all means at their disposal to achieve this objective. Local actors, often with apparently conflicting roles, exercise their influence through these intensely localized economic and bureaucratic structures. This helps to explain the intensity and diffuse nature of local transactional networks, within structures and across space, and accounts for the lesser importance of linkages with external economies and the dynamics of agglomeration.

Ultimately, however, I am less concerned with the simple unfolding of the social relations of production across space than with the means whereby local actors, through their transactional networks, construct industrial space by utilizing certain administrative and institutional structures. These transactional networks and institutional structures must be carefully analysed in order to understand and explain enterprise location and the reconstitution of local space in the lower Yangzi delta. The conceptual framework proposed here, provides a preliminary checklist of the main elements which underlie spatial economic restructuring in the lower Yangzi delta. It also serves to uncover, and then suggests methodologies to evaluate, the critical linkages between the underlying processes and mechanisms and the specific consequences of regional economic transformation in the delta. A detailed analysis of each of the key elements of this transformation is undertaken in the following chapters.

Notes

1. Douglass, M. (1995a) Viewpoint – bringing culture in: locality and global capitalism in East Asia. *Third World Planning Review* 17 (3), viii; McGee, T. G. (1995b) Geography and development: crisis commitment and renewal. *Cahiers de géographie du Québec* 39 (108); Massey, D. (1993b) Questions of locality. *Geography* 78 (2), 147.
2. Ettlinger, N. (1994) The localization of development in comparative perspective. *Economic Geography* 70 (2), 144.
3. Massey, D. (1993b) op. cit., p. 147.
4. Ibid.; Little, D. (1989) *Understanding Peasant China: Case Studies in the Philosophy of Social Science*. New Haven: Yale University Press, p. 25.

5. Peet, R. (1994) Review of 'Beyond the impasse: new directions in development theory.' *AAAG* 84 (2), 340.

6. Ibid., p. 341; Escobar, A. (1984–85) Discourse and power in development: Michel Foucault and the relevance of his work to the third world. *Alternatives* 10; Peet, R. and Watts, M. (1993) Introduction: development theory and environment in an age of market triumphalism. *Economic Geography* 69 (3); Watts, M. (1993) Development 1: power, knowledge, discursive practice. *PIHG* 17 (2).

7. See for example: Peet, R. (1993) Reason, space, modernity: The future of development geography. *Association of American Geographers Annual Meeting*, Atlanta. In a more recent, though distinctly non-Foucauldian critique, McGee highlights the 'considerable disillusionment' within the geography of development debates. He draws particular attention to the assumption that classical and Marxist theories of economic development would bring about the 'condition of "development"'. See: McGee, T. G. (1995b) op. cit., pp. 527–528.

8. Ibid.

9. Ibid., p. 8; Chambers, R. (1983) *Rural Development: Putting the Last First*. Harlow: Longman.

10. Schuurman, F. J. (Ed.) (1993a) *Beyond the Impasse: New Directions in Development Theory*. London: Zed.

11. Brown, L. A. (1988) Reflections on third world development: Ground level reality, exogenous forces, and conventional paradigms. *Economic Geography* 64 (3).

12. Ibid., pp. 267–268.

13. In the context of this study, unless otherwise stated, 'local' will always refer to small scale usually 'rural' areas and is meant to be distinguished from what I later call 'city driven' factors. This is necessary because of the now standard dualisms frequently assumed in the conventional models that I wish to challenge here.

14. Brown, L. A. (1988) op. cit., p. 263.

15. Ibid.

16. Notions of how urban and rural are defined and how this influences the theoretical frameworks for development are discussed later. As will become clear, the precise definitions are less important than underlying assumptions regarding how they relate to each other.

17. Notable exceptions include: Baker, J. and Pedersen, P. O. (Eds.) (1992) *The Rural–urban interface in Africa: Expansion and Adaption*. Uppsala: The Scandinavian Institute of African Studies; Cronon, W. (1991) *Nature's Metropolis: Chicago and the Great West*. New York: Norton; Funnell, D. C. (1988) Urban–rural linkages: Research themes and directions. *Geografiska Annaler* 70 B (2); Potter, R. B. and Unwin, T. (Eds.) (1989) *The Geography of Urban–rural interaction in Developing Countries*. London: Routledge.

18. Potter, R. B. and Unwin, T. (Eds.) (1989) op. cit., p. 11.

19. Lipton, M. (1977) *Why Poor People Stay Poor: A Study of Urban Bias in World Development*. London: Temple.

20. Rondinelli, D. A. (1983) *Secondary Cities in Developing Countries: Policies for Diffusing Urbanization*. Beverly Hills: Sage; Rondinelli, D. A. (1985) *Applied Methods of Regional Analysis: The Spatial Dimensions of Development Policy*. Boulder: Westview; Stohr, W. B. and Taylor, D. R. F. (Eds.) (1981) *Development from Above or Below? The Dialectics of Regional Planning in Developing Countries*. Chichester: Wiley.

21. Limited theoretical and policy insights are revealed in: Baker, J. and Pedersen, P. O. (Eds.) (1992) op. cit.; Potter, R. B. and Unwin, T. (Eds.) (1989) op. cit.

22. Funnell, D. C. (1988) op. cit., p. 273.

23. Ibid., p. 268.
24. For just two examples which discuss the situation in southern Jiangsu from this perspective see: Lee, Y. S. (1991) Rural non-agricultural development in an extended metropolitan region: The case of southern Jiangsu. In N. Ginsburg, B. Koppel and T. G. McGee (Eds.) *The Extended Metropolis: Settlement Transition in Asia*. Honolulu: University of Hawaii Press; Pannell, C. W. and Veeck, G. (1991) China's urbanization in an Asian context: Forces for metropolitanization. In N. Ginsburg, B. Koppel and T. G. McGee (Eds.) op. cit.
25. A la Harvey, D. (1985) *The Urbanization of Capital: Studies in the History and Theory of Capitalist Urbanization*. Oxford: Basil Blackwell; see also Funnell, D. C. (1988) op. cit.
26. Preston, D. (1975) Rural–urban and inter-settlement interaction: Theory and analytical structure. *Area* 7 (3); Rondinelli, D. A. (1983) op. cit.; Unwin, T. (1989) Urban–rural interaction in developing countries: A theoretical perspective. In Potter, R. B. and Unwin, T. (Eds.) op. cit.
27. Koppel, B. (1991) The rural–urban dichotomy reexamined: Beyond the ersatz debate? In N. Ginsburg, B. Koppel and T. G. McGee (Eds.) op. cit., p. 47.
28. Corbridge, S. (1982) Urban bias, rural bias, and industrialization: An appraisal of the works of Michael Lipton and Terry Byres. In J. Harris (Ed.) *Rural Development: Theories of Peasant Economy and Agrarian Change*. London: Hutchinson.
29. This approach is inspired by: Shue, V. (1988) *The Reach of the State: Sketches of the Chinese Body Politic*. Stanford: Stanford University Press; also see: Leung, C. K. (1993) Personal contacts, subcontracting linkages, and development in the Hong Kong – Zhujiang delta region. *AAAG* 83 (2), p. 297.
30. Storper, M. and Walker, R. (1989) *The Capitalist Imperative: Territory, Technology, and Industrial Growth*. New York: Basil Blackwell, p. 1.
31. Ibid.
32. Gregory, D. (1981) Alfred Weber and location theory. In D. R. Stoddart (Ed.) *Geography, Ideology and Social Concern*. Oxford: Basil Blackwell; Harvey, D. (1985) op. cit.; Massey, D. (1973) Towards a critique of industrial location theory. *Antipode* 5 (1); Sayer, A. (1985) Industry and space: a sympathetic critique of radical research. *Environment and Planning D: Society and Space* 3; Smith, N. (1989) Uneven development and location theory: Towards a synthesis. In R. Peet and N. Thrift (Eds.) *New Models in Geography: The Political-economy Perspective*. London: Unwin.
33. For an excellent summary see: Smith, N. (1989) op. cit., pp. 145–152.
34. Ibid., p. 155.
35. Massey, D. (1979) In what sense a regional problem? *Regional Studies* 13 (2); Massey, D. (1984) *Spatial Divisions of Labour: Social Structures and the Geography of Production*. New York: Methuen; See also Smith, N. (1989) op. cit.
36. Massey, D. (1993a) Classics in human geography revisited: 'Spatial divisions of labour', author's response. *PIHG* 17 (1).
37. Massey, D. (1984) op. cit., p. 120.
38. Martin, R. (1993) Classics in human geography revisited: 'Spatial divisions of labour', commentary 1. *PIHG* 17 (1); Sayer, A. (1985) op. cit.; Smith, N. (1989) op. cit.
39. Smith, N. (1989) op. cit., pp. 154–155.
40. Gregory, D. (1989) Areal differentiation and postmodern human geography. In D. Gregory and R. Walford (Eds.) *Horizons in Human Geography*. London: Macmillan.
41. Storper, M. (1987) The new industrial geography, 1985–1986. *Urban Geography* 8 (6), p. 593.

42. Scott, A. J. (1987) *Industrial Organization and Location: Division of Labour, the Firm, and Spatial Process.* Department of Geography, UCLA. Cited in Ibid., p. 588.
43. Walker, R. (1988) The geographical organization of production systems. *Environment and Planning D: Society and Space* 6 (3).
44. See especially: Sayer, A. and Walker, R. (1992) *The New Social Economy: Reworking the Division of Labour.* Cambridge: Blackwell; Scott, A. J. (1988a) Flexible production systems and regional development. *IJURR* 12 (2); Storper, M. and Scott, A. J. (Eds.) (1992) *Pathways to Industrialization and Regional Development.* London: Routledge; Storper, M. and Walker, R. (1989) op. cit.
45. Rees, J. (1989) Regional development and policy. *PIHG* 13 (4); Rees, J. (1992) Regional development and policy under turbulence. *PIHG* 16 (2).
46. Walker, R. (1989) A requiem for corporate geography: New directions in industrial organization, the production of place and the uneven development (sic). *Geografiska annaler* 71B (1).
47. Dicken, P. and Thrift, N. (1992) The organization of production and the production of organization: Why business enterprises matter in the study of geographical industrialization. *TIBG* 17, p. 288.
48. Storper, M. (1987) op. cit., p. 592.
49. Walker, R. (1988) op. cit., p. 385.
50. Scott, A. J. (1986) Industrialization and urbanization: A geographical agenda. *AAAG* 76 (1).
51. Pudup, M. B. (1992) Industrialization after (de)industrialization: A review essay. *Urban Geography* 13 (2), p. 194; See also Jacobs, J. (1984) *Cities and the Wealth of Nations: Principles of Economic Life.* New York: Random.
52. Cronon, W. (1991) op. cit.; Pred, A. R. (1966) *The Spatial Dynamics of US Urban Industrial Growth, 1860–1914.* Cambridge: MIT Press; Pudup, M. B. (1992) op. cit., p. 194; Scott, A. J. (1988b) *Metropolis: From the Division of Labour to Urban Form.* Berkeley: University of California Press; Walker, R. (1988) op. cit., p. 408.
53. Pudup, M. B. (1992) op. cit., p. 195.
54. Kwok, R. Y. W. (1992) Urbanization under economic reform. In G. E. Guldin (Ed.) *Urbanizing China.* Westport: Greenwood, p. 73; Pannell, C. W. (1992) The role of great cities in China. In G. E. Guldin (Ed.) op. cit., p. 36.
55. Lovering, J. (1990) Fordism's unknown successor: A comment on Scott's theory of flexible accumulation and the re-emergence of regional economies. *IJURR* 14 (1); Lovering, J. (1991) Theorizing postfordism: Why contingency matters (a further response to Scott). *IJURR* 15 (2); Scott, A. J. (1991a) Flexible production systems: Analytical tasks and theoretical horizons – A reply to Lovering. *IJURR* 15 (1); Scott, A. J. (1991b) A further rejoinder to Lovering. *IJURR* 15 (2).
56. O hUallachain, B. (1993) Industry geography. *PIHG* 17 (4); Sayer, A. (1989) Postfordism in question. *IJURR* 13 (4); Sayer, A. and Walker, R. (1992) op. cit.
57. Phelps, N. A. (1992) External economies, agglomeration and flexible accumulation. *TIBG* 17 (1).
58. Leung, C. K. (1993) op. cit.
59. For a superb overview of the development of urban planning in China see: Yeh, A. G. O. and Wu, F. L. (1999) The transformation of the urban planning system in China from a centrally-planned to transitional economy. *Progress in Planning* 51 (3), pp. 173–195. A useful survey of other work focusing on Chinese urbanization is found in Chan, K. W. (1994a) *Cities with Invisible Walls: Reinterpreting Urbanization in Post-1949 China.* Hong Kong: Oxford

University Press, pp. 7–18; Yan, X. P. (1995) Chinese urban geography since the late 1970s. *Urban Geography* 16 (6); See also: Geographical Society of China (Ed.) (1990) *Recent Development of Geographical Science in China*. Beijing: Science Press, especially chapters by: Li, W. Y., pp. 197–203; Shen, D. Q. and Cui, G. H., pp. 204–213; and Wu, C. J., pp. 1–17; Kirkby, R. J. R. (1985) *Urbanization in China: Town and Country in a Developing Economy 1949–2000 AD*. London: Routledge; Pannell, C. W. (1980) Geography. In L. A. Orleans (Ed.) *Science in Contemporary China*. Stanford: Stanford University Press; Pannel, C. W. (1990) China's urban geography. *PIHG* 14 (2); Wei, D. Y. H. (1999) Regional inequality in China. *PIHG* 23 (1); Yeung, Y. M. and Zhou, Y. X. (1991) Human geography in China: Evolution, rejuvenation, and prospect. *PIHG* 15 (3); Zhang, L. and Zhao, S. X. B. (1998) Re-examining China's 'urban' concept and level of urbanization. *China Quarterly* 154.

60. Wu, C. J. (1990) Territorial management and regional development. In Geographical Society of China (Ed.) op. cit.

61. Fei, X. T. (1984) Xiao chengzhen da wenti (Small towns, a big issue). *Liaowang (Outlook)*. January; Fei, X. T. (Ed.) (1986) *Small Towns in China: Functions, Problems and Prospects*. Beijing: New World Press.

62. Shen, D. Q. and Cui, G. H. (1990) Urban geography and urban planning. In Geographical Society of China (Ed.) op. cit., p. 210.

63. Feng, Y. F. (1983) Fazhan xiao chengshi shi woguo chengshihua weiyi zhengque de daolu ma? (Is the development of small cities China's only correct road to urbanization?). *JJDL* 3 (2); Li, B. R. (1983) Woguo chengzhenhua daolu wenti de taolun (A discussion on China's road to urbanization). *CSGH* 6 (2); Ma, Q. Y. (1983) Woguo chengzhenhua de tedian ji fazhan qushi de chubu fensan (A preliminary analysis of characteristics and development trends of China's urbanization). *JJDL* 3 (2).

64. Ibid.

65. Bai, D. M. (1981) Weixing cheng nengqi kongzhi shiqu guimo de zuoyong ma? (Are satellite towns a useful means of controlling the population in urban districts?). *Jianzhu xuebao (Architectural Journal)* (4).

66. Feng, Y. F. (1983) op. cit.

67. Ibid., p. 138.

68. Hu, B. L. (1991) *Industrial Guidance in the Urbanization Process*. Asian Institute of Technology, Bangkok. Unpublished manuscript.

69. Ibid., pp. 4, 7–8.

70. Ibid., p. 11.

71. Ibid., p. 12.

72. Ibid., p. 4.

73. Ibid., p. 18.

74. Cai, Q. M., Zhao, P. S. and Jiang, M. K. (1991) Butong fazhan jieduan xiangzhen qiye yu nongye neizai guanxi chutan (Exploration of the internal relationship between rural enterprises and agriculture at different developing periods). *JSJJTT* (2); Xu, Y. M. and Wu, Q. (1990) Shinianlai xiangzhen qiye lilun yanjiude huigu (Ten year review of research on rural enterprise theory). *JSJJTT* (10).

75. Cai, Q. M., Zhao, P. S. and Jiang, M. K. (1991) op. cit., pp. 42–43; Xu, Y. M. and Wu, Q. (1990) op. cit., pp. 18–19.

76. Cai, Q. M., Zhao, P. S. and Jiang, M. K. (1991) op. cit., p. 39; He, B. S. (1991) *Jiangsu nongcun feinonghua fazhan yanjiu (Research on Rural Non-agricultural Development in Jiangsu)*. Shanghai: Shanghai People's Publisher, pp. 30–66.

77. He, B. S. (1991) op. cit., pp. 92–105.

78. Lin, F. R., Wang, Z. D. and Tang, Q. L. (1992) Guanyu nongye quyu zonghe

kaifa wogan lilun wentide tantao (Inquiry into certain theoretical issues of the comprehensive development of rural areas). *JJDL* 12 (3).

79. Huang, M. D. (1993) *Chengzhen tixide jiegou yu yanhua: Lilun fanxi yu shizheng yanjiu (The Structure and Evolution of Urban Systems: Theoretical Analysis and Case Study)*. Unpublished Ph.D. dissertation: East China Normal University, pp. 81–82.
80. Ibid.
81. Shi, Y. S. (1992) Xiangcun dilixue fazhande huigu yu zhanwang (Development of rural geography: Retrospect and prospect). *DLXB* 47 (1); Shuai, J. P. (1993) Woguo xiangzhen qiye fada diqude fazhan dui nongyequ weide yinxiang (Influence of China's flourishing rural enterprise development on agricultural areas). *DLYJ* 12 (3); Yang, C. Y. (1992) Xiangzhen gongye chengzhang yu fazhan zhanlue yanjiu (Research on the growth and development strategy of rural industry). *JJDL* 12 (1).
82. Li. W. Y. (1990) Recent development of industrial geography in China. In Geographical Society of China (Ed.) op. cit.; Lu, D. D. (1990) *Zhongguo gongye bujude lilun yu shijian (China's Industrial Distribution: Theory and Practice)*. Beijing: Science Press.
83. Gong, F. X. (1992) *Zhongguo qinggongye jingji wenti tansuo (Exploring the Problem of China's Light Industrial Economy)*. Beijing: Economic Science Press; Lu, D. (1992) *Zhongguo gongye jingjide gaige yu fazhan (China's Industrial Economic Reform and Development)*. Beijing: Economic Management Press; Zhou, S. L. and Chen, J. G. (1992) *Zhongguo gongyede fazhan yu gaige (China's Industrial Development and Reform)*. Beijing: Economic Management Press.
84. Yang, W. Y. (1992) Jingji dilixue: Kongjian jingjixue yu quyu kexue (Economic geography: Spatial economics and regional science). *DLXB* 47 (6).
85. Lu, D. D. (1991) Woguo gongye buju yanjiu qude quanmian zhongda jinzhan (Seeking overall significant progress in China's industrial location research). *JJDL* 11 (2); Shi, Q. W. and Wu, W. (1992) Gongye buju: Zai buju lun (Industrial location and relocation theory). *JJDL* 12 (2); Yang, K. Z. (1993) Zhongguo diqu gongye jiegou bianhua yu quji chengzhang he fengong (Changes in China's regional industrial structure and its effect on regional growth and specialization). *DLXB* 48 (6).
86. Li, W. Y. (1990) op. cit., p. 202; Peng, Q. (1993) Chanye jiegoude chengzhang yu jingjiqude kuozhang (Development of industrial structure and the expansion of economic regions). *DLYJ* 12 (1), p. 80; Yang, W. Z. (1991) Chanye jiegou, chanye buju, chanye zhengce yitihua wenti (Industrial structure, industrial location, industrial policy: Problems of integration). *JJDL* 11 (1).
87. Li, W. Y. (1990) op. cit., p. 199; Liang, R. C. (1992) Lun gongyequde xingcheng yu fazhan (On the formation and development of industrial regions). *DLKX* 12 (4); Zhou, Y. X. and Yang, Q. (1995) Geographical analysis of the industrial economic return of Chinese cities. *Urban Geography* 16 (6).
88. Lin, J. B. (1993) Guanyu kaifaqude jige wenti (On the problems of development zones). *JJDL* 13 (2); Special Zones Office of the State Council (1991) *Zhongguo yanhai chengshi jingji jishu kaifaqu (China's Coastal Municipal Economic and Technological Development Zones)*. Beijing: State Council; Wei, X. Z. (1991) Guanyu gaojishu chanye jiqi yuanqu fazhande yanjiu (Research on the development of high technology industrial parks). *JJDL* 11 (1).
89. Li. W. Y. (1986) Developing regional industrial systems in the Chinese People's Republic. In F. E. I. Hamilton (Ed.) *Industrialization in Developing and Peripheral Regions*. London: Croom Helm; Liang, R. C. (1989) Gongyequde dengji leixing jiqi jiegou tezhengde tantao (Inquiry into the categories and

structural features of industrial areas). *DLXB* 44 (1); Shen, X. P. (1987) Shilun gongyequ gongye qiye chengzu bujude jingji xiaoguo he zuijia guimade queding (Discussion on the economic effect of the location of industrial enterprises and the determination of optimum size). *DLXB* 42 (1).

90. Huang, M. D. (1991) Xiandai qiye zuzhide quwei xuanze jiqi kongjian yingxiang (Organization of location choice of modern enterprises and their spatial influence). *JJDL* 11 (4); Li, X. J. (1991) Guanyu gongsi dili yanjiude jige wenti (Some problems in the research of firm geography). *JJDL* 11 (3); Li, X. J. (1993) Chanye lianxi yu nongcun gongyehuade qiye fenxi (Analysis of industrial linkages and rural industrialization enterprises). *JJDL* 13 (2).

91. Fei, H. P. (1993a) Qiye yu quyu jingji xietiao fazhan yanjiu (Research on coordinating enterprises and regional economic development). *JJDL* 13 (3); Fei, H. P (1993b) Duochang qiye kongjian yanhua moshi yanjiu (Study of the models of the spatial evolution of multi-plant enterprises). *DLKX* 13 (4).

92. Fei, H. P. (1993b) op. cit., pp. 329–330.

93. Liang, R. C. (1992) op. cit., p. 343.

94. Shen, D. Q. (1988) Changjiang liuyu kaifade zhengtixing, jieduanxing yu leixingxing (The periodicity, typicality and overall development of the Yangzi River valley). In Y. F. Si (Ed.) *Zhongguo Kexueyuan Nanjing Dili yu Hupo Yanjiusuo jikan* (*Memoirs of the Chinese Academy of Sciences Nanjing Institute of Geography and Limnology*, Vol. 5). Nanjing: People's Press, pp. 99–100.

95. Sun, Y. S. and Lin, Y. Z. (1988) Nongcun chengzhenhuade guochengji qileixing (Processes and types of rural urbanization). *JJDL* 8 (1). The article refers to the *Sunan* (southern Jiangsu) model characterized by medium to large size township and village collective enterprises; the Wenzhou (located in coastal Zhejiang) model characterized by small scale individual and household enterprises; and the *Subei* (northern Jiangsu) model characterized by a lower level of rural development of mixed collective and individual and household enterprises.

96. Xu, Y. M. and Wu, Q. (1990) op. cit.

97. Ibid., p. 18.

98. This perspective is reinforced by discussions with informants and my research collaborators.

99. Huang, M. D. (1993) op. cit., p. 107.

100. Ibid.

101. He, B. S. (1991) op. cit., pp. 42–51; Ho, S. P. S. (1994) *Rural China in Transition: Non-agricultural Development in Rural Jiangsu, 1978–1990*. Oxford: Clarendon, pp. 61–63; Ning, Y. M. and Yan, Z. M. (1993) Woguo zhongxin chengshide bupingheng fazhan ji kongjian kuosande yanjiu (The uneven development and spatial diffusion of China's central cities). *DLXB* 48 (2), p. 103; Pang, X. M. (1992) An analysis of the role of cooperations [sic] between urban and rural industries in the development of rural industry in China. *The Journal of Chinese Geography* 3 (1); Zeng, Z. G. and Lu, C. (1989) Jiangsusheng xiangcun jingji leixingde chubu fenxi (Preliminary analysis of rural economic types in Jiangsu Province). *DLYJ* 8 (3); Zhang, F. B. (1988) Jingjiangxian duiwai jingji he shehuide diyu lianxi (External socio-economic regional interaction in Jingjiang County). In Si, Y. F. (Ed.) op. cit.

102. Gu, C. L. *et al.* (1993) Zhongguo dachengshi bianyuanqu texing yanjiu (Study of the special characteristics of the fringes of China's mega-cities). *DLXB* 48 (4); Zhou, Y. X. The metropolitan interlocking region in China: A preliminary hypothesis. In N. Ginsburg, B. Koppel and T. G. McGee (Eds.)

op. cit. See also Wang, S. F. (1991) Chengzhenhua yu quyu jingji fazhan (Urbanization and regional economic development). *JJDL* 11 (1).

103. Gu, C. L. and Chen, Z. G. (1994) Zhongguo dadushi kongjian zengzhang xingtai (Metropolitan spatial growth patterns in China). *CSGH* 18 (6); Shen, D. Q. and Cui, G. H. (1990) op. cit., pp. 209–210.

104. Kirkby, R. J. R. (1985) op. cit., p. 252.

105. Hu, X. W. (1994) Jiaqiang duiquyu he chengshi fazhande guihua yu tiaokong (Strengthening the planning and readjustment of urban and regional development). *CSGH* 18 (2); Wang, S. F. (1991) op. cit.; Zhao, J. X. and Xu, C. X. (1992) Woguo quyu jingji zengzhang zhengcede lilun tantao (Theoretical inquiry into China's policy of regional economic growth). *JJDL* 12 (3).

106. Wei, Y. H. (1993) Zhongguo quyu fazhan yanjiu: Zhuyao yiti he jinqi jinzhan (Research on China's regional development: Major topics and recent progress). *JJDL* 13 (4); and for an excellent discussion on a unified theory of 'dual' structures see Yang, K. Z. (1992) Eryuan quyu jiegou lilunde tantao (Inquiry into theories of dual regional structures). *DLXB* 47 (6).

107. Li, M. B. (1983) Woguo chengzhen fazhande zhanwang (China's urban development and prospects). *Chengxiang jianshe (Urban–rural Construction)* 12 (1), p. 16.

108. Kirkby, R. J. R. (1985) op. cit., p. 243.

109. Lin, F. R., Wang, Z. D. and Tang, Q. L. (1992) op. cit.; Miao, C. H. (1994) Quyu chengxiang gongyede xietiao fazhan zhanlue (Strategies for coordinating the development of urban and rural industries). *JJDL* 14 (2).

110. Sui, Y. Z. (1992) Chengxiang ronghe xitongde SD dongtai guotu guihua chutan (Study of the SD territorial planning for the city-countryside fusion system). *JJDL* 12 (4); Wang, S. F. (1991) op. cit.

111. Chen, J. Y. and Hu, B. L. (1991) Chengshihua renkou yu laodongli wenti yanjiu (Urbanization, population and labour force research problems). In B. C. Zhang, J. Y. Chen and Y. X. Zhou (Eds.) *Zhongguo chengshihua daolu hongguan yanjiu (Macro-research on China's Road to Urbanization)*. Harbin: Heilongjiang People's Press, p. 89.

112. Ibid., p. 92.

113. Ibid., p. 102; Liu, D. H. and Ma, M. (1991) Renwen dilixue yuqi duiguotu guihua lilun yanjiude gongxian ji fazhan wenti (Theoretical research contributions of human geography to the problems of development of territorial planning). *JJDL* 11 (4), pp. 16–17.

114. Duan, X. M. (1993) Nongcun gaige he fazhan mianlinde xin wenti (Facing the new problems of rural reform and development) *ZGNCJJ* (8), p. 19; Zhang, L. J. (1989) *Chengxiang yitihua zhilu (The Path Towards Urban–rural Symbiosis)*. Beijing: Rural Reading Materials Press.

115. Human Geography Research Office (1990) *Jiangnan xiangcun chengshihua bijiao yu fazhan yanjiu (Comparative and Development Research of Rural Urbanization in Southern Jiangsu)*. Nanjing: Nanjing Normal University, Department of Geography.

116. Koppel, B. (1991) op. cit. Koppel also shows how conventional analysis of rural and urban is anchored to other dichotomies: agricultural and industrial; socialist and capitalist; public and private; equity oriented and growth oriented; bottom-up and top-down.

117. Ibid., p. 48.

118. McGee, T. G. (1991a) The emergence of 'desakota' regions in Asia: Expanding a hypothesis. In N. Ginsburg, B. Koppel and T. G. McGee (Eds.) op. cit., p. 3.

119. Ibid. The term is coined from the Bahasa Indonesian words for village (*desa*) and for town (*kota*) and is intended to invoke a conceptualization of

landscapes neither clearly rural nor urban, but incorporating elements of the two.

120. By 'open door' I refer not only to the policy of opening to the outside world, but also to the liberalization of the domestic economy referred to by the Chinese variously as 'socialism with Chinese characteristics', or a 'socialist market or commodity economy'.

3 The lower Yangzi delta: historical geography and contemporary patterns of change

This chapter will explore the nature of spatial economic restructuring in the lower Yangzi delta. The analysis presented here is framed by three objectives. The first is an explicit response to the perspective emphasized in the previous two chapters which insisted that the importance of locality and the circumstances of place be more carefully considered in the processes of development. Hence, the first sections of Chapter 3 will explore the critical historical conditions into and from which recent changes in the lower Yangzi delta have been imbricated. This provides the necessary context for the second objective which includes engaging in a detailed examination of the contemporary patterns of spatial economic transformation. Analysis of these patterns across the wider area of Jiangsu and Shanghai will also highlight the way in which the lower Yangzi delta is distinguished from the surrounding region. The third objective of this chapter is to position Kunshan, first, within the most dynamic spatial economic restructuring that has occurred throughout the delta, and second, in relation to the elaboration in subsequent chapters about particular elements of mega-urbanization.

The chapter begins with a survey of the natural environment and its relationship to the spatial economic structure of the lower Yangzi delta. Particular emphasis is placed upon commercialization and the growth and spatial proliferation of rural non-agricultural activities, and urban development through the Late Imperial and Republican periods. The second section briefly discusses the pre-reform (1949–1978) political economy which sets the stage for a detailed review of the reforms since 1978 and the resulting transformation of the rural economy. The fourth section examines recent spatial economic patterns in the delta and highlights specific features not adequately explained by the conventional wisdom of urban and regional development. The chapter concludes by introducing particular circumstances of spatial economic restructuring in Kunshan as a quintessential example of the local character of regional change.

The lower Yangzi delta from the Late Imperial period

Central to this study is the assumption that spatial economic patterns, the structure of human agency, and the natural environment form a highly interdependent system. Focusing specifically on the lower Yangzi delta permits sustained analysis of the interrelationships among the various dimensions of this region as an integrated entity. While such an approach cannot adequately portray the full complexity of all of China, it can provide important insights into the processes of contemporary regional transformation. I will, however, endeavour to include some comparative references to the rest of China in general and to the northern part of Jiangsu Province (*Subei*) in particular.

Natural environment and spatial economic structure

The lower Yangzi delta, including Nantong, Taizhou, and Yangzhou in the north, Nanjing and Zhenjiang in the west, the Lake Tai region of Changzhou, Wuxi and Suzhou to the south, and Shanghai to the southeast is roughly shaped as a shallow basin sloping towards Lake Tai (see Map 3.1). The lowest part of the basin between Lake Tai and Kunshan is 1.7 to 3 metres above sea level. The surrounding area slopes upwards to the north and east to an average of 6 metres. Between Changzhou and Nanjing the land rises to between 20 and 50 metres with a few points reaching just over 400 metres. The immediate vicinity of the cities of Nanjing and Yangzhou are on the deltaic plain of the Yangzi River averaging between 2 to 10 metres above sea level. Rainfall across the region averages between 950 and 1,150 millimetres per year with the greatest proportion falling between May and August. The average annual temperature is 15 to 16°C with a mean temperature in January of 3° and in July of 28°C, and an average of 230 frost-free days.[1] Linked to the interaction between the Yangzi River and ocean tides, and the sinking and inundation of the central part of the lower delta, the region has seen repeated expansion and contraction of lakeshore, rivers and drainage, and oceanfront.

Competing forces of silting and erosion and flooding and reclamation created the delta's distinctive topography upon which emerged a regional space economy characterized by interaction and linkages among three broadly defined sub-regions.[2] The first is the high-lying outer ridge areas of present day east, central and north Shanghai Municipality, the three northernmost counties of Suzhou and most of Nantong (see Map 3.1). This coastal deltaic plain consists of well drained percolating alluvial (or paddy) soils where the dominant crop historically was cotton. Output of both raw cotton and cloth supplied the low-lying areas of the central basin. While cotton remains the local speciality modern agriculture includes winter cropping of rape-seed (canola) and wheat, and rice during the

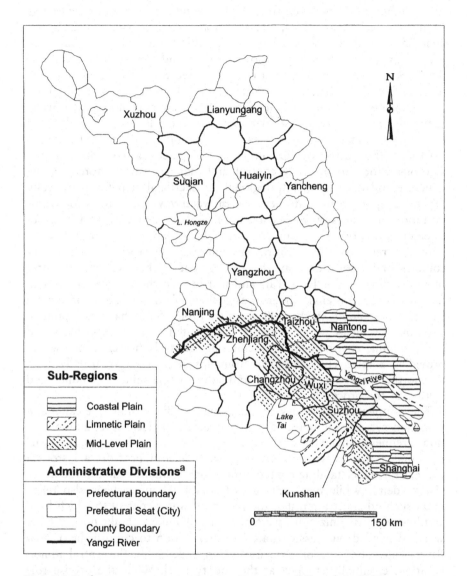

Map 3.1 Prefectures, counties and cities: Jiangsu and Shanghai, 1998.
Note
a For a detailed explanation of the hierarchy of administrative units in China see Appendix 2.
Source: Adapted from: *SHNJ 1998*, p. 41, Map appendix; *ZGXZHC 1997*, pp. 27–29.

summer. The lowest-lying area of the central basin, a limnetic plain of poorly draining paddy soils, developed an interdependent system of wet and dry agriculture. Wet rice was grown in fields surrounded by prominent embankments to prevent inundation. Reinforcing these embankments were mulberry bushes which supported thriving local sericulture. Earnings from silk largely financed imports of cotton and cloth. Middle-lying areas, including the southwest part of present day Shanghai, Kunshan and the vicinity of the city of Suzhou, most of Wuxi and Changzhou, and along the banks of the Yangzi River to Nanjing (see Map 3.1), are comprised of a mid-level limnetic and deltaic plain. As these areas required no embankments, yet were easily irrigated, they grew rice almost exclusively, supplying the other two areas with surplus grain. Today, rice is a highly productive summer crop along with winter crops of wheat and canola.

Clearly, the success of agriculture in the lower Yangzi delta required vigorous efforts to precisely control and manage water. Moreover, the structure and intensity of intraregional transactional activities historically depended upon an intricate network of waterways and canals for transportation. The density of this irrigation and transport network was six to eight times greater than in the north China plain before the post-1949 efforts to restructure the natural environment.[3] Presently, across the six counties of Suzhou, for example, 16 per cent of the total area is water (not including any of Lake Tai) and in Kunshan the proportion rises to 22.3 per cent.[4] This environment was ecologically more stable with a mere twenty major floods in the 500 years to 1900.[5] Some have also pointed out how this dense water network contributed to a more stable social and economic environment by facilitating relatively higher incomes, and providing a relatively safe haven from uprisings and war, usually from the north, absorbing population and advanced farming techniques and culture in the process.[6]

The complexity of the task of managing and maintaining the canal and irrigation system was reflected in the structure of local level administration. Frequently haphazard and inconsistent over the centuries, the issue of water control is worth mentioning here since it provides a historical context for understanding contemporary local administration in the lower Yangzi delta. While the taxation and corvée labour systems also relied upon such administration it is the nature of water control to which local administrative organizations were most clearly linked. Unlike north China, which depended on massive state led intervention to control the Yellow River, state water control in the lower Yangzi delta, like the central administration, essentially stopped at the county level. While the precise role that small communities historically played in water control is the subject of continuing debate, it is clear that what emerged in the delta was a system in which localities were left to fend for themselves until the situation degenerated into widespread inundation. With the divergence of local interests, long-term regional degeneration of water control was virtually unavoidable, only periodically slowed by central government efforts in response to disaster.[7] Yet the fact of strong local interests and the organizational structures through which they acted, remained a prominent characteristic throughout. Thus, the scale of water control projects in the lower Yangzi delta, usually too small for state concern and too large for individual households, necessarily resulted in a complex set of interrelationships, driven at the community level (township and village), between the central state, peasants, and beginning around 1350, the urbanizing mercantile and landowning elites.

Rural–urban relations and the urban penumbra

Sustained high levels of agricultural output and abundant water transport led to a highly commercialized rural economy in the lower Yangzi delta. The basis for this transformation was the introduction of cotton cloth and silk. In the 500 years or so of late imperial China cotton cloth replaced hemp as the material of choice among peasants while silk became popular among the expanding merchant class and other well-off urbanites. These developments also resulted in the commercialization of grain in the delta during this period. Today, extensive commercialization has also occurred in other traditional agricultural activities such as animal husbandry and aquaculture.

Commercialization of cotton and sericulture, and marketization of grain contributed to a dramatic growth in the number of small towns in the lower Yangzi delta during the Late Imperial period. Linked to the marketing of cloth, silk, and rice this region became the most highly urbanized and commercialized in China by the late nineteenth century. In the mid-fourteenth century, on the eve of the founding of the Ming Dynasty (1368), one part of the delta, including the six counties of present day Suzhou, the former Jiading and Baoshan Counties – now both incorporated into Shanghai's urban districts – contained only four towns. This increased to sixty-seven by the early seventeenth century and to ninety by the mid-nineteenth century (late Qing Dynasty).[8] For Kunshan during the same period the corresponding numbers of towns was zero, nine and fifteen respectively. Today there are twenty administratively designated towns in Kunshan. While southern Jiangsu became the most highly commercialized and urbanized region in China, by the late nineteenth century only 10.6 per cent of the population lived in towns of 2,000 or more.[9] Meanwhile, the walled city of Suzhou probably became the largest metropolis in China based on the cotton cloth processing and silk weaving industries.[10]

While the increasing involvement of peasants in the commercialization of the delta contributed to the proliferation of small towns, a number of related factors acted to keep by far the greatest proportion of the population residing in the countryside. Relatively stable and productive agriculture stimulated population growth which in turn exerted pressures on food production and per-capita incomes. An increasing proportion of labour in excess of that needed for cultivation assumed a greater share of the household's productive activities in agricultural sidelines to offset these pressures. Notwithstanding the vicissitudes of increasingly influential market conditions, the household economy in the delta became relatively more stable with a given unit of land thus able to support more people. Moreover, since small towns emerged mainly as centres of commercial activities, with the exception of a certain amount of silk and cotton cloth production, most processing activities were dispersed throughout the countryside.[11]

The increasing peasant population was so well-linked to higher level markets that the standard periodic market towns, which supplied a range of daily necessities and around which socio-economic life in most of rural China was organized, did not exist in the lower Yangzi delta.[12] By the end of the nineteenth century a complex system of markets, commercial services, and production had emerged that enabled peasants to engage in non-agricultural production without having to leave the farm. While small towns in southern Jiangsu served the immediate community and were linked to external markets, they also catered to the rapidly expanding rural consumer market.[13] Expanding commercialization and marketization in the delta, and the transformation of the peasant economy and growth of small towns which accompanied them, were based on a highly effective transactional network. Yet the efficiency of local level productive activities and per-capita incomes over the same period eventually either stagnated or declined.[14] It is important to emphasize here that commercialization in the delta, while resulting in dramatic change, did not, in the long-run, lead to transformative development.

The rise of new industries and of large and small cities with the penetration of international capitalism through the late nineteenth century and the Republican period, added a further dimension to change in the lower Yangzi delta. While some claimed that the rural economy remained to a large extent unaffected by the development of urban capitalism in China others have clearly shown how it fundamentally reshaped peasant production.[15] The basic change which left virtually no peasant household untouched, was the switch from weaving cloth with home-spun yarn to the use of machine-spun yarn produced in urban mills made from locally produced cotton and silk. The fact that this new system of production sustained involutionary commercial growth and contributed to the growth of many towns and the decline of a few others, is less important to this study than the way in which urban areas became linked to the peasant economy. These interrelationships relied upon commercial services, especially the trade and investment activities of merchants and their organizational and transactional networks. Profiting mainly from the circulation of capital in the exchange of goods and not from investment in production, these activities did nevertheless stimulate the proliferation and modernization of agricultural sidelines and household based processing activities.[16]

This helps to explain the lower Yangzi delta's rather underdeveloped urban hierarchy through this period described so well in Skinner's seminal study.[17] Along with larger cities such as Suzhou and Nanjing, the region became crowded with many smaller towns deeply linked to the peasant economy, without a commensurate growth in small and medium sized cities. Regional prosperity and urbanization in this underdeveloped hierarchy of settlements was seen to be more 'general' throughout the delta.[18] Even the explosive growth of Shanghai after its founding as a Treaty Port in 1842, did not diminish the economic and cultural prosperity of the delta, although by many measures Shanghai quickly surpassed older cities like Suzhou.[19]

The transformation of sericulture and cotton production during the Late Imperial and Republican periods, characterized by the proliferation of small scale transactional activities, embedded small towns and large cities within an extensive network of reciprocal exchange relationships. This meant that rural communities assumed a greater variety of roles and, as the density of villages and small towns in the lower Yangzi delta increased, their functional integration with the larger cities became increasingly complex. Such integration tied large cities to the growing concentration of rural populations in what Marmé describes as the 'urban penumbra'.[20] With the transformation and expansion of agricultural sidelines then, major cities emerged as part of 'an area of widely diffused urbanness', a region with whose fortunes their own prosperity tended to move in tandem.[21] The role of cities in the lower Yangzi delta, therefore, needs to be placed in the context of a fundamentally endogenous rural transformation of rather long duration.

Pre-reform political economy

Widespread 'socialist transformation' implemented in China following 'Liberation' in 1949 was characterized by a process of collectivization in which agriculture became independent of individual small-holdings, private ownership was reduced, and the means of production were socialized. Along with land reform in the early 1950s, which resulted in the redistribution of land and tools of production to poorer households, agricultural sideline production in the lower Yangzi delta continued to develop rapidly.[22] By 1955 there was another large scale movement under way to reorganize the peasant economy into agricultural producers' cooperatives and handicraft cooperatives, the latter being mostly relocated into towns and administratively separated from agriculture. The commensurate emphasis on the production of grain and on the development of large scale urban industrial enterprises led to the stagnation of small scale non-agricultural production in the countryside. In 1958 the process of collectivization culminated with the policies of the Great Leap Forward and the almost overnight establishment of people's communes (*renmin gongshe*) loosely based on the former townships in terms of population and spatial extent. Constituent brigades (*shenchan dadui*), roughly equivalent to administrative villages of perhaps

200 to 400 households, and production teams (*shenchan xiaodui*), which in the delta approximated the old natural village (*zhuang*) of between thirty to fifty households, became responsible for all aspects of rural life under the unified management of communes. Since specific tasks were determined and assigned to small production groups (*shenchan xiaozu*) comprised of one to a few households, all but a few of the most rudimentary family chores had become collectively organized.

A new policy for rural industrialization in China also emerged at this time which encouraged communes and brigades to establish enterprises to produce industrial goods. While the central objective was to serve agriculture and the mechanization and electrification of farming, industrial production was also supposed to meet the demands of the peasants for daily necessities and provide materials and local processing to support China's industrial development. A large number of highly inefficient enterprises were subsequently established in the countryside which resulted in the enormous waste of human and material resources. Considerable disruption in agricultural production also occurred as rural areas concentrated on local non-agricultural activities precipitating disastrous food shortages.[23] The government responded to the crisis in 1960 by implementing a nation-wide programme of retrenchment and adjustment of rural industry. Many commune and brigade enterprises were ordered closed and strict requirements were placed on the proportion of rural labour to be allocated to agriculture. In addition, a large number of peasants who had moved to cities to join the urban industrial workforce were returned to the countryside.

While informants frequently referred to this period as the 'three difficult years' many also highlighted aspects of the Great Leap Forward which contributed to the later prosperity of rural industrial development in southern Jiangsu. While many commune and brigade enterprises were forced to close or, as with the handicraft cooperatives in the mid-1950s, were relocated to urban areas, a sizeable amount of rural industrial infrastructure was created. This, combined with the experience that many farmers gained from rural industrialization during the Great Leap Forward, and the newly acquired skills of those who were forced to return from urban state enterprises, contributed to a build-up of physical and human capital in rural areas. Generally speaking however, except during the first part of the Great Leap Forward, national policies towards rural industry remained highly restrictive through the early to mid-1960s.

During the decade of the Cultural Revolution (1966–1976), rural industry came to be viewed as a way of directing resources into agriculture by supporting local self-sufficiency in the material inputs needed for irrigation, mechanization, electrification and application of chemical fertilizers.[24] Although some communes and most brigades were allowed to operate small collective factories, any enterprises that might divert resources from farming or activities not in direct support of agriculture were vigorously discouraged. Furthermore, in the frenzied ideological icon-oclasm of the day individual and even commune and brigade enterprises were frequently attacked as the 'tail of capitalism'. In the context of central government policies to focus on 'grain first' this led to considerable pres-sure to restrict rural non-agricultural development.

In spite of the highly centralized and uniform organizational structure of the collective period after 1949 rural communities and local leadership often had a great influence on rural industrialization. Local and regional authorities in southern Jiangsu often resisted and sometimes, with great political risk, successfully circumvented national campaigns to shut down or readjust commune and brigade enterprises and to concentrate on agri-cultural production. In the early 1960s, for example, while most of China struggled unsuccessfully to feed itself, the crisis in the lower Yangzi delta was less severe. With relatively higher agricultural productivity, more advanced rural industrialization, and among the nation's highest density of rural population, a national retrenchment policy that treated all regions equally was viewed as unnecessarily severe in the delta.

Again in the early 1970s intense debate erupted locally about how to adopt the spirit of a national campaign to concentrate on grain produc-tion. In the end, several counties in southern Jiangsu unofficially permitted, and even encouraged, the establishment of commune and brigade enter-prises, protecting those not specifically related to the support of agriculture. Relying on the expertise of returned urban workers, the experience gained during the Great Leap Forward, and taking advantage of the general short-ages of industrial goods in the countryside precipitated in part by work stoppages in urban production during the Cultural Revolution, commune and brigade enterprises in places like Kunshan continued to expand and proliferate counter to the prevailing official policy.[25] Thus, on the eve of reforms in the late 1970s the southern Jiangsu countryside was industri-ally more advanced than other rural regions in China.

Two other aspects of the collective period are worth mentioning here because of how they became important in the more recent transforma-tion in the delta. First, numerous informants referred to various mass campaigns during which urban workers were returned to the countryside, and in the later stages of the Cultural Revolution in the early 1970s, when many urban youths were 'sent up to the mountains and down to the countryside'. Many of these individuals, for various reasons elaborated upon in the next chapter, often ended up living in rural townships in places such as Kunshan. In addition to technological and some manage-ment skills they also brought social networks and contacts with family, friends and former colleagues in cities like Shanghai and Suzhou. The second aspect relates to the underlying influence collectivization had upon the development of local level administrative structures in the delta. The state had forced a shift in economic decision making from the household level to production teams and their commune and brigade organizations.

In addition to directing virtually every detail of agricultural and industrial production and procurement, communes and brigades were also responsible for negotiating economic relations with the centre. In a parallel development that occurred with the establishment of the National Rural Industry Administration in 1976, communes and brigades, which later provided the organizational foundation for township and village governments, began to set up formal structures to strengthen the administration and management of local industrial enterprises. As will be demonstrated later, rural industrial production in southern Jiangsu was to remain largely under the control of townships and villages and their constituent administrative organizations.

Reforms and transformation in the rural economy

The death of Mao, and the end of the Cultural Revolution with the arrest of the Gang of Four in 1976, signalled the beginning of a reassessment of the policies that affected the rural economy and precipitated a rapid expansion in rural industrial activities. In 1976 and 1977 rural gross industrial output in Jiangsu grew by 48 and 54 per cent respectively.[26] While this growth continued through the interregnum it was not until the Third Plenary of the Eleventh Central Committee of the Chinese Communist Party (CCP) in December 1978, when Deng Xiaoping began to consolidate his power, that the first of a series of resolutions regarding the rural economy was formally adopted.[27] The resulting reforms implemented in the late 1970s and early 1980s led to a deregulation of rural non-agricultural activities and reduced central and local government control of agriculture.

Changes in agriculture

This reduced direct government control in agriculture was most evident in the establishment of the household or production responsibility system (*baogan daohu*) which had been widely adopted in Jiangsu by 1983. While land was still owned collectively, management decisions regarding production were left to individual households. After meeting certain fixed obligations based on state procurement, surplus output could be retained for consumption or disposed on the market. Much has been made of the return to household organization in farming, particularly in terms of its supposedly superior incentives in producing dramatic increases in crop yields.[28] Across Jiangsu, total output from cultivation and crop yields per unit area in fact stagnated into the late 1980s and early 1990s. Unit area yields of staple grains, for example, actually showed a marginal average annual decline between 1984 and 1993. The same is also true for cotton, while the unit area yields of oil bearing seeds increased at an annual average rate of only 1 per cent during the same period.[29]

Two other parallel developments in the rural economy occurred in the early 1980s which contributed to the transformation in the countryside. First, the production responsibility system brought about crucial changes in the former collective workpoints system of remuneration which had greatly diluted incentives for hard work and the use of spare-time auxiliary labour for farming and off-farm employment. Direct payment of workers, pay based on performance, profit related bonuses, and piece rate wages became the norm and had a dramatic impact on incentives and efficiency in the agricultural and rural non-agricultural sectors. Second, the capacity to make more flexible and efficient use of labour increased with the relaxation of restrictions on the expansion of non-agricultural activities by rural communities associated with the abolition of commune structures and their replacement by township and village administrations by 1984. The simultaneous development of all rural activities was seen as the most effective way of increasing efficiency in agricultural production and for absorbing underemployed labour released from collective agriculture. Thus, as Huang has suggested, the rural change of greatest long-term importance in post-reform Jiangsu was the deinvolution of crop production that came with the diversification of the rural economy through rural industrialization and the expansion of sideline activities, and not the turn to marketized farming as is commonly assumed.[30]

Table 3.1 shows changes in the gross value of agricultural output (GVAO) and the sectoral distribution of agriculture in Jiangsu for selected years between 1978 and 1998. While the GVAO grew from RMB 14.05 billion to RMB 34.79 billion between 1978 and 1993, nearly 70 per cent of this increase occurred in sectors outside cultivation.[31] Aquaculture (primarily fish and shrimp raising) and animal husbandry (mostly poultry and pigs), accounted for 27 and 9 per cent respectively of the increase in GVAO over the period 1978 to 1993. A further 33 per cent of the increase came from growth in household sidelines or so-called petty commodity production, including handicrafts, and simple food processing such as the production of *doufu* and related products (see Plate 3.1). More significantly, the proportion of GVAO from such sidelines increased from under 2 per cent in 1978 to over 20 per cent in 1993 reflecting a 35 per cent average annual increase in the value of output. Meanwhile, the proportions from aquaculture (2.3 to 6.2 per cent) and animal husbandry (15.8 to 22.3 per cent) showed only modest growth over the same period.[32] Taken together the combined growth in agricultural activities outside crop production resulted in a decline in the proportion of GVAO from cultivation from over 80 per cent in 1978 to about 50 per cent in 1993, despite substantial increases in the state procurement prices for major crops over the same period (see Table 3.1). For the period between 1993 and 1998 the GVAO grew a further 32.6 per cent. However, growth in the value of activities outside cultivation stagnated or declined, led by a precipitous decline in the output value of animal husbandry. This was largely the result of over-capacity in the sector which led to a decline in prices and a subsequent decrease in the value of output. The relative opening up of procurement prices in the major crops sectors, combined with bumper harvests, meant that cultivation accounted for more than 117 per cent of the growth in total agricultural output value in Jiangsu between 1993 and 1998 (see Table 3.1).

Agricultural productivity also exhibited wide spatial variation. Map 3.2 plots agricultural output value per *mu* of arable land for Jiangsu and Shanghai for 1995 as an indicator of relative agricultural productivity.[33] With one or two notable exceptions the region of the lower Yangzi delta including Suzhou, Wuxi, Changzhou, Shanghai and the immediate vicinity of Nanjing were agriculturally more productive than most of the rest of Jiangsu. Unit area output values here were 1.8 to 3.5 times that of most of the northern part of Jiangsu. Ganyu County north of the city of Lianyungang in northeast Jiangsu was located in the heart of the province's petro-chemical producing region and benefited from easy access to chemical fertilizers, which helps to explain why it falls within the highest category of agricultural productivity. Ganyu and other counties along the coast such as Sheyang in Yancheng Prefecture and several counties in Nantong Prefecture, are well known for their aquaculture and fishing

Table 3.1 Total agricultural output and sectoral distribution: Jiangsu, 1978–1998 (selected years) (billion RMB (1980 constant values))

Year	Total (%)	Cultivation (%)	Husbandry (%)	Sidelines (%)	Aquaculture (%)
1978	14.05 (100)	11.27 (80.2)	2.22 (15.8)	0.24 (1.7)	0.32 (2.3)
1981	15.73 (100)	12.30 (78.2)	2.81 (17.9)	0.14 (0.9)	0.48 (3.0)
1985	22.98 (100)	15.65 (68.1)	4.73 (20.6)	1.82 (7.9)	0.79 (3.4)
1988	26.91 (100)	16.60 (61.7)	5.50 (20.4)	3.57 (13.3)	1.25 (4.6)
1991	27.12 (100)	15.82 (58.3)	6.16 (22.7)	3.76 (13.9)	1.39 (5.1)
1993	34.79 (100)	17.78 (51.1)	7.75 (22.3)	7.10 (20.4)	2.16 (6.2)
1996	44.7 (100)	28.40 (63.5)	2.32 (5.2)	10.41 (23.3)	3.57 (8.0)
1998	46.13 (100)	31.10 (67.4)	1.92 (4.2)	8.92 (19.3)	4.19 (9.1)

Sources: Calculated from: *JSTJNJ 1992*, pp. 93–95, 107; *JSTJNJ 1994*, pp. 131, 134; *JSTJNJ 1997*, p. 187; *JSTJNJ 1999*, pp. 148–149.

Plate 3.1 Household sideline production. Preparing *baiye doufu* (100 leaves doufu), Dianshanhu Town, Kunshan.

Plate 3.2 Office farmers. Peasants in office attire fertilizing rice seedlings, Tongxin Village, Kunshan.

which also helps to explain their relatively high levels of agricultural productivity. Furthermore, with the exception of Huaiyin City in *Subei*, all urban districts fall into the highest categories of agricultural production. Most urban districts in Jiangsu and Shanghai include small areas of arable land cultivated with labour intensive cash crops, especially vegetables, for urban consumption which explains their relatively high levels of agricultural productivity. Interestingly, Kunshan falls within only the third highest category of agricultural productivity. Variations in the distribution of surplus labour may partly explain this classification. Since no such data were available, population density was a reasonable proxy for surplus labour in the countryside. Map 3.3 plots population density across Jiangsu and Shanghai for 1998. Population density in Kunshan, compared to other parts of the delta, was a relatively low 679 people per square kilometre. Therefore, in terms of GVAO per-capita, Kunshan was actually one of the most productive areas in all of Jiangsu.[34]

The introduction of Map 3.3 provides the opportunity to examine the demographic context of the patterns of spatial economic change discussed in more detail later. Parts of the lower Yangzi delta, including most of Shanghai, Suzhou, Wuxi, Changzhou and two counties in Zhenjiang along the south bank; three counties in Yangzhou and Taizhou and most of Nantong along the north bank, were the most heavily populated in the region with densities ranging from 750 to 1260 people per square kilometre. All but two of the urban centres fall into the highest category, with average city densities ranging from as low as 1390 in Huaiyin in *Subei* to well over 10,000 in Shanghai. The extensive region of relatively high population density along the north bank of the lower Yangzi delta resulted from a combination of historically productive agriculture, which was able to foster and sustain a greater population and a rather underdeveloped settlement hierarchy. Except for Nantong City (population 639,600), there were no other urban settlements of significant size to absorb large numbers of the local population. On the other hand, the presence of more concentrated urban centres such as Suzhou (population 1,077,500), Wuxi (population 1,102,100) and Changzhou (population 856,100) helps to explain the slightly lower densities in parts of the south bank region in the vicinity of these cities. That Kunshan and a few adjacent counties show relatively lower densities is partly explained by the presence of extensive waterways and lakes for which the density data presented in Map 3.3 did not compensate.[35] With an aggregate population of nearly three million in 1998, Shanghai's suburban counties fell mostly into the highest categories of population density. The high degree of coincidence of the patterns illustrated in Maps 3.2 and 3.3 confirms the traditional relationship between high levels of agricultural productivity and greater population. I will return to these figures again later, but for the time being they provide the initial empirical evidence that circumstances in the lower Yangzi delta distinguish it from the surrounding region.

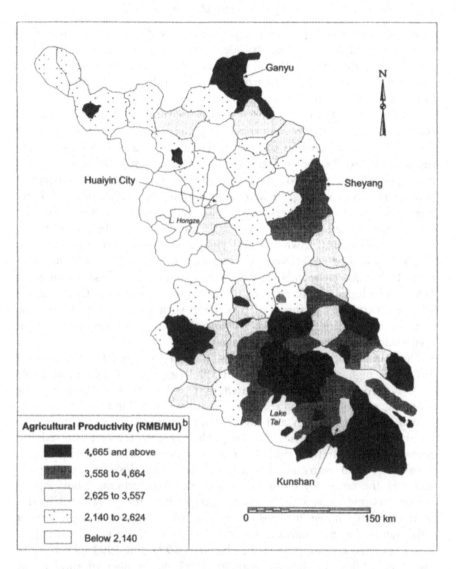

Map 3.2 Agricultural output value per *mu* of arable land: Jiangsu and
        Shanghai, 1995.[a]

Notes
a The 1995 administrative boundaries have been retained for this map.
b 1995 current values; 15 *mu* = 1 hectare.

Sources: Calculated from *HDDTNJ 1996*, pp. 105–122, 185–190; *SHTJNJ 1996*, pp.
165, 170; *SZTJNJ 1996*, p. 81.

Township and village enterprises: new shapes, old patterns

Although the central government provided little direct support to industrial development in the countryside, either by way of tax concessions, subsidies, or investments, the adoption of reform measures since 1978 has significantly improved the environment for rural non-agricultural activities. The deregulation of rural activities 'released a tremendous amount of productive and entrepreneurial energy in rural areas that had previously been constrained by central planning and tight government control.'[36] This is clearly reflected in the data presented in Table 3.2 which show the sectoral distribution of total output and the number of enterprises in rural Jiangsu for selected years since 1978. The term rural enterprise (*xiangzhen qiye* or *nongcun qiye*) unless otherwise indicated, will hereafter refer to all collectively (*jiti qiye*) and privately (*siying qiye*) or individually owned (*geti qiye*) industrial enterprises at or below the township level. The term township and village enterprise will largely denote enterprises owned collectively by township and village level administrations. Unless otherwise indicated most data presented for these designations will also include a small number of cooperative enterprises (*hezuo qiye*), and new variations in forms of ownership such as foreign and domestic joint ventures, joint households (*lianhu qiye*) and associations and joint ownership by different administrative units.

The number of rural enterprises in Jiangsu increased from 56,500 in 1978 to a high of nearly 105,000 in 1988 (see the last column in Table 3.2). A national campaign initiated in October 1988 to 'improve the economic environment and rectify the economic order' in response to overheated industrial growth and high inflation, resulted in a decline in the number of rural enterprises that year. The squeeze on credit and reduced access to raw materials during the two year recessionary period which followed, forced many rural enterprises either to close or amalgamate, and saw the return of many laid-off workers to farming. Many of the informants interviewed in the lower Yangzi delta region referred to this period of retrenchment in a positive way, emphasizing how it led to greater efficiency in the rural industrial sector.[37] Figures for the number of enterprises resumed a more gradual rise between 1991 and 1993 increasing to just over 99,000. In the five years to 1998 the number of rural enterprises in Jiangsu had decreased to just under 64,500 reflecting efforts to amalgamate and create enterprise groups (*jituan*) to increase efficiency. Meanwhile, rural GVIO increased at an annual average rate of 32 per cent between 1978 and 1993 (see Table 3.2). This compares with output values from all agriculture which increased an average of only 3 per cent annually over the same period.[38] In the five years to 1998 rural GVIO had almost tripled to RMB 960.45 billion. This figure for Jiangsu Province represents a staggering 18 per cent of the nation's total value of rural industrial output![39]

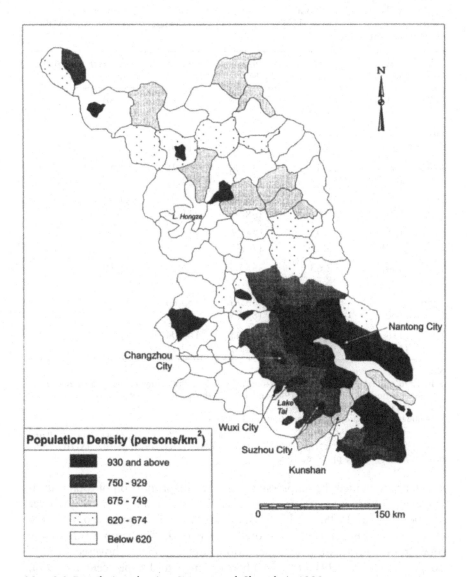

Map 3.3 Population density: Jiangsu and Shanghai, 1998.
Sources: Calculated from: *HDDTNJ 1996*, pp. 185–198; *JSTJNJ 1999*, pp. 366–368, *SHTJNJ 1999*, p. 26.

Changes in agriculture and the growth of rural non-agricultural activities have also facilitated a dramatic sectoral restructuring of the entire rural economy in Jiangsu. The total value of output increased from RMB 21.45 billion in 1978 to RMB 1,116.47 billion in 1998 (see Table 3.2).[40] More significant was the change in the sectoral distribution of output

Table 3.2 Total value of output, sectoral distribution and the number of industrial enterprises: rural Jiangsu, 1978–1998 (selected years) (billion RMB (1980 constant values)[a]

Year	Total (%)	Agriculture (%)	Industry (%)	Other [b] (%)	Industrial enterprises (× 1,000)
1978	21.45 (100)	13.21 (61.6)	6.28 (29.3)	1.96 (9.1)	56.50
1981	30.78 (100)	14.94 (48.5)	12.47 (40.5)	3.37 (11.0)	58.05
1985	68.12 (100)	21.84 (32.1)	38.00 (55.8)	8.28 (12.1)	81.56
1988	130.31 (100)	25.51 (19.6)	89.78 (68.9)	15.02 (11.5)	104.93
1991	167.50 (100)	25.94 (15.5)	126.36 (75.4)	15.20 (9.1)	93.90
1993	394.10 (100)	32.63 (8.3)	355.01 (90.1)	6.46 (1.6)	99.10
1996	874.19 (100)	44.64 (5.1)	745.71 (85.3)	83.84 (9.6)	91.14
1998	1,116.47 (100)	49.98 (4.5)	960.45 (86.0)	106.04 (9.5)	64.47

Notes
a In 1996 official figures for the gross output value of rural industry were calculated using a new method. The figures for 1996 and 1998 in this table have been adjusted to compare with data from earlier periods.
b Includes construction, transportation, and commerce

Sources: The number of enterprises for 1978 from Ho (1994) p. 19; other data calculated from: *JSSSN 1949–1989*, p.136; *JSTJNJ 1992*, p. 124; *JSTJNJ 1994*, p. 147; *JSTJNJ 1997*, p. 199; *JSTJNJ 1999*, pp. 146, 160.

which accompanied this impressive growth. The proportion of total output from agriculture declined from nearly 62 per cent in 1978 to just over 4.5 per cent in 1998, while the share from industry grew from 29 per cent to over 86 per cent over the same period. The proportion of the total from construction, transportation, and commerce hovered around 10 per cent until 1991 after which it declined to 1.6 per cent by 1993. The proportion of total output in these categories had increased again to about 10 per cent by 1998. Rural industrial growth was responsible for nearly 90 per cent of the increase in total output over the period 1978 to 1998.[41]

This shift from agricultural to industrial and other non-agricultural activities in rural Jiangsu is also reflected in the sectoral distribution of rural labour as illustrated in Table 3.3. The total number of employees in rural industry rose from 2.03 million in 1978 to a high of 5.62 million in 1988, declining thereafter to 4.63 million by 1998.[42] This parallels the

Table 3.3 Total labour force and sectoral distribution: rural Jiangsu, 1978–1998 (selected years) (number of workers in millions) [a]

Year	Total (%)	Agriculture (%)	Industry (%)	Other[b] (%)
1978	21.94 (100)	18.94 (86.3)	2.03 (9.3)	0.97 (4.4)
1981	22.31 (100)	19.83 (88.9)	1.74 (7.8)	0.74 (3.3)
1985	24.68 (100)	17.03 (69.0)	4.81 (19.5)	2.84 (11.5)
1988	26.14 (100)	16.21 (62.0)	5.62 (21.5)	4.31 (16.5)
1991	26.79 (100)	17.40 (65.0)	5.06 (18.9)	4.33 (16.1)
1993	26.74 (100)	16.26 (60.8)	5.40 (20.2)	5.08 (19.0)
1996	26.58 (100)	15.30 (57.6)	5.16 (19.4)	6.12 (23.0)
1998	26.72 (100)	15.31 (57.3)	4.63 (17.3)	6.78 (25.4)

Notes
a In 1996 official figures for rural labour were calculated using a new method. The figures for 1996 and 1998 in this table have been adjusted to compare with data from earlier periods.
b Includes construction, transportation and commerce

Sources: The number of employees for 1978 from Ho (1994) p. 19; other data calculated from: *JSSSN 1949–1989*, p. 136; *JSTJNJ 1992*, p. 78; *JSTJNJ 1994*, pp. 33, 129; *JSTJNJ 1996*, p. 163; *JSTJNJ 1997*, p. 182; *JSTJNJ 1999*, pp. 64, 144.

pattern revealed in Table 3.2 for the total number of rural industrial enterprises. The most obvious change was the decline in the share of the rural labour force employed in agriculture from 86.3 per cent in 1978 to 57.3 per cent in 1998, nearly all of which came from decreases in the number of peasants engaged in cultivation.[43] The proportion of rural labour working in industry increased from about 9 per cent in 1978 to over 20 per cent in 1993, decreasing thereafter to 17.3 per cent by 1998. Meanwhile employment in other sectors increased from 4.4 per cent in 1978 to 25.4 per cent in 1998. The construction, transportation, and commercial sectors accounted for over 70 per cent of the growth in this latter category.

Patterns of rural employment also exhibited wide spatial variation. Map 3.4 plots the available data for non-agricultural employment as a proportion of the total rural labour force for Jiangsu and Shanghai in 1998. In most of the south bank region of the lower Yangzi delta, including all of Shanghai, Suzhou and Wuxi, and the administrative units between Changzhou, Zhenjiang and Yangzhou Cities, including Wujin, Jingjiang

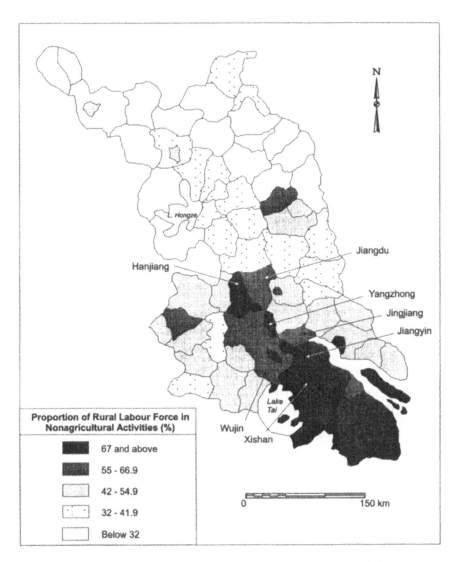

Map 3.4 Non-agricultural employment as a proportion of the rural labour
force: Jiangsu and Shanghai, 1998.[a]

Note
a Data presented for Shanghai were calculated for the municipal region as a whole.

Sources: Calculated from: *JSTJNJ 1999*, pp. 369–371; *ZGNCTN 1999*, pp. 44–45.

(in Taizhou), Yangzhong, Jiangdu and Hanjiang (all labelled on Map 3.4),
more than 55 per cent of the rural labour force was engaged in non-
agricultural activities corresponding to the two darkest categories illustrated. The single county level outlier is Jianghu just to the north of

Yancheng City, where 56.4 per cent of rural labour is engaged in non-agricultural employment. In at least four county level units, including two each in Wuxi and Suzhou Prefectures, nearly 75 per cent or more of the rural labour force was employed in the non-agricultural sectors. In fourteen county level units in *Subei*, on the other hand, the proportion dips to below 30 per cent. Not surprisingly, all urban areas in the lower Yangzi delta exhibited high proportions of rural labour outside agriculture. However, since city districts include only a tiny number of officially designated local rural residents, the classifications illustrated for urban areas should not be considered significant.[44]

Taken from the official Chinese statistical sources, these figures for Jiangsu and Shanghai need to be considered in the context of first-hand field observations and interview data which reveal that the sectoral divisions of rural labour were not as straightforward as these figures imply. While the absolute number of rural workers included a small proportion who have moved to work in urban areas (especially in construction), the official statistics conceal the fact that there was much occupational overlap and dual employment. Many of those employed primarily in agriculture, for example, spent at least part of their working time engaged in non-agricultural activities. More significant, was the fact that rural workers were frequently released from the factories and other non-agricultural activities during the particularly busy stages of cultivation (see Plate 3.2).

Development of rural enterprises in Jiangsu has also been accompanied by growth in trade and commercial activities. New procurement and marketing channels were established, initially as a result of the increase in agricultural and sideline products sold directly to end users, and later to the increased rural production and consumption of manufactured goods. Rural residents were also gradually permitted to engage in the transport and sale of certain goods, and in many areas to establish residence in small market towns for commerce and services if they supplied their own rations for grain. Rural retail sales of consumer goods in Jiangsu, as one measure of such activity, increased from RMB 5.71 billion in 1978 to RMB 88.46 billion in 1998 accounting for 40 per cent of total provincial retail sales for that year.[45] A further indication of the vigour of rural commerce was the rise in the volume of agricultural production sold by farmers directly to urban residents, increasing from RMB 183 million in 1978 to RMB 28.9 billion in 1998, accounting for 12.9 per cent of that year's total volume of retail sales for the province.[46]

Official sanction of township and village industries, individual and institutional entrepreneurship and a commensurate rise in commercial and trading activities in the countryside, have led to a revitalization of the marketing and commercial functions of small towns. While the magnitude and extent of the spatial economic restructuring that has fuelled this revitalization is a relatively recent phenomenon, historical evidence reviewed in the first part of this chapter suggests that these developments have resulted in a recapturing of former transactional networks in addition to the creation of new ones. Thus, while many aspects of the shapes of this restructuring may be new, in terms of ownership, types of industries and enterprise structure, the patterns of location and the institutional context of non-agricultural activities were consistent with historical patterns of commercialization and the development of small towns in the lower Yangzi delta – the 'new shapes, old patterns' in the title of this section. Each of these issues mentioned above constitute key elements of the rural transformation and mega-urbanization identified in Figure 2.2.

Rural residents and community governments responded aggressively to the new opportunities that emerged within a more permissive and flexible reform environment. This release of energy at the grass-roots level, manifested most clearly in the shift of resources from agriculture, especially cultivation, to more profitable non-agricultural activities, was the underlying cause of spatial economic restructuring in rural Jiangsu through the 1980s and 1990s.[47] As will be discussed in the following section, however, rural non-agricultural activities are not evenly distributed throughout the region.

Spatial economic patterns in the lower Yangzi delta

Changes in the lower Yangzi delta reflect an evolution of the regional space economy whereby industry and other non-agricultural activities have been integrated into areas of the countryside that were also among the nation's most productive agricultural regions. Some of the highest income households in China were found in these areas, benefiting from nearby markets for their produce along with burgeoning urban and rural demand for locally produced goods, and services such as transportation and construction. As extensive commercial and market transactions proliferated at the fringe of large urban conurbations like Shanghai, the distinction between urban and rural economies has become less clear. This section will discuss the emergence of particular patterns of rural industrial activity across Jiangsu and Shanghai which highlight these features.

The spatial distribution of 1998 rural per-capita net incomes for Jiangsu and Shanghai are plotted in Map 3.5. Work by Veeck has demonstrated that growing per-capita incomes show a strong positive relationship to locational variations in non-agricultural employment opportunities.[48] Since, industrial employment was the most significant factor in income determination, Map 3.5 shows where industrial activity was relatively important. It was a zone in the southern part of the lower Yangzi delta between Nanjing and Shanghai, especially around the Lake Tai cities of Suzhou, Wuxi and Changzhou (often referred to by the Chinese as *Suxichang* taken from the names of each city), and parts of Zhenjiang. Rural per-capita net incomes here averaged double or more those of the northern part of Jiangsu indicating the relative importance of rural indus-

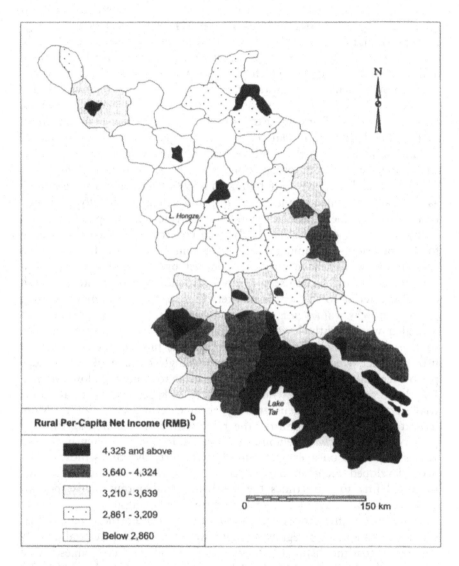

Map 3.5 Rural per-capita net income: Jiangsu and Shanghai, 1998.[a]
Notes
a Data presented for Shanghai are for the municipal region as a whole.
b 1998 current values.
Sources: *JSTJNJ 1999*, p. 437; *SHTJNJ 1999*, p. 56.

trial activity. As with data on agricultural productivity, the high level classification of urban areas should not be considered significant. The second
and third highest classifications for the four counties in coastal Yancheng
Prefecture probably resulted from the presence of comparatively profitable

coastal fishing, and extensive aquaculture and salt production, combined with relatively low population densities (see Map 3.3). As expected, average rural per-capita net incomes in Shanghai Municipality were relatively high.

The spatial patterns for rural per-capita net income are largely confirmed and reiterated in Map 3.6 which plots the available data for rural industrial output. Somewhat surprising, however, was the relatively lower rankings of all but one county adjacent to the city of Nanjing (population 2.76 million). Rural industry was less vigorous here than proximity to Jiangsu's largest industrial centre might suggest. Except for Jiangning County immediately to the south of Nanjing City, values for rural industrial output in the four other counties of the prefecture averaged only slightly more than RMB four billion in 1998. These values were as low as the least developed counties in *Subei* and cannot be wholly explained by the fact that the Yangzi River bisects the region. Development of rural industry in these counties has likely been constrained by factors relating to the 'primacy' of Nanjing City (the provincial capital). Investment in rural industry may have also been limited by potential earnings from employment in the service sector, in construction, or from intensive cash cropping catering to the nearby market. These same factors may also help to explain why values for rural industrial output in two counties in Shanghai were slightly lower than the highest level categorization. The southernmost administrative unit in Shanghai is Jinshan, the city's newest urban district, where industry is overwhelmingly dominated by the huge petro-chemical facility located there. This helps to explain its low ranking. For the municipality as a whole, however, 24.8 per cent of total industrial output value was generated by rural enterprises in 1997.[49] More importantly, Map 3.6 confirms the relative intensity of non-agricultural activity in the *Suxichang* region near Lake Tai in southern Jiangsu. Output values here were on average twenty-five to thirty-five times those of the least developed areas in *Subei*. Xishan, the richest county in China, produced fifty to sixty times the rural industrial output of the poorest counties in Huaiyin and Suqian in north central Jiangsu.

In addition to the pronounced difference between northern Jiangsu and the lower Yangzi delta region, spatial patterns of rural industrial activity also reveal that the distinction between urban and rural economies within the most developed areas of the delta was becoming less clear. Map 3.7 plots the gross value of industrial output (GVIO) across Jiangsu and Shanghai for 1998. Once again, the Lake Tai region of *Suxichang* exhibits among the highest levels of industrial activity. More interesting, however, is that county level jurisdictions here show levels of industrial activity that in most cases equalled or exceeded those of the nearby cities of Suzhou, Wuxi and Changzhou. The GVIO in these areas averaged 87 per cent of comparable values in the urban districts. Moreover, in 1998 for example, the average per-capita GVIO in the six counties of Suzhou (RMB 46,216) significantly exceeded that in Suzhou City (RMB 42,206). The 1998

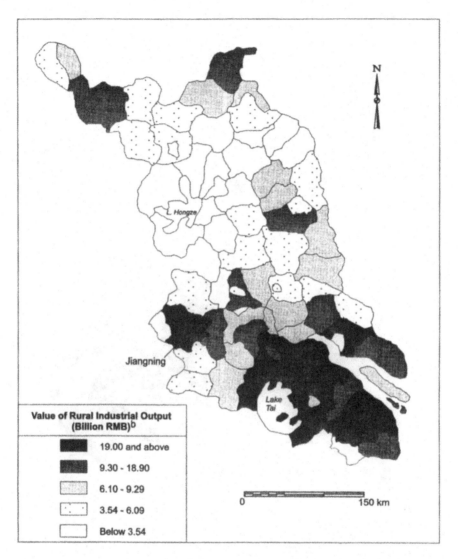

Map 3.6 Rural industrial output: Jiangsu and Shanghai, 1997.[a]

Notes

a Data for the two southernmost administrative units in Shanghai (Jinshan District and Fengxian County) were estimated based on the available data (see below).

b 1997 current values.

Sources: *JSXZQN 1998*, pp. 198–201; *SHNJ 1998*, pp. 446–500.

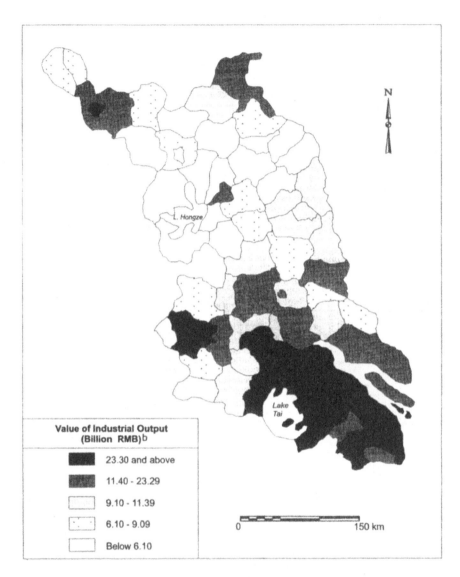

Map 3.7 Gross value of industrial output: Jiangsu and Shanghai, 1998.[a]

Notes

a Data preseted for Shanhai do not include output from industrial enterprises (mostly private) below the village level.

b 1998 current values.

Sources: *JSTJNJ 1999*, pp. 384–386; *SHTJNJ 1999*, p. 173.

average per-capita GVIO in the three counties of Wuxi (RMB 53,488) was nearly equivalent to that in Wuxi City (RMB 55,788).[50] Figures for average per-capita GVIO in the counties of Wuxi and Suzhou also exceeded the comparable value for Shanghai (RMB 40,282).[51]

It may be possible to suggest that the relative inefficiency of the urban industrial sector, dominated as it is by state owned enterprises, partly explains the lower values here for per-capita GVIO. However, similar data calculated for per-capita GDP, which should accommodate the relatively more important higher value added sectors in urban areas, does not always bear this out. The 1998 average per-capita GDP in the six counties of Suzhou was RMB 22,489. This is significantly greater that the comparable figure for Suzhou City (RMB 18,426). In fact, only one county (Wuxian, RMB 16,990) had a per-capita GDP lower than the nearby city of Suzhou.[52] While some counties in Shanghai also show high levels of gross output, they were in all cases dwarfed by the nearly RMB 600 billion produced by the city's urban industrial complex in 1998. Also of interest in this context were the relatively low values of output in several counties near the city of Nanjing. In 1992 for example, the GVIO in the five counties of Nanjing never amounted to more than 9 per cent that of the urban area. The 1992 per-capita GVIO in the five counties surrounding Nanjing City was only RMB 3733, equivalent to 24 per cent of that in the nearby urban districts (RMB 15,534).[53] With the exception of Jiangning, immediately to the south of Nanjing city proper, the 1998 spatial patterns for the region illustrated in Map 3.7 have remained largely unchanged. While issues of urban primacy and constraints on local investment in rural industrial activity may be relevant for these areas, it seems clear that mere proximity to large urban conurbations did not result in the sort of rural economic transformation which was occurring in the *Suxichang* region of the delta.

Although non-agricultural growth has occurred in all parts of Jiangsu and Shanghai, variations in the pace of industrial development emphasize how regional differences have widened. Map 3.8 plots per-capita increases in industrial output across Jiangsu and Shanghai for the six years between 1985 and 1991 during one of the most intensive phases of economic change in China. *Suxichang* again comprised the greatest contiguous extent of county level jurisdictions with the largest increases. Values for per-capita growth here were ten to twenty times larger than most areas of *Subei*. In fact, the magnitude of the increases in this part of the lower Yangzi delta were on average seven to ten times larger than total per-capita output values for the least developed parts of northern Jiangsu, especially Xuzhou, Suqian, Lianyungang, Huaiyin and Yanchen. The only significant outlier in this pattern was Yizheng County to the west of Yangzhou City. Well situated on the north bank of the Yangzi River, Yizheng was an important transshipment centre for petroleum from the northern Jiangsu oil fields.[54] As a result, the production of synthetic fabrics and chemicals became well

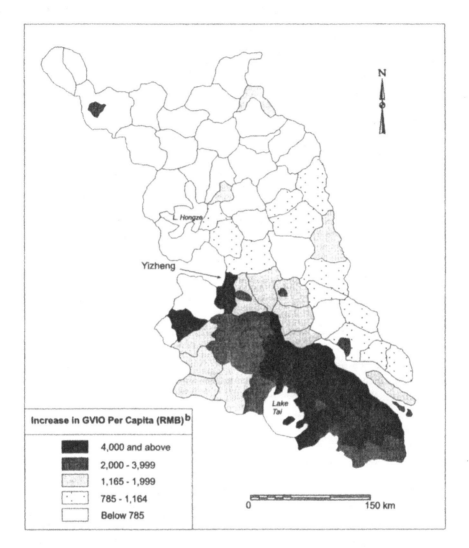

Map 3.8 Industrial output per-capita increase, 1985–1991: Jiangsu and Shanghai.[a]

Notes
a The 1991 administrative boudaries have been retained for this map.
b 1980 constant values.

Sources: Calculated from *HDDTNJ 1992*, pp. 270–273, 365–377; *JSSN 1949–1989*, pp. 382, 384–396; *JSSXJJ 1992*, pp. 429–430, 453–454; *JSTJNJ 1992*, pp. 135, 138; *SHJGQD*, pp. 2–3; *SHTJNJ 1986*, pp. 58, 108; *SHTJNJ 1992*, pp. 105, 107; *WXTJNJ 1992*, pp. 326–331.

developed in this area and probably account for its large increase. The patterns illustrated in Map 3.8 strongly suggest that, compared with other regions, industrial enterprises in *Suxichang* were either more efficient or tended to engage in more productive activities or both.

What was it about the countryside here that has led to significantly higher levels of rural industrial development? Moreover, is it possible to delineate the spatial extent of such a highly productive non-urban region? The concept of mega-urbanization proposed in Chapter 2 suggests that there are a number of processes and outcomes that could be examined to help answer these questions. While the preceding analysis was able to clearly establish the existence of particular patterns of transformation, the intention was not to explicitly demarcate a mega-urban region as defined at the end of Chapter 2.[55] However, it is possible to say with some certainty at this point, that at least *Suxichang*, most of Shanghai and parts of Zhenjiang are likely to be included within such a region. More importantly, this analysis has highlighted patterns that, first of all, distinguish this region from other areas, and second, appear to be inconsistent with conventional expectations. The two most obvious of these patterns were the presence of industrial development in areas of the countryside that equalled or, in many cases, exceeded levels of industrial development found in nearby cities, and the persistence of areas near large cities like Nanjing and Shanghai that did not seem to have benefited by proximity to vibrant urban economies to the same extent as other regions.

With regard to the first observation, it is worthwhile noting that the most intense rural industrial development largely coincided with areas that exhibited among the highest levels of agricultural productivity (compare Map 3.2 with any or all of Maps 3.5 to 3.8). This is not surprising in the Chinese context where productive agriculture leads to greater population densities and pressures on arable land which stimulated the development of off-farm activities. The resulting rise in rural incomes also increased local demand for manufactured goods and services and linked prosperous agriculture to the growth of rural non-agricultural activities. With respect to the second point, I remain less sanguine than most about the supposedly central role of large cities and other exogenous forces as they affected the rural restructuring observed in the lower Yangzi delta. The evidence presented thus far, in the context of the historical geography of the region, strongly suggests that there were other processes and mechanisms linked to locality, the transactional environment, and the geography of production that were also at work here. Conceptualized under the rubric of mega-urbanization proposed in Chapter 2, these processes and mechanisms need to be further analysed to understand and explain how they drive the region's spatial economic transformation. This undertaking will also provide insights into the means by which the spatial extent of the lower Yangzi delta mega-urban region may be more precisely defined for the purpose of management and planning.

The final section of this chapter, will introduce some of the key characteristics of the transformation that has occurred in Kunshan. The objective is to position Kunshan in the context of the lower Yangzi delta and to justify the detailed case studies in the following three chapters which address specific elements of the conceptual framework of mega-urbanization.

At the edge of Shanghai: Kunshan to the fore

Kunshan epitomizes at once the depth of change, the profound problems, and tantalizing prospects of spatial economic transformation in China's lower Yangzi delta. Yet the most rapid rural industrialization did not begin here until the mid-1980s, several years behind other counties in *Suxichang*. With an average of more than 1 *mu* of arable land per person in Kunshan, the pressures to diversify into non-agricultural activity were less intense since per-capita output value from agriculture was relatively high. Areas such as Jiangyin in Wuxi, on the other hand, where arable land per person was under 0.7 *mu*, had already been vigorously promoting non-agricultural development since the early 1980s.[56] Informants in Kunshan frequently claimed, however, that despite the later start, industrial development was beginning at a higher level and therefore, was advancing more rapidly than in other areas more famous for their development.[57] Whatever the case, it was clear that since the mid-1980s Kunshan, like other parts of the lower Yangzi delta, has undergone dramatic industrial growth and rural restructuring.

The first stage of this transformation is revealed in Part A of Table 3.4 which plots the available data for the increase and sectoral distribution of total output in Kunshan for selected years between 1980 and 1992. Total output in Kunshan grew from RMB 690 million in 1980 to RMB 16.23 billion in 1992.[58] While the share of output from construction, transportation, and commerce remained unchanged at about 13 per cent, the proportion from industry rose from about half in 1980 to more than four-fifths in 1992. Meanwhile, the proportion from agriculture decreased from 34 per cent in 1980 to 5.5 per cent in 1992. Average annual growth of the GVIO in Kunshan was over 35 per cent for the period accounting for 98.3 per cent of the increase in the gross value of agricultural and industrial output (GVAIO).[59] While total output for China also showed rapid growth, the changes in sectoral distribution were less dramatic (see Part B of Table 3.4). Year on year growth in China's GVIO over the period averaged 14 per cent, accounting for 90 per cent of the total increase in the GVAIO.[60] Annual growth in the GVAO in Kunshan averaged only 5 per cent between 1980 and 1992, while agriculture across China grew 6.2 per cent annually and still accounted for more than 16 per cent of the nation's total output in 1992.[61]

Data for growth and restructuring in Kunshan for the period 1988 to 1998 are presented in Part A of Table 3.5.[62] Total GDP rose from RMB

Table 3.4 Total value of output and sectoral distribution: Kunshan and China, 1980–1992 (selected years) (billion RMB (Current values for the year shown))

Year	Total (%)	Agriculture (%)	Industry (%)	Other ᵃ (%)
		Part A: Kunshan		
1980	0.69 (100)	0.23 (33.6)	0.36 (52.1)	0.10 (14.3)
1985	2.00 (100)	0.37 (18.3)	1.28 (64.0)	0.35 (17.7)
1990	7.40 (100)	0.76 (10.3)	5.74 (77.5)	0.90 (12.2)
1992	16.28 (100)	0.90 (5.5)	13.26 (81.4)	2.12 (13.1)
		Part B: China		
1980	853.4 (100)	192.3 (22.5)	515.4 (60.4)	145.7 (17.1)
1985	1658.2 (100)	361.9 (21.8)	971.6 (58.6)	324.7 (19.6)
1990	3803.5 (100)	766.2 (20.2)	2392.4 (62.9)	644.9 (16.9)
1992	5584.2 (100)	908.5 (16.3)	3706.6 (66.4)	969.1 (17.3)

Notes
a Includes construction, transportation, and commerce.

Sources: Calculated from: *JSSSN 1949–1989*, pp. 382, 394, 398; *JSTJNJ 1990*, pp. 30–31; *SZTJNJ 1989*, pp. 15, 32–33; *SZTJNJ 1991*, pp. 38–39; *SZTJNJ 1993*, pp. 40–41; *ZGTJNJ 1993*, p. 50.

1.63 billion in 1988 to RMB 15.05 billion in 1998. The share of GDP from industry showed a modest increase from 45.4 per cent to 53 per cent, while growth in the share of GDP from construction, transportation and commerce increased from 28.9 per cent to 39.3 per cent in Kunshan over the same period. Meanwhile, the proportion of GDP from agriculture declined significantly from 25.7 per cent in 1988 to just 7.7 per cent in 1998. Comparable data presented in Part B of Table 3.5 show much less intensive, though still significant, restructuring for China as a whole over the same period. Perhaps the most noteworthy phenomenon is that nearly one-fifth of the nation's total GDP is still attributed to the agricultural sector. This is well over twice the proportion in Kunshan which sits in the heart of one of the nation's most productive agricultural regions. Per-capita gross domestic product in Kunshan in 1998 was RMB 25,625, the fourth highest in Jiangsu behind three other areas in Suzhou and Wuxi, and six to ten times larger than the seventeen least developed counties in the province.[63] The GVAIO per-capita in Kunshan in 1998

Table 3.5 Gross domestic product and sectoral distribution: Kunshan and China, 1988–1998 (selected years) (billion RMB (current values for the year shown))

Year	Total (%)	Agriculture (%)	Industry (%)	Other[a] (%)
Part A: Kunshan				
1988	1.63 (100)	0.42 (25.7)	0.74 (45.4)	0.47 (28.9)
1991	2.44 (100)	0.46 (18.9)	1.36 (55.7)	0.62 (25.4)
1993	6.04 (100)	0.58 (9.6)	3.13 (51.8)	2.33 (38.6)
1996	11.43 (100)	1.15 (10.0)	6.10 (53.4)	4.18 (36.6)
1998	15.05 (100)	1.16 (7.7)	7.98 (53.0)	5.91 (39.3)
Part B: China				
1988	1492.83 (100)	383.10 (25.7)	577.72 (38.7)	532.01 (35.6)
1991	2161.78 (100)	528.86 (24.5)	808.71 37.4	824.21 (38.1)
1993	3463.44 (100)	688.21 (19.9)	1414.38 (40.8)	1360.85 (39.3)
1996	6788.46 (100)	1384.42 (20.4)	2908.26 (42.8)	2495.78 (36.8)
1998	7955.30 (100)	1429.90 (18.0)	3354.10 (42.2)	3171.30 (39.8)

Notes
a Includes construction, transportation and commerce.
Sources: Calculated from *KSTJNJ 1989*, p. 10; *KSTJNJ 1991*, p. 8; *KSTJNJ 1993*, p. 21; *KSTJNJ 1996*, p. 21; *SSB (1999)*, p. 1; *SZTJNJ 1997*, pp. 40–41; *SZTJNJ 1999*, pp. 42–43; *ZGTJNJ 1998*, p. 55; *ZGTJNJ 1999*, p. 55.

was RMB 55,969, fifth highest in Jiangsu and six to ten times that of the fifteen least developed counties in the province.[64]

However, as will be demonstrated below, the rapid growth of industrial activity in Kunshan has neither required nor resulted in a commensurate shift in residential urbanization.[65] That is not to say that there has been little or no mobility of local labour and population. In fact, significant proportions of the officially designated peasant population either resided in or commuted on a daily basis to work in or near the town centres.[66] According to the official statistical classification 20.2 per cent of the population in Kunshan in 1992 was considered non-agricultural (*fei nongye renkou*).[67] This administrative designation conceals the numbers actually residing in the built-up township centres, but it does provide a useful baseline. Combined with data provided by informants it is possible to estimate an adjusted level of urbanization in Kunshan of approximately 25 to 30 per cent.[68] While there have been many attempts to generate longitudinal estimates of urbanization for all of China the same is much more difficult for small jurisdictions such as Kunshan.[69] Data in the most recent gazetteer does suggest, however, that Kunshan was probably about 12 to 15 per cent urbanized on the eve of reforms in the late 1970s.[70] While the level of urbanization in Kunshan has increased from perhaps 12 to 30 per cent in the twenty or so years of reform since 1978, it is important to clarify the nature of this transition. First, approximately 60 per cent to 70 per cent of the urban population in Kunshan in 1996 resided in nineteen small towns outside the largest central urban settlement.[71] Second, from 1978 to 1996 these small towns, which grew on average from about 2,000 to 5,000 people, accounted for nearly 90 per cent of the growth in Kunshan's urban population over the same period.[72] The level of urbanization, its rate of increase, and the structure of urban settlement in Kunshan strongly suggest that rapid industrial growth here has not resulted in large scale urban agglomeration. This finding becomes even more significant when we consider that the 1998 per-capita GVIO in Kunshan (RMB 51,945) and per-capita GDP (RMB 25,675) were both substantially larger than the figures for Suzhou City (RMB 42,206 and RMB 18,426 respectively) which was at least 90 per cent urban![73]

Other indicators are also instructive. Industrial land-use, for example, comprised an average of 40 per cent of the area of town seats, while 7 per cent of all of Kunshan was considered built-up in 1992.[74] In addition to at least two national level and more than two dozen county and town level special development zones, all twenty towns had designated industrial areas (though not always contiguous), while more than 60 per cent of the 463 villages had areas to which they referred as industrial districts.[75] In 1998 there were 3,498 registered industrial enterprises in Kunshan accounting for more than 53 per cent of total GDP and employing 151,100 of the 340,700 strong workforce.[76] To emphasize the intensity of non-agricultural development in Kunshan, add to this the several thousand commercial organizations which employed 28,900 people, construction units with 15,600 labourers, a transport and telecommunications sector with 13,100 employees, and other tertiary level activities which employed a further 18.4 per cent of the workforce.[77] All this in an area with the nation's highest unit area yields of staple grains (6,990 kg/hectare), including rice (8,310 kg/hectare) and wheat (4,695 kg/hectare), and other agricultural products such as canola (2,040 kg/hectare), vegetable greens (14,550 kg/hectare) and melons (19,665 kg/hectare).[78] It is noteworthy that Kunshan, along with other rural areas of the lower Yangzi delta, have retained their critical importance in a national context as agricultural producer regions while at the same time undergoing rapid industrialization.

These preliminary findings establish Kunshan as part of the most dynamic spatial economic restructuring occurring in the region. For this reason, understanding and explaining the processes and mechanisms working at the local level in Kunshan is to appreciate trends of mega-urbanization across the entire lower Yangzi delta. The next part of this book will focus on the specific circumstances in Kunshan which drive local non-agricultural development in general, and which determine enterprise location and the emergence of related physical and institutional infrastructure in particular.

Notes

1. She, Z. X. (Ed.) (1991) *Taihu liuyu ziran ziyuan ditu ji* (*Lake Tai Basin Natural Resources Atlas*). Beijing: Science Press, Plates 9, 10; Wang, C. F. (Ed.) (1990) *Jiangsu sheng ditu ce* (*Atlas of Jiangsu Province*). Guangdong: Guangdong Map Publisher, Plates 6–8.
2. The information presented here is based on an analysis of several historical studies, atlases and gazetteers: Bell, L. S. (1992) Farming, sericulture, and peasant rationality in Wuxi County in the early twentieth century. In T. G. Rawski and L. M. Li (Eds.) *Chinese History in Economic Perspective*. Los Angeles: University of California Press; Hu, H. Y. (1947) A geographical sketch of Kiangsu Province. *Geographical Review* 37 (4); Huang, P. C. C. (1990) *The Peasant Family and Rural Development in the Yangzi Delta, 1350–1988*. Stanford: Stanford University Press; KSXZ (1990). Shanghai: Shanghai People's Publishers; She, Z. X. (Ed.) (1991) op. cit., Plates 3, 4, 8–10, 18, 23; Wang, Y. C. (1992) Secular trends of rice prices in the Yangzi delta, 1638–1935. In T. G. Rawski and L. M. Li (Eds.) op. cit.
3. Huang, P. C. C. (1985) *The Peasant Economy and Social Change in North China*. Stanford: Stanford University Press, Chapter 3.
4. Calculated from *SZTJNJ 1992*, p. 11.
5. The north China plain was subject to flooding almost every year. Huang, P. C. C. (1990) op. cit., p. 43.
6. Huang, M. D. (1993) *Chengzhen tixide jiegou yu yanhua: Lilun fenxi yu shizheng yanjiu* (*The Structure and Evolution of Urban Systems: Theoretical Analysis and Case Study*). Unpublished Ph.D. dissertation: East China Normal University, Shanghai, pp. 80, 81.
7. Huang, P. C. C. (1990) op. cit., alludes to a long standing debate in China that focuses attention upon the need to coordinate local efforts in the lower Yangzi delta for regional benefit. Major flood events in 1991, 1995 and 1998 that I call 'administrative floods' have again highlighted how lack of adequate cooperation between Shanghai, Jiangsu and Zhejiang exacerbated the innundations. See, for example, Gao, A. M. (1992) Jiangsu sets its growth strategy. *China Daily*, 26 March, p. 4. For many years geographers at East China Normal University have been predicting just such disastrous events. In the conclusion I will raise specific issues relating to administrative structure, jurisdiction, and power that must be resolved to overcome the local squabbling which bedevils regional coordination.
8. Wang, J. F. (1984) Ming Qing Jiangnan shizhen jiegou ji lishi jiazhi chutan (Jiangnan cities and towns during the Ming and Qing Dynasties: Their structure and historical value). *Huadong shifan daxue xuebao: Zhexue shehui kexue ban.* (*Journal of East China Normal University: Philosophy and social sciences edition*) (1), p. 75.

9. Skinner, G. W. (1977) Regional urbanization in nineteenth-century China. In G. W. Skinner (Ed.) *The City in Late Imperial China*. Stanford: Stanford University Press.

10. Huang, P. C. C. (1990) op. cit., p. 48; Mote, F. W. (1973) A millennium of Chinese urban history: Form, time, and space concepts in Soochow. *Rice University Studies* 59 (4), p. 43, claims that Suzhou was never China's largest city; Johnson, L. C. (1993) Preface. In L. C. Johnson (Ed.) *Cities of Jiangnan in Late Imperial China*. Albany: State University of New York Press, p. x, suggests, on the other hand, that Suzhou was the largest and most prosperous city in the Empire in the late imperial period.

11. Shih, J. C. (1992) *Chinese Rural Society in Transition: A Case Study of the Lake Tai Area, 1368–1800*. Berkeley: Institute of East Asian Studies, pp. 81–82.

12. Skinner, G. W. (1985) Rural marketing in China: Revival and reappraisal. In S. Plattner (Ed.) *Markets and Marketing*. Lanham: University Press of America.

13. Densely populated rural areas of the lower Yangzi delta were tied directly to higher level markets by an excellent network of navigable canals. Through an agency system and widespread boat ownership, small towns via hundreds of agent boats could supply tens of thousands of rural households; See especially: Fei, X. T. (1939) *Peasant Life in China*. London: Routledge, pp. 101–102; Marmé, M. (1993) Heaven on earth: The rise of Suzhou, 1127–1550. In L. C. Johnson (Ed.) op. cit., p. 34.

14. Huang, P. C. C. (1990) op. cit., 11–18 passim, describes two patterns of development in the peasant economy of the delta in Late Imperial times: 'intensification' in which output or output value expands at the same rate as labour input; and 'involutionary growth' and 'involutionary commercialization' (based on the famous study from Geertz, C. (1963) *Agricultural Involution: The Process of Ecological Change in Indonesia*. Berkeley: University of California Press) in which total output expands, but at the cost of diminished marginal returns.

15. Hou, C. M. (1963) Economic dualism: The case of China, 1840–1937. *Journal of Economic History* 23 (3); Murphey, R. (1977) *The Outsiders*. Ann Arbor: University of Michigan Press.

16. Huang, P. C. C. (1990) op. cit., pp. 133–136; Shih, J. C. (1992) op. cit., pp. 120–125.

17. Skinner, G. W. (1977) op. cit.; Skinner's lower Yangzi urban region also included parts of northern Zhejiang Province including Hangzhou and Ningbo; Also referred to in Pannell, C. W. and Veeck, G. (1989) Zhujiang delta and Sunan: A comparative analysis of regional urban systems and their development. *Asian Geographer* 8 (1 and 2), p. 137.

18. Mote, F. W. (1973) op. cit., p. 44.

19. Ibid., p. 47; According to Skinner, G. W. (1977) op. cit., p. 238, in 1843 Shanghai was ranked fourth in the lower Yangzi delta urban system after Suzhou, Hangzhou and Nanjing.

20. Marmé, M. (1993) op. cit., p. 38.

21. Rowe, W. T. (1993) Introduction. In L. C. Johnson (Ed.) op. cit., p. 12.

22. Across China the output value of such sideline production nearly doubled to RMB 2.2 billion in the five years to 1954. See: Byrd, W. A. and Lin, Q. S. (1990) China's rural industry: An introduction. In W. A. Byrd and Q. S. Lin (Eds.) *China's Rural Industry: Structure, Development, and Reform*. Oxford: Oxford University Press, p. 9; Ho, S. P. S. (1994) *Rural China in Transition: Non-agricultural Development in Rural Jiangsu, 1978–1990*. Oxford: Clarendon, p. 13.

23. Estimates vary, but most observers agree that perhaps 20–30 million Chinese died during the 1960–1962 famine.

24. Known as the 'four transformations' (*sihua*) they were linked to the development of the 'five small industries' (*wu xiao gongye*) – locally run enterprises that utilized lower level technology to produce iron and steel, cement, energy, chemical fertilizers and agricultural machinery. For more discussion regarding why China promoted small-scale industry to modernize agriculture see: American Rural Small-Scale Industry Delegation (1977) *Rural Small-scale Industry in the People's Republic of China.* Berkeley: University of California Press, Chapters 1, 4, 9; Sigurdson, J. (1977) *Rural Industrialization in China.* Cambridge: Council on East Asian Studies, Harvard University, Chapters 1, 6.

25. Research in other parts of the lower Yangzi delta, especially near Wuxi, confirms this finding. See: Byrd, W. A. and Lin, Q. S. (1990) op. cit., p. 7.

26. *JSSSN 1949–1989*, p. 138; According to Ho, S. P. S. (1994) op. cit., p. 19, commune and brigade enterprise output across China for the same period increased by an annual average of 38 per cent.

27. For a superb review of the political economy of this period see Lieberthal, K. (1995) *Governing China: From Revolution Through Reform.* New York: Norton.

28. Croll, E. (1994) *From Heaven to Earth: Images and Experience of Development in China.* London: Routledge, Chapter 2; Huang, P. C. C. (1990) op. cit., p. 319.

29. *JSTJNJ 1992*, pp. 107, 111, 112; *JSTJNJ 1994*, pp. 134, 137, 138.

30. Huang, P. C. C. (1990) op. cit., p. 17–18.

31. Cultivation includes all crop production in the standard Chinese statistical categories including staple grains, cotton, silk, oil seeds and so on.

32. The figure for Forestry (one of the five standard statistical categories for agriculture in China) has been excluded since in all cases it never comprised more than 1 per cent of the GVAO in Jiangsu.

33. The data for 1995 were used since this was the most recent year that figures on the area of arable land were reported for all units. The most recent figures report the area of land actually sown (*bo zhong*) which is much larger than the area for arable land due to double and triple cropping. The five classifications of values plotted in this map, and in subsequent Maps 3.2 and 3.4 to 3.8, were determined as follows: Data for the county level units was ranked and categorized initially into five classifications divided at each of the twentieth, fortieth, sixtieth, and eightieth percentiles. In all but one case (Map 3.7) the data for each of the fourteen sets of urban districts (thirteen prefectural seats in Jiangsu plus Shanghai City) were excluded for the purpose of determining each of these percentile divisions. In some cases data for the four suburban counties in Shanghai Municipality were also excluded when determining classification intervals. For example, data for agricultural productivity in Map 3.2 was categorized without including the values from Shanghai. This seems reasonable if we consider the somewhat special circumstances which lead to higher output values for the suburban counties in Shanghai which have greater opportunities to engage in higher value production of cash crops for the enormous urban market within this administrative jurisdiction. In other cases, such as the population density figures illustrated in Map 3.3, values for Shanghai were included when determining the intervals. Finally, classification intervals were sometimes adjusted slightly to reflect the existence of obvious statistical and spatial clustering.

34. Veeck, G. (1991) Regional variations in employment and income in Jiangsu Province. In N. Ginsburg, B. Koppel and T. G. McGee (Eds.) *The Extended Metropolis: Settlement Transition in Asia.* Honolulu: University of Hawaii Press, p. 166. Veeck also suggests, however, that environmental conditions

and land quality are more effective estimators of agricultural productivity than labour since the large surplus rural work force in many areas keeps per-capita output values low. Thus, I have calculated output value per unit area of arable land to provide a more reliable comparison of agricultural productivity over space.

35. I was able to locate surface water area figures for only Changzhou and Suzhou. Thus, Kunshan for example, with water covering 22.3 per cent of its administrative area, would yield a corrected population density figure of 874 people per square kilometre.
36. Ho, S. P. S. (1994) op. cit., p. 27.
37. Interview notes.
38. Calculated from: *JSTJNJ 1992*, pp. 93–95, 107; *JSTJNJ 1994*, pp. 131, 134.
39. Calculated from: *ZGNCTN 1999*, p. 297.
40. Prior to 1993 these values were called total social product (*shehui zong chanzhi*) and referred to the gross output value of the material products sectors. See Appendix 1.
41. Although data are compared in constant values and state procurement prices in the agricultural sector rose sharply during this period, widespread price deregulation in most industrial sectors has probably inflated the relative value of output from industry. Even when this is taken into consideration, however, it is clear that the growth of rural industry was the most significant component of rural restructuring in Jiangsu.
42. The figures here for the number of employees refers to the actual number of workers employed in rural enterprises which may include people with official registration above the township level and/or from other areas.
43. *JSTJNJ 1988*, p. 125; *JSTJNJ 1991*, p. 91; *JSTJNJ 1992*, p. 78, 101; *JSTJNJ 1994*, p. 33, 129; *JSTJNJ 1999*, p. 144.
44. For more details about this phenomenon see Appendix 2.
45. *JSTJNJ 1999*, p. 236.
46. Ibid.
47. This point is repeatedly emphasized by Ho. For example see: Ho, S. P. S. (1994) op. cit., pp. 27, 29, 47.
48. Veeck, G. (1991) op. cit.
49. *SHTJNJ 1998*, pp. 179, 222–225.
50. Calculated from: *JSTJNJ 1999*, pp. 363–367, 384–385.
51. Ibid., pp. 427, 441, 446. The data calculated for Shanghai were for the municipal region as a whole.
52. Calculated from: *JSTJNJ 1999*, pp. 363–367, 384–385.
53. *HDDTNJ 1993*, pp. 230–231. For a more detailed discussion of the spatial patterns in the early 1990s see: Marton, A. M. (1995c) Mega-urbanization in southern Jiangsu: Enterprise location and the reconstitution of local space. *Chinese Environment and Development* 6 (1 and 2).
54. Veeck, G. (1991) op. cit., p. 167.
55. I prefer the term 'mega-urban region' or 'mega-urbanization' in this context to capture the nature of the processes at work in the lower Yangzi delta. Terms such as 'extended metropolitan region', on the other hand, imply that the spatial economic transformation is primarily driven by the growth and expansion of city based processes of metropolitanization that are pushing out into the adjacent countryside. While such processes are still important, clearly I wish to place greater emphasis on the local factors driving rural restructuring in the delta.
56. Interview notes.
57. Ibid.

58. Data for total output (or total social product of the material products sectors as it was called then) for Kunshan was unavailable in constant prices. However, growth rates for industrial and/or agricultural output discussed below are determined from data compared in real terms.
59. Calculated from: *KSTJNJ 1989*, p. 9; *KSTJNJ 1991*, p. 7; *JSSXJJ 1993*, pp. 59, 83; *JSSSN 1949–1989*, pp. 317–318, 393–394; *SZTJNJ 1991*, p. 15; *SZTJNJ 1992*, p. 15.
60. Calculated from: *ZGTJNJ 1993*, pp. 50–51.
61. Ibid.; See note 54.
62. After 1992 China's official statistics no longer calculated total social product figures. Thereafter, figures based on conventional GDP calculations were reported. Since neither total output nor GDP figures were reported across the entire period 1978 to 1998, I have created the separate, but overlapping, Tables 3.4 and 3.5 to illustrate the dramatic growth and restructuring in Kunshan and China.
63. *JSTJNJ 1999*, p. 427
64. Ibid., p. 429.
65. This finding is consistent with numerous recent studies which have examined industrialization and urban growth for all of China. For example: Yan, X. P. (1995) Chinese urban geography since the late 1970s. *Urban Geography* 16 (6), p. 474 refers to several Chinese studies which demonstrate how the shift of rural labour into non-agricultural activities has largely occurred in situ. Yan also claims, however, that this occupational transfer without significant migration into urban centres is only a transitional stage. More will be said about this assertion in the conclusion. Wu, H. X. Y. (1994) Rural to urban migration in the People's Republic of China. *The China Quarterly* 139, p. 692 has also clearly demonstrated how China's non-agricultural share of gross domestic product has grown much faster than its urban share of both total population and employment.
66. Informants in Shipai and Bacheng townships in Kunshan, for example, reported that daytime populations rose from 4,000 to 10,000 and 1,500 to 8,000 persons respectively, for each township seat. (Interview notes.) This is consistent with survey data reported in a study from Nanjing Normal University which shows daytime populations in four township seats across the lower Yangzi delta ranging between 24 per cent to 209 per cent larger than the resident populations. See: Nanjing Normal University, Department of Geography (1990) *Jiangnan nongcun juluo yu chengshihua yanjiu: Sunan fada diqu nongcun chengzhenhua tujing tantao (Jiangnan Rural Agglomeration and Urbanization Research: Methods of Inquiry into Southern Jiangsu Rural Urbanization)*. Nanjing: Nanjing Normal University, Department of Geography, p. 17. On any given day then, approximately a quarter to one half the total population of some towns in Kunshan, and elsewhere in the delta, commute to work in the town seat.
67. *HDDTNJ 1993*, p. 330; Also see Appendix 2. Individuals designated as non-agricultural (with urban registration) resided almost exclusively in urban administrative areas. As such they had access to certain benefits such as subsidized grain and other food commodities, and social welfare. However, since the beginning of reforms, the original intent and influence of these administrative designations has weakened.
68. Interview notes; and *KSTJNJ 1991* p. 14. For example: While officially classified non-agricultural residents in Shipai, Penglang and Diandong townships in Kunshan numbered 1,641, 1,870, and 1,578 persons respectively in 1991, local informants estimated the actual number of residents of these township seats to be 4,000, 6,000, and 4,000 respectively. By 1998, the official figure

for the non-agricultural population in Kunshan was 30 per cent of the total. However, the official figure still conceals much about the actual residential location of the non-agricultural population. See: *SZTJNJ 1999*, p. 51.

69. Criteria for what constitutes a city or town in China, related definitions of urban, and changing administrative boundaries have fluctuated greatly since 1949 leading to wide variations in the estimates of the proportion of the population considered urban. For example see: Chan, K. W. (1987) Further information about China's urban population statistics: Old and new. *The China Quarterly 109*; Chan, K. W. (1988) Rural–urban migration in China, 1950–1982: Estimates and analysis. *Urban Geography 9* (1); Chan, K. W. (1994) Urbanization and rural–urban migration in China since 1982: A new baseline. *Modern China 20* (3); Chan, K. W. and Xu, X. Q. (1985) Urban population growth and urbanization in China since 1949: Reconstructing a baseline. *The China Quarterly 104*; Goldstein, S. (1990) Urbanization in China, 1982–1987. *Population and Development Review 16* (4); Kirkby, R. J. R. (1985) *Urbanization in China: Town and Country in a Developing Economy 1949–2000 AD*. London: Routledge; Lee, Y. S. (1989) Small towns and China's urbanization level. *The China Quarterly 120*; Ma, L. J. C. and Cui, G. H. (1987) Administrative changes and urban population in China. *AAAG 77* (3); Based on the 1990 census the most recent generally accepted estimate for the level of urbanization in China is 26.2 per cent. See: The National Population Census Office (1991) *Zhongguo disici renkou pucha de zhuyao shuju* (*Major Figures of the Fourth Population Census of China*). Beijing: State Statistical Publishers, pp. 76, 83; Yu, D. P. (1995) Heli duliang diqu chengshihua shuiping de silu (Considerations for the rational measure of regional urbanization levels). *Renkou yu jingji* (*Population and Economics*) (5), p. 42 provides an adjusted times series which suggests that China was 27.6 per cent urban in 1992. The most recent contribution to this discussion is from: Zhang, L. and Zhao, S. X. B. (1998) Re-examining China's 'urban' concept and level of urbanization. *China Quarterly 154*, p. 376–377. They show an adjusted time series which suggests that China was 33 per cent urbanized in 1995.

70. KSXZ (1990), pp. 131–141; As with other estimates based on the official statistics for non-agricultural population, this value needs to be placed within the context of shifting definitions and mass campaigns that often dramatically affected urban and rural populations at the local level. The official non-agricultural population in Kunshan comprised between 16 to 18 per cent of the total from 1949 to 1960 after which it declined gradually, reaching 10 per cent in the late 1960s and where it remained until the late 1970s.

71. Calculated from the same figures used above to estimate the true level of urbanization. Interview notes; and *KSTJNJ 1991*, p. 14; *KSTJNJ 1996*, p. 31.

72. Calculated from: Ibid.; KSXZ (1990), pp. 131–141. Several recent studies provide evidence for similar findings across China: Li, M. H. (1994) Woguo renkou qianyi de liuxiang (China's migration flow). *Renkou yanjiu* (*Population Research*) 18 (3), p. 51; Wang F. (1993) Woguo 'sanpu' zi 'sipu' jian shizhen renkou zhenzhang goucheng fenxi (Structural analysis of China's urban population growth between the third and fourth census). *Renkou yanjiu* (*Population Research*) 17 (4), pp. 16–17 shows that between 1985 and 1990, more than 55 million people migrated permanently from rural areas to townships and towns within the same county. This was 4.1 times the number who migrated from provincial, prefectural, and county level units to cities and towns outside those jurisdictions; Wu, H. X. Y. (1994) op. cit., p. 697; Zhu, J. M. (1993) Zhongguo dacheng shiqu renkou zhenzhang de feizhongxinhua yanjiu (A study of the non-centralization of population growth in China's large urban areas). *Renkou yanjiu* (*Population Research*) 17 (6), pp. 29–30. Meanwhile,

Xu, X. Q., Ouyang, N. J. and Zhou, C. S. The changing urban system of China: New developments since 1978. *Urban Geography* 16 (6) show that between 1978 and 1990 small and very large cities grew the most rapidly. However, since they have apparently excluded nearly 150 million urban people from their analysis of city growth, it is possible to infer that a substantial proportion of growth in the urban population of China has occurred in small towns (see their Table 3, p. 497).

73. Calculated from: *JSTJNJ* 1999, pp. 363–367, 384–385.
74. Interview notes.
75. Ibid.; *China Daily* (1991a) Kunshan races on fast track. 27 October, p. 4; Kunshan People's Government (1992) *Banhao nongcun gongye xiaoqu: Tigao fazhan xiangzhen qiye* (*Good Management of Rural Industrial Zones will Improve the Development of Rural Enterprises*). Kunshan: Kunshan People's Government; Zhang S. C. (1996) *Kunshan fazhan guiji jishi* (*A Record of Kunshan's Course of Development*). Nanjing: Jiangsu People's Press, p. 160.
76. *JSTJNJ* 1999, pp. 369, 381; *SZTJNJ* 1999, p. 60.
77. *SZTJNJ* 1999, p. 60.
78. Calculated from: *KSTJNJ* 1996, p. 96.

4 Transforming the Kunshan countryside: structure of local government and relationship to enterprises

In Chapter 2 I argued that the conceptual framework proposed for understanding and explaining mega-urbanization in the lower Yangzi delta should necessarily privilege local circumstances. I also suggested the need to examine the details of local institutional structures as they related to larger patterns and trends and, more specifically, to consider the activities of industrial enterprises in their institutional and transactive contexts. The processes by which institutional structures are linked to regional economic development in China are complex, usually ill-defined, and frequently quite puzzling. By undertaking an analysis that is sensitive to local cultural and historical circumstances, however, particular insights can reveal how spatial economic change is affected by evolving institutional structures, and conversely, uncover the socio-political consequences of recent reforms and the resulting transformation of the rural economy.

This chapter explores the relationships between the changing structure of community administration, the development of rural non-agricultural enterprises, and the emergence of institutional structures which managed local economic activity in Kunshan. The first section begins with a review of the recent changes in community administration and how they related to the wider hierarchy of authority and jurisdiction in China. The latter part of this section discusses how reforms in public finances stimulated local development imperatives and the emergence of rural industrial enterprises. These issues are related to the spatial proliferation of rural industrial enterprises introduced in the second section. Details of how community governments in Kunshan formalized local institutional structures and the means by which local cadres were able to influence town and village development are discussed in the third section. The chapter concludes with a summary that highlights key elements of mega-urbanization, as conceptualized in Chapter 2, to illustrate how particular findings from this analysis of the structure of local government and its relationship to enterprises challenges conventional views of regional development in China.

Bifurcation of the functions of local government

Community administration

On 27 July 1989 Kunshan was administratively reclassified from a county (*xian*) to a county level city (*xianji shi*).[1] Having met certain criteria which accorded it economically more developed status, the new designation was intended to promote further industrialization and urban construction. The inclusion of large areas of the Kunshan countryside into 'city' status (the former county boundary remained unchanged) was aimed at better integrating rural and urban sectors at the local level. Able to deal more directly with the province, Kunshan also experienced less interference from intermediate levels of administration since, with reclassification, it became equal in planning terms to the prefectural level city of Suzhou.[2] This increased autonomy included greater authority to collect and retain tax revenues from enterprises and to locally approve higher values of external investment in Kunshan. More than anything else, local authorities emphasized how 'city' status carried greater prestige than the county designation. Since Kunshan became 'more famous', outsiders would be more willing to invest here, and as a city, they could set higher standards for themselves.[3] When pressed for further details one CCP official referred to the new television station and a new ticket office for the Shanghai based China Eastern Airlines – the only one outside Shanghai at the time. In addition, more passenger and freight trains could stop in Kunshan which was 'good for opening-up to the outside'.[4]

Kunshan's city designation also changed its internal relationship with its twenty townships, the lowest level of the urban administrative hierarchy. By 1990 all twenty had been elevated from township (*xiang*) to designated town (*jianzhi zhen*) status.[5] As with the county level reclassification, designated towns in Kunshan acquired new authority to raise funds for local development.[6] In addition, they were also supposed to receive county (now city) level allocations for town construction. In practice, however, these funds were inadequate, so town governments increasingly turned to other more substantial and stable sources of revenue. Under the official notion of 'town leading the development of the countryside', towns were to act as a 'bridge' to revenue generating opportunities in areas of the countryside directly under their jurisdiction.[7]

Map 4.1 illustrates the location of town seats, their respective administrative regions, and Kunshan's 463 villages. Village level administrative boundaries are not shown. In addition to their respective government functions, Yushan and Chengbei town seats formed the built-up core of Kunshan, including the municipal (Kunshan) government seat, and were administered as a single urban unit by the Kunshan level bureaucracy.[8] The municipal government also directly administered at least five specialized state farms in Zhoushi, Zhengyi and Penglang towns, the Special Economic

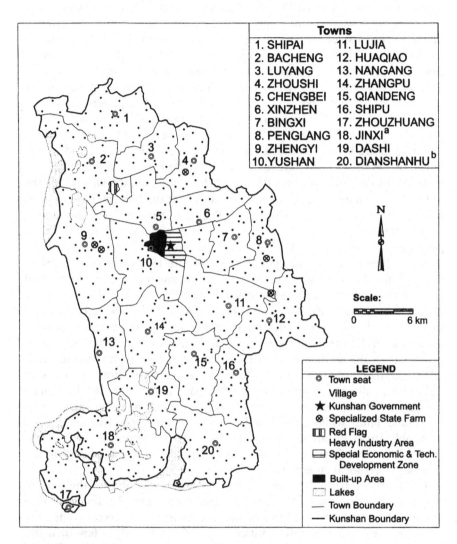

Towns	
1. SHIPAI	11. LUJIA
2. BACHENG	12. HUAQIAO
3. LUYANG	13. NANGANG
4. ZHOUSHI	14. ZHANGPU
5. CHENGBEI	15. QIANDENG
6. XINZHEN	16. SHIPU
7. BINGXI	17. ZHOUZHUANG
8. PENGLANG	18. JINXI[a]
9. ZHENGYI	19. DASHI
10.YUSHAN	20. DIANSHANHU[b]

LEGEND

◎ Town seat
· Village
★ Kunshan Government
⊗ Specialized State Farm
▥ Red Flag Heavy Industry Area
▱ Special Economic & Tech. Development Zone
■ Built-up Area
▭ Lakes
— Town Boundary
— Kunshan Boundary

Scale:
0   6 km

Map 4.1 Kunshan: administrative divisions, 1998.

Notes
a Formerly Chenmu.
b Formerly Diandong.

Sources: Adapted from: *KSSDMT* (1993); *KSXZ* (1990), unpaginated preface; *SZTJNJ* 1999, p. 14.

and Technological Development Zone just to the east of Yushan Town, and the Red Flag (*Hong Qi*) Industrial Area in Bacheng, jointly administered with Yushan. While the administrative boundaries illustrated in Map 4.1 were spatially distinct, they also embodied complex overlapping, and often conflicting, patterns of authority, jurisdiction and power that were much less clear. This was true not only of different levels in the administrative hierarchy, but also of the various agencies at any given level. Understanding the nature of how these patterns were constructed, negotiated, and operationalized in Kunshan reveals much about the processes and characteristics of local development. Before proceeding, however, it is necessary to provide an administrative context over and through which such patterns emerged.

Table 4.1 outlines the structure and development of the Kunshan administration between 1978 and 1997. Only the main units of local government in Kunshan are listed. Excluded are the numerous sub-sections and subordinate offices of the local bureaucracy. Also excluded are the chief decision-making and executive bodies sitting atop these bureaux, the various organs of the CCP, and grass-roots organizations such as the Political Consultative Committee, and the local Congress of People's Deputies.[9] The table illustrates, therefore, changes in the broad mid-level administration of the local government bureaucracy. The first two columns for 1978 and 1985 illustrate the changes which occurred between the late 1970s when central planning remained dominant to the mid-1980s by which time the reforms had become well established. The last column for 1997 outlines the most recent elements of community administration in the period often referred to as market socialism. Two fundamental trends are apparent: the enormous expansion in the size and range of responsibilities of the local bureaucracy; and what might be described as the corporatization of the bureaucratic-administrative mid-section of the Kunshan government. Both trends were linked to the disengagement of the central government from local administration and the reduction of state allocations which financed many of its functions. Thus, while central and provincial authorities still determined local obligations through economic and administrative policies and regulations, their financing and implementation at the county level and below were a largely local enterprise.

The term 'enterprise' is used deliberately here to connote the way in which local government in Kunshan bifurcated into the dual roles of community administration, and owner and manager of several companies and corporate-like economic entities. Table 4.1 lists only a few of these. By the end of 1997 there were at least 100 companies directly or indirectly affiliated with some part of the Kunshan level government bureaucracy. Some of these firms emerged as a result of the partial commercialization and marketization of government functions within the old state run command economy structures. The most important of these companies became integral components of the various industrial and commercial bureaux and related exchange and distribution organizations under the Planning and Economic Commissions (see Table 4.1). These companies also provided a significant proportion of the financing for their respective administrative organizations, including supplementary bonuses for state employees and the full salaries of other bureaucrats not covered by state

Table 4.1 Structure and development of community administration in Kunshan, 1978–1997

1978 (central planning)	1985 (reform)	1997 (market socialism)
County Government Office	County Government Office	Municipal Government Office[a]
Civil Affairs Bureau	Civil Affairs Bureau	Civil Affairs Bureau[a]
		Civil Affairs Industrial Company[a]
		Administrative Organs Mgmt. Bureau
Culture and Education Bureau	Culture and Education Bureau	Culture Bureau
		Education Bureau
		School Industries Supply and Sales Sect.
Personnel Bureau	Personnel Bureau	Personnel Bureau[a]
	Labour Bureau	Labour Bureau
		Labour Services Company
		Employment Management Office
	Statistics Bureau	Statistics Bureau
		Price Bureau
Financial Services Bureau	Financial Services Bureau	Finance Bureau
		Jiangsu and Suzhou Accounting Offices
		Audit Bureau
	Tax Bureau	Local Tax Bureau
		National Tax Bureau
Public Security Bureau	Public Security Bureau	Public Security Bureau
	Justice Bureau	Justice Bureau
Grain Bureau	Grain Bureau	Grain Bureau[a]
		Cereals and Edible Oils Sup. and Sales Co.
	Food Office	Food Company
Agriculture Bureau	Agriculture Bureau	Agriculture Bureau[a]
		Agricultural Products and Materials Co.
Water Conservancy Bureau	Water Conservancy Bureau	Water Conservancy Bureau
Agricultural Machinery Bureau		Agricultural Machinery Company[a]
Economic Diversification Mgmt. Bureau	Economic Diversification Mgmt. Bureau	Economic Diversification Mgmt. Bureau[a]
		Diversification Management Corporation[a]
		Sideline Products Office
Planning Committee	Planning Committee	Planning Commission
Industry Bureau	Industry and Commerce Bureau	Industry and Commerce Administration and Management Bureau

Table 4.1 (continued)

1978 (central planning)	1985 (reform)	1997 (market socialism)
		Industry Supply and Sales Company
No. 2 Industry Bureau	Industrial Company	No. 2 Industrial Supply and Sales Co.
Commerce Bureau	Commerce Bureau	Commerce Bureau
Finance and Trade Office		Commercial Corporation
		Commercial Inspection Bureau
		Commercial Market Construction Office
Supply and Sales Office	Supply and Sales Office	Supply and Sales Cooperation Office
		Supply and Sales Corporation
Goods and Materials Bureau	Goods and Materials Bureau	Goods and Materials Bureau
		Goods and Materials Management Co.
		Coal and Petroleum Company
	Economic Commission	Economic Commission[a]
		Industrial Wholesale Company
		Chemical, Pharmaceutical and Construct. Materials Industries Bureau[a]
		Chemical and Pharmaceutical Supply and Sales Company
		Construction Materials Company
		Machinery, Electronics and Metallurgical Industries Bureau[a]
		Mach., Electronics, and Metallurgical Co.
		Textiles Bureau[a]
		Textiles Company[a]
		Light Industry Bureau
		Light Industry Company
	Rural Industry Bureau	Rural Industry Bureau[a]
	Economic Cooperation Commission	Economic Cooperation Commission[a]
		Economic and Technical Cooperation Off.
		Economic and Technical Cooperation and Development Company

1978 (central planning)	1985 (reform)	1997 (market socialism)
		Economic System Reform Commission[a]
		Economic Research Centre[a]
		Foreign Economic Relations and Trade Commission
Foreign Trade Bureau	Foreign Trade Bureau	Foreign Trade Company
		Suzhou Customs Office
		Special Economic and Technological Dev Zone (SETDZ) Mgmt. Committee[a]
		SETDZ Agriculture, Industry and Commercial Corporation
		Industrial Trade Corporation
		Tertiary Industry Office
		Tourism Bureau
		Economic Development Corporation
	Basic Construction Bureau	Urban and Rural Construction Bureau[a]
		Public Parks Construction Office
		Land Management Bureau
		Real Estate Development Administration
Public Health Bureau	Public Health Bureau	Public Health Bureau
Transportation Bureau	Transportation Bureau	Transportation Bureau[a]
		Transportation Corporation[1]
Post and Tele-communications Bureau	Post and Tele-communications Bureau	Post and Tele-communications Bureau
Science Committee	Science and Technology Committee	Science and Technology Commission
Sports Committee	Sports Committee	Sports Committee
		Sanitation Committee
		Social Safety Management Committee
Birth Control Office	Birth Control Office	Birth Control Committee
		Standards and Measures Bureau
		Reception Bureau
		Investigations Bureau
	Nationalities and Religious Affairs Section	Nationalities and Religious Affairs Sect.
	Foreign Affairs Office	Foreign Affairs Office[a]

Table 4.1 (continued)

1978 (central planning)	1985 (reform)	1997 (market socialism)
	Overseas Chinese Affairs Office	Overseas Chinese Affairs Office
		Overseas Chinese Construction Office
		Senior Citizens Office
	Archives Bureau	Archives Bureau
		Local Gazetteer Office
	Environmental Protection Office	Environmental Protection Bureau
		Environmental Protection Industry Supply and Sales Company
	Electricity Supply Bureau	Electricity Supply Bureau
	Broadcast and Television Bureau	Broadcast and Television Bureau
		Broadcast and Television Company
	Staff and Workers Education Office	Staff and Workers Education Office[a]
	Suzhou Television University	Suzhou Television University
	Salt Industry Company	Salt Industry Company
	Tobacco Speciality Sales Bureau	Tobacco Speciality Sales Bureau
		Tobacco Company
		Cigarettes, Sugar and Liquor Company
	Weather Station	Weather Bureau
	Insurance Company	Insurance Company
People's Bank of China	People's Bank of China	People's Bank of China
Agricultural Bank of China	Agricultural Bank of China	Agricultural Bank of China
	People's Construction Bank of China	People's Construction Bank of China
	Industrial and Commercial Bank	Industrial and Commercial Bank
		Bank of Communications

Note
a Interviewed.

Sources:
Several interviews; *Kunshan dianhua haobu 1996* (*Kunshan Telephone Directory 1996*).
Kunshan: Post and Telecommunications Bureau; *Kunshan xianzhi* (1990) (*Kunshan County Gazetteer*). Shanghai: Shanghai People's Publishers, pp. 254–264, 514–517.

allocations.[10] Other companies were created solely in order to increase extrabudgetary revenues for the benefit of their respective bureaux and/or their clients, engaging in activities largely unrelated to the administrative functions of local government. The Civil Affairs Bureau, for example, operated several enterprises in this category including a chemical factory and plastic works which employed more than 200 workers, 90 per cent of whom were handicapped.[11] In addition to the numerous small school-based factories which were part of the educational infrastructure and labour curriculum, the Education Bureau also operated a large and very successful enterprise with nearly 1,000 workers that manufactured children's bicycles, tricycles and strollers.

Table 4.1 also illustrates the emergence of specialized organizations which were created to manage and promote exchange and distribution for the large number of enterprises which were not part of the planned economy. Agencies such as the Rural Industry Bureau, the Economic Cooperation Commission, and the Economic and Technical Cooperation and Development Office facilitated access to the means of production, technical and management expertise, and markets necessary for the successful development of local industrial enterprises. The nature of these linkages, interactions and interrelationships, and the institutional parameters which embodied them, are discussed in more detail below and in the two chapters which follow. Suffice it to say at this point that the emergence of these organizations and their affiliated corporate-like entities, reflected dramatic changes in the local space economy.

This transformation has, of course, not gone unnoticed by the central government. As a result, two other very important organizations were established in Kunshan as part of a nationwide effort to undertake structural reform: the Economic System Reform Commission (*Ti gai hui*); and the Economic Research Centre (see Table 4.1).[12] Both concentrated their efforts on investigating and implementing strategies for separating government administration (and by default the CCP) from the economy. While the corporatization of government bureaucracy in Kunshan was linked to the dramatic growth and structural changes in the local economy, the official view was that the overlap of government administrative and economic functions was unhealthy in the long term. In addition to the large number of local government run companies, the fact that agencies such as the Bank of Communications and other banks, which were supposed to operate on purely commercial criteria, were considered part of the local administration, suggests that the practical realities of separating government and the economy were profoundly more complex (see the bottom of Table 4.1).

At the town and village levels, overlap of civil administration, CCP affairs, and management of the economy was even more apparent. Town and village CCP secretaries often served in government bureaux and frequently held directorships in the town's Economic Commission or related companies.[13] Criteria used to assess the performance of these local cadres and, therefore, their level of remuneration, have become increasingly linked to the success of local economic development and the welfare of local residents.[14] Combined with fiscal pressures to increase the revenue base and to raise extrabudgetary funds for local economic development and social welfare, it was easy to see why town and village governments in Kunshan vigorously encouraged the expansion of rural non-agricultural activities.[15]

Ownership and management of enterprises

The rights and responsibilities of the various levels of government were officially most clearly articulated in terms of the fiscal and budgetary system.[16] In practice, the precise functioning of community level governments depended largely upon their ability to generate extrabudgetary revenues. In Kunshan, collectively owned town and village industrial enterprises became the most important source of such revenues. Development and management of these enterprises significantly enhanced the economic and administrative power and autonomy of local governments. Part A of Table 4.2 presents the public financial revenues and expenditures at the town level in Kunshan from 1989 to 1996. The proportion of total town revenues from extrabudgetary sources rose from 31.3 per cent in 1989 to 45.7 per cent in 1991, rising further to 48.4 per cent by 1996. Seventy-five per cent of extrabudgetary revenues over the period 1989 to 1996 was comprised of funds transferred directly to local governments from town enterprises. Approximately 80 per cent of budgetary revenues between 1989 and 1996 were generated by various taxes and fees collected from town enterprises. These amounts, combined with the extrabudgetary revenues transferred directly from enterprises to town governments accounted for 80 to 90 per cent of total revenues between 1989 and 1996 (see Table 4.2).[17] Other extrabudgetary sources included locally collected fees for education and training and special agricultural taxes. Town government spending showed a similar pattern with extrabudgetary expenditures comprising 65.1 per cent of the total in 1991. Town enterprises provided funds for 76.4 per cent of extrabudgetary expenditures in 1991. This is slightly lower than the 80.5 per cent figure for 1989, although the absolute value of such expenditures increased 71 per cent over the same period, accounting for 71.3 per cent of the increase in total extrabudgetary spending.[18] By 1996 the proportion of total expenditures from extrabudgetary sources had decreased to 52.7 per cent. However, the proportion of extrabudgetary expenditures financed by town enterprises had risen to 83 per cent by 1996. Moreover, since total expenditures had nearly quadrupled between 1991 and 1996, the absolute value of the contributions to expenditures from town enterprises was impressive (see Table 4.2).

Part B of Table 4.2 shows the distribution of 1996 extrabudgetary expenditures from town enterprise raised funds. Social welfare expenditures

Table 4.2 Town level public finances in Kunshan

Part A: Revenues and Expenditures, 1989–1996 (million RMB)

| | Total | Budgetary | Extrabudgetary | |
			Town enterprises	Other
		Revenues[a]		
1989	108.55	74.57	24.78	9.20
1990	125.64	79.26	31.73	14.65
1991	139.46	75.73	47.21	16.52
1992	198.73	109.43	64.60	24.70
1993	294.88	199.89	69.01	25.98
1994	284.49	177.48	76.65	30.36
1995	266.81	145.46	91.17	30.18
1996	291.07	150.34	104.86	35.87
		Expenditures[a]		
1989	47.45	17.07	24.46	5.92
1990	70.36	26.00	33.21	11.15
1991	83.94	29.32	41.75	12.87
1992	121.48	40.14	61.76	19.58
1993	161.51	77.17	64.57	19.77
1994	189.90	88.29	76.43	25.18
1995	217.94	94.96	96.75	26.23
1996	247.46	117.14	108.07	22.25

Part B: Distribution of Extrabudgetary Expenditures From Funds Transferred by Enterprises, 1996 (million RMB)

		(%)
Total	108.07	(100)
Enterprise development	2.60	(2.4)
Social welfare (Education, health, culture, etc.)	7.88	(7.3)
Government and related administration	60.15	(55.7)
Agriculture	10.04	(9.3)
Other	27.40	(25.3)

Note
a The figures represent funds actually collected and spent for that year. Budgetary surpluses were transferred to higher levels of government. The differences between extrabudgetary revenues and expenditures were listed as net current account balances.

Sources *KSTJNJ 1989*, pp. 219–221; *KSTJNJ 1991*, pp. 160–163; *KSTJNJ 1993*, pp. 127–129; *KSTJNJ 1995*, pp. 76–78; *KSTJNJ 1996*, pp. 68–69.

included spending on culture, education and health, and public services such as community centres, retirement homes and pensions. Both the absolute value and share of such expenditures in 1996 were down significantly from 1991 when RMB 12.86 million, over 30 per cent of extrabudgetary expenditures financed by town enterprises, went to social welfare. It is likely that the difference was made up for by increased budgetary revenues raised through taxes and fees from booming local enterprises, although there were no data available to confirm this. Meanwhile, government related administration, which included bonuses and salaries for town cadres not covered through state allocations, accounted for the largest proportion of extrabudgetary expenditures comprising nearly 56 per cent of the total. Payments to support agriculture, while still significant, garnered only about half the share they received in 1991. Other expenditures included enterprise and business expenses such as management and consulting fees paid to relevant bureaux as well as other costs normally associated with operating enterprises. These official figures concealed other more dubious government spending on such things as banquets, liquor and cigarettes and travel. While officially disallowed in China, such expenditures were an integral part of government and enterprise operations. Local governments also disguised other financial arrangements within such extrabudgetary ambiguities. Town governments, for example, were not permitted to run budgetary deficits. However, in Kunshan many towns financed local initiatives by securing sizeable bank loans indirectly through local enterprises. Moreover, by fudging enterprise expenditures, town and village governments reduced the tax burden on their collectively owned enterprises, thereby leaving more funds available for discretionary spending.[19]

Economic power and management authority in Kunshan were manifest through the operation of collectively owned community enterprises concentrated at the town and village levels.[20] Under the supervision of the Kunshan Rural Industry Bureau every town established an industrial corporation to oversee the operations of all town and village run industrial enterprises. In addition to its supervisory role, the Rural Industry Bureau provided a range of business services to the town industrial corporations and directly to rural enterprises. The Bureau also regulated and approved the development of enterprises and often acted on their behalf to seek the necessary permission from other parts of the Kunshan administration, such as the Land Management and Environmental Protection Bureaux, for the construction of factories in the countryside. More importantly, the Rural Industry Bureau would facilitate investment and exchange relationships, technological and management cooperation and the training of workers and managers.[21] Another more specific mandate of the Bureau was to promote the development of rural industries that were linked directly to the agricultural sector and which would benefit local farmers.[22] The Bureau itself had thirty-nine employees, only twelve of whom were funded through state allocations. The bulk of the administration, including the twenty-seven non-state employees, was funded through consulting fees collected from rural industrial enterprises and industrial corporations, and the revenues generated by six enterprises owned by the Bureau.

Town industrial corporations acted primarily as the branch of town governments that actually owned and operated town enterprises. These corporations, which also existed in many villages, functioned like holding companies with a board of directors who determined enterprise activities in consultation with managers and town governments. Town and village governments, for example, selected directors for their industrial corporations who would then appoint factory managers. There was, of course, much overlap of responsibility in these respective positions since local government officials frequently served as directors or deputy heads in the industrial corporations and were sometimes intimately involved in the day to day operations of specific enterprises.[23] As long as these enterprises made money, however, managers and the section heads they appointed usually operated with minimal interference from local governments.

Similar to the Kunshan Rural Industry Bureau, industrial corporations also fulfilled other roles relating to the provision of certain services. These included market research for villages that intended to establish an enterprise, advice on the design and implementation of accounting systems, and the allocation and training of workers and management personnel. Similar to an industrial association, the corporation provided 'member' enterprises access to services and expertise for a fee.

Through their supply and sales organizations the industrial corporations also negotiated access to inputs and markets for local enterprises. With the authority, representation, political connections and entrepreneurial savvy of the town government supporting them, industrial corporations in Kunshan facilitated linkages between local enterprises and factory managers, emerging markets, the agricultural sector and, most importantly, the partially reformed command economy structures. In this context even the names of towns became important since the industrial corporations and many local enterprises bore the same name. Thus, the town of Chenmu in southern Kunshan, which means 'old tomb' and is not an auspicious name for doing business, became Jinxi – 'bright and beautiful brook' – in 1993. That same year, the town of Diandong ('East of Dian' [Lake]) became Dianshanhu ('Dianshan Lake') Town for the same reason (see Map 4.1).[24] In addition to its economic functions, the town industrial corporation also provided 'guidance' for the implementation of workplace safety regulations, labour standards including salaries, environmental protection rules and supervised the finances and accounting practices of enterprises. Moreover, the industrial corporation had the power to force enterprise mergers or break-ups if circumstances were deemed appropriate.[25]

Taken together, the administrative, regulatory and economic functions of the town industrial corporations were said to provide the 'internal engine of development'.[26] Although town and some village governments had similar companies in the construction, commercial and services sectors, in value terms they were less important than local industrial corporations. More about the precise transactional relationships and interactions will be discussed below, but it is clear at this point that such organizations embodied complex overlapping, apparently conflicting roles and responsibilities. The nature of the way in which these functions were negotiated and balanced reveals much about the underlying processes and mechanisms driving local development. Informants in Kunshan and other parts of the lower Yangzi delta, repeatedly emphasized the importance of local industrial organizations and the way in which town and village governments 'stimulated' and 'encouraged' investment in local enterprises and the development of production and marketing linkages. The particular institutional parameters to which these comments referred, parallel the historical patterns of local administration outlined in Chapter 3. I refer especially to the emergence of largely autonomous community level bureaucracies, linked primarily to the water management imperatives of late imperial times, which underlie contemporary patterns of administrative jurisdiction and power.

One of the more obvious outcomes of these patterns was the severe restrictions placed upon the development of household and individual level and private industrial enterprises in Kunshan. Under the pre-reform planned agricultural system, Kunshan, like other counties in the Lake Tai region, was under pressure to fulfil high farm production targets and government purchasing quotas. To ensure these obligations were met, local governments banned production teams and individuals from engaging in non-farm activities. They were compensated for this limitation by payments from commune and brigade enterprises through a system of workpoints.[27] However, the abolition of transfers from industrial enterprises to production teams and the shift to direct payment of workers with implementation of the household responsibility system in agriculture in the early 1980s, eliminated powerful disincentives for factory labour. The concomitant substitution of inefficient triple cropping with higher yielding better quality grain and cash crops generated higher farm incomes, stimulated local demand for manufactured goods and released labour from agriculture to work in the newly more productive and rapidly expanding rural industrial enterprises. Thus, by 1984 the ban on production team (by then reorganized into village small groups, joint households and associations or small cooperatives) run factories and other private or individual enterprises was lifted. Within a year, however, these privately run industries were posing stiff competition for commune and brigade (by then township and village) enterprises for markets, skilled personnel and raw materials. Although private industrial enterprises were legally tolerated, measures were put in place by the late 1980s in Kunshan which severely restricted access to loans and subsidized inputs, tightly controlled labour allocation and wage levels, and created a formidable and costly administrative and regulatory environment.[28] The profitability of township and village industries meant that local authorities were reluctant to encourage the development of private enterprises, thus prohibitive obstacles against the development of sizeable ones have persisted. Only in sectors such as commerce, transportation and food services, that did not compete directly with township and village industries, were private enterprises allowed to flourish. These factors served to reinforce the concentration of economic and administrative power, ownership, and management authority at the town and village levels and helps to explain the proliferation of industrial activities into all corners of the Kunshan countryside.

Spatial proliferation of enterprises

Since all town and village governments wished to develop their own enterprises as a source of extrabudgetary revenues this led to the scattering of factories across the countryside. While a number of these enterprises were located in or near the town seats, most were built among the rice paddies, wheat fields, and canola crops (see Plates 4.1 and 4.2). The locational distribution of town and village enterprises was closely linked to the structure of ownership and the territorial extent of the respective administrative jurisdictions.[29] The most important group of enterprises in Kunshan included town and village level industries, which together comprised 69.8 per cent of the 2,205 industrial enterprises and 59.8 per cent of the gross value of industrial output in 1996.[30] This latter value for the share of output from town and village level enterprises is down from the comparable share of 70 per cent in 1990. As will be demonstrated below, however, this decline in share is partly explained by the rapid growth in other non-state sector enterprises located in Kunshan, and not by a decline in the absolute value of industrial output from town and village enterprises, which, in fact, grew in real terms by 217.3 per cent in the six years to 1996. Town and village level enterprises included collectives (396), village factories (745), domestic joint ventures and cooperatives (252), and sino-foreign joint ventures (147) scattered throughout rural Kunshan. It turns out that virtually all of the town and village level industrial enterprises were established in rural locations within the jurisdictions of their respective administrative units.[31] Of the 132 wholly foreign owned industrial enterprises, which accounted for 30.3 per cent of gross output value in 1996, ninety-one were located in the Special Economic and Technological Development Zone (see Map 4.1). The fifty-nine state owned enterprises were located in or near the built-up core of Yushan Town, in a few towns, and in the Red Flag Industrial Area, and were responsible for only 6.8 per cent of total industrial output in Kunshan, down from 14 per cent in 1990. Kunshan also had four joint stock enterprises in 1996. Most of the 470 private enterprises were established in Kunshan's then 466 villages and accounted for only 1.5 per cent of total industrial output. None of the figures for the number of enterprises listed above include the 997 small scale, largely rural, household based individual industrial enterprises which were listed separately in the official statistics. If these latter enterprises, and the figures for private enterprises cited above, are combined, together they accounted for 45.8 per cent of the total number of enterprises, but only 2.2 per cent of total industrial output in 1996. While this share of output is up from 0.9 per cent in 1990, the figures seem to confirm the marginalization of such enterprises

Plate 4.1 Rural enterprises. Shipai Town, Kunshan.

Plate 4.2 Surgical glove factory. Yushan Town, Kunshan.

described in the previous section. In 1998 Kunshan had a total of 3,498 registered industrial enterprises. Of these 3,303 were classified as rural, and together they generated 61 per cent of the total industrial output of RMB 30.52 billion that year.[32]

Across China in 1996, state owned enterprises comprised only 1.4 per cent of the total number of enterprises and accounted for 28.5 per cent of total industrial output, down sharply from 54.6 per cent in 1990. Collectively owned township and village enterprises made up 11 per cent of the total number of industrial enterprises in 1996 and generated 27.7 per cent of total output. Meanwhile, individually owned enterprises (the overwhelming majority of which were located in rural areas) comprised 77.8 per cent of the total number of industrial enterprises in China in 1996 and were responsible for 15.5 per cent of the total output, up from only 5.4 per cent in 1990.[33] By the end of 1998 the number of state owned enterprises across China had decreased to only 0.8 per cent of the total, although they still generated 28.2 per cent of total industrial output. Rural township and village level enterprises (including collectives, individual, and other types of enterprises) made up 83 per cent of the nations 7.97 million enterprises, giving some indication of their spatial proliferation. Rural township and village run enterprises (excluding individual enterprises) accounted for at least 32.2 per cent of the nation's total industrial capacity in 1998, up from 20.2 per cent in 1990.[34]

Linked to the desire of each administrative jurisdiction to maximize local productive opportunities, the sectoral structure of industry across towns and villages in Kunshan has also diversified. Figure 4.1 illustrates the sectoral distribution of the number of enterprises, employees and output values of the enterprises surveyed in Kunshan in 1992. While textiles and related activities were the most important sector, accounting for 34 per cent of output value, 31.1 per cent of employees, and 25.9 per cent of the number of enterprises, chemical, metal fabrication, machinery, building materials and consumer goods industries also proliferated.[35] This sectoral breakdown of industrial activities closely parallels the distribution of such activities across the entire *Suxichang* region.[36] Informants referred to numerous examples of how town and village governments, anxious to achieve the same success as neighbouring communities, invested in virtually identical activities.[37] In addition to the development of broadly similar industrial structures across the region, this spontaneous and haphazard growth created enormous problems related to the provision of infrastructure, duplication and the waste of capital and land. With typical Chinese panache, allusions to such conditions were captured in a local slogan: *cun cun dianhuo, chu chu maoyan* (in every village fires stir, and everywhere is belching smoke) (see Plate 4.1).[38] While such industrial development was 'comprehensive' and relatively successful at the local scale, in regional terms (county level and higher) it remained 'irrational' and spatially scattered.[39]

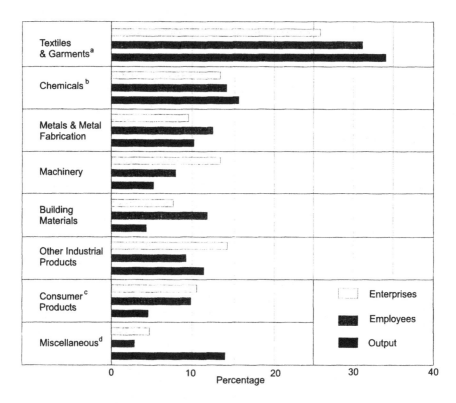

Figure 4.1 Sectoral distribution of enterprises, employees and output: Kunshan.

Notes

a Includes weaving and dyeing, and the production of cloth.
b Includes industrial chemicals, pharmaceuticals, paints, dyes, etc.
c Includes household appliances, shoes, toys, furniture, etc.
d Includes a very large honey manufacturer and a large food commodities trading firm, each responsible for 7.3 per cent and 6.5 per cent respectively of the total output of the enterprises surveyed, in addition to several smaller service companies engaged in transportation, vehicle repair, etc.

Source: Calculated from the enterprise survey data.

In conceptual terms, the diverse structure and spatial proliferation of industrial activities in Kunshan provides further evidence that the rural transformation observed here occurred largely as a response to intensely localized development imperatives, rather than serving merely the exigencies of external (metropolitan) demand or other exogenous forces.[40] The resulting density of residential, industrial, and agricultural land use in rural Kunshan is evident in Plate 4.3. The view is to the west across Chengbei and Xinzhen Towns. It illustrates the classic linear patterns and architecture of southern Jiangsu villages, the rich agricultural lands typical of the region and examples of some township enterprises. As will be shown in the next chapter, most of the fields in the middle-ground have since been converted into village run industrial enterprises. Official concern with the loss of such highly productive land prompted the creation of specially designated agricultural protection zones in several towns in Kunshan (see Plate 4.4).[41] The sign shown in Plate 4.4 outlines the distribution of land quality and the proclamation from the Shipai Town People's Government that decreed its preservation for agricultural production. That such measures were necessary in one of China's richest farming regions says much about the proliferation of non-agricultural activities and hints at the inherent tensions and conflicts which underlie the spatial economic transformation in Kunshan. The means by which these issues were negotiated and resolved, and the institutional structures that emerged to control and manage the local economy are introduced in the next section.

Formalizing local institutional structures in a partially reformed command economy

In addition to demonstrating the inadequacy of conventional approaches which emphasize the role of external economies in regional development, the findings presented thus far highlight the need to understand the way in which specific cultural, political and historical circumstances led to the emergence of institutional structures which controlled and managed economic activity in Kunshan. As will be demonstrated below, these localized structures or modes of domination embodied stratification by bureaucratic hierarchy rather than by market competition and opportunity. These realities in Kunshan should be distinguished from the social stratification and variations in the modes of production motifs advocated in the conventional wisdom.[42]

Capitalism with Chinese characteristics

What emerged during the pre-reform period as local strategies and sub-cultures of economic (and political) survival had blossomed by the late 1980s into a kind of bureaucratic capitalism whereby 'socialist wheeler dealers' pertinaciously served local interests while enhancing their own power.[43] This power was manifest and exercised in several ways. The power and prestige of local cadres in Kunshan was based upon their capacity to negotiate their community's relationship and obligations to the centre. These interactions occurred through personal relations or *guanxi* and via intensely localized administrative and institutional structures that represented local interests. Kunshan was thus able to accumulate resources for its own development by engagement with, and manipulation of the partially reformed command economy structures. Kunshan and community level bureaucrats would reinterpret and distort the rules of the planned economy and bend the guidelines of state managed finance to 'make full

Plate 4.3 Restless landscapes. Chengbei and Xinzhen Towns, Kunshan.

Plate 4.4 Agricultural land protection zone. Shipai Town, Kunshan.

use of the official policies in as flexible a way as possible' to benefit local development.[44] The most common refrain heard in this regard was 'above there is policy, below we have strategy' (*shang you zhengce, xia you jice*, or sometimes *duice* – 'countermeasures'). One especially perceptive informant referred to *cabian qiu* – the phenomenon in ping-pong whereby a player attempts to direct the ball as close as possible to the opponent's edge of the table without going off.

The multiple roles and interests of local governments also meant that issues of enterprise scale and location were often decided administratively for what might otherwise be seen as marginal investments. Numerous officials interviewed throughout the lower Yangzi delta, as well as in Kunshan, spoke passionately about local initiatives, particularly with respect to major infrastructural investments, despite obvious duplication or disarticulation with similar endeavours in neighbouring jurisdictions. When pressed to explain how such investments were considered economically viable, local officials referred to specific means by which they could guarantee the success of such initiatives. These included administrative decrees that forced enterprises within their jurisdiction to purchase locally produced goods, to utilize local services or infrastructure, and the implementation of various administrative barriers to 'protect' these local investments from outside competition.[45]

The spatial economic implications of such intense localism were reflected in the emergence of what some have termed 'palace economies', in which economic efficiencies were subordinated by administrative imperatives linked to areas of jurisdiction, authority and power.[46] Taken together, these factors contributed to the downward dispersion of economic power away from the centre. Clearly, this trend was also prone to deep distortion and corruption within conditions I have elsewhere labelled 'capitalism with Chinese characteristics'.[47] As a result, Kunshan was able to manage its economy as a discrete, autonomous entity and to strongly influence the way it related to the regional, national and global economies.

Individual interactions and interrelationships

The success of community development largely depended upon the expertise, experience, and entrepreneurial savvy of local cadres, workers, and other individuals. The management and technical skills that had built up in Kunshan over the years was thus drawn upon to support the development of local enterprises. Such expertise sometimes came from local residents who had been sent earlier to work in cities, but who were returned to the countryside in the 1960s and 1970s. In addition to their particular skills and experience, they also brought social connections and networks that would become important later in terms of obtaining market information and other assistance. Informants in Kunshan also referred to another group of individuals, who emerged from the political campaigns of the Cultural Revolution, who played an important role in local development. Between 1968 and 1976 more than a million Shanghai youths were rusticated to remote parts of China.[48] Although some have since been permitted to return to Shanghai most were not, so many of them chose to settle in places nearby such as Kunshan.[49] The establishment of numerous successful local enterprises was directly associated with these individuals and their families who provided links not only with Shanghai, but also with the region and units to which they had been sent earlier. One of many notable examples was a group of several dozen Shanghai natives returned from Chengdu in Sichuan Province who set up a factory in Chengbei Town to manufacture watch components.[50] Between 1987 and 1989 the Kunshan government even had an office in the capital of Guizhou Province in southwest China that facilitated such arrangements.[51]

It also became clear early in the fieldwork that several prominent officials in Kunshan were formerly high ranking PLA commanders who had been transferred by choice to key civilian posts (*zhuanye*). One such individual who was recognized for his superb administrative and entrepreneurial skills in the military arrived in Kunshan in 1988 and was, by 1991, a vice-director of the Municipal Civil Affairs Bureau.[52] Promoted by 1993 to the directorships of the Kunshan Economic System Reform Commission and the Economic Research Centre, he was also deeply involved in a number of local development activities including promoting Kunshan as part of a trade and investment delegation in his former military region in China's northeast.

Enterprises in Kunshan also took advantage of every available opportunity to establish linkages with technical and management expertise from outside the region. Senior and retired cadres from enterprises and bureaux in Shanghai, for example, were hired on a contract basis to provide advice, expertise, and were sometimes invited to invest in local enterprises. Famous for its fishing, Kunshan attracted many older Shanghai experts who were recruited quite literally while casting from the banks of local waterways.[53] Supplementing meagre pensions from state enterprises with attractive benefits, many lived in Kunshan to run factories full-time, or commuted regularly as 'weekend engineers' (*zhoumo gongchengshi*).[54] Other economic interactions emerged largely from personal connections and other social relationships.[55]

Coinciding with a critical change of leadership in 1984, the Kunshan government began encouraging enterprises and individuals to find ways of establishing linkages outside the region. By 1985 the county government had established a special office under the auspices of the new Economic Cooperation Commission to promote technical, management, investment, and production and marketing cooperation (see Table 4.1). While Shanghai, and later the new zone in Pudong across the Huangpu River near downtown Shanghai, were the main focus of such endeavours, by 1992 the Kunshan government also had representative offices in

Nanjing, Beijing and Shenzhen which facilitated local linkages. In addition, by 1997 there were hundreds of other town, village, enterprise, and individual agents and representatives located throughout China.[56] A key element of the reform changes in Kunshan highlighted by local informants was this 'opening-up' to the outside and a fundamental shift in outlook initiated by the new mayor in 1984.[57] While the imperatives and outcomes of community development in Kunshan remained intensely localized, many had come to recognize the value of external linkages and cooperation. By the early 1990s, the Kunshan level bureaucracy and town and village governments had established institutional structures to promote, control and manage this increasingly interactive transactional environment.

Horizontal and vertical linkages

Transactional linkages, and other economic interrelationships relevant for local economic development in Kunshan, were cultivated along two sometimes intersecting streams (*shuang gui, shuang cheng* – literally 'double tracks, double levels').[58] The first included horizontal linkages (*hengxiang lianxi*) arising largely from the kind of relationships described in the previous section. Seen more as commercially based arrangements that crossed regions and administrative boundaries, these linkages also tended to eschew bureaucratic hierarchies taking advantage of opportunities to 'capture' talent, capital, information, and markets within and outside Kunshan.[59] While often pursued and promoted through local government institutional structures, the development of such linkages relied less on the functional relationships of government bureaucracy than on the connections between individuals, enterprises and local collective entities.

A village in Lujia Town, for example, became aware of three engineers in Shanghai who had designed a specialized machine tool, but were denied the opportunity to develop the device by their state run factory. The three resigned and were attracted to Lujia to establish what became a highly successful local enterprise. Even though most of the initial capital investment came from the village collective, the Shanghai engineers retained 30 per cent ownership of the enterprise.[60] Informants also referred to several examples of military third front enterprises who wished to establish a 'window' into coastal markets and gain access to the technology and expertise necessary to convert their factories to civilian consumer production. Often finding it too difficult to set up in places like Shanghai or Suzhou many were attracted to the more 'receptive' administrative environment in Kunshan.[61] Kunshan also had an office in Pudong that specifically targeted domestic and foreign investors who were experiencing difficulties establishing enterprises in the new zone. Kunshan boasted several advantages especially in terms of its less cumbersome administrative and regulatory environment and, by many indications, a superior level of infrastructural attributes.[62]

The second type of interaction cultivated by the local government was referred to as vertical linkages (*zhongxiang lianxi*).[63] These linkages followed the bureaucratic and administrative hierarchy more closely than did horizontal linkages. While they were also frequently based on personal connections and *guanxi*, the resulting transactional relationships relied on negotiated access to, and sometimes subversion of, the partially reformed command economy structures. It is clear from Table 4.1 that a large number of institutional structures emerged in Kunshan to manage and manipulate these linkages. Those concerned with specific industrial sectors, for example, were hived off from the Economic Commission in the early 1990s.[64]

The Kunshan Machinery, Electronics and Metallurgical Industries Bureau, and the Textiles Bureau were both established in 1991 to strengthen linkages with the respective provincial and prefectural level bureaux responsible for these sectors (see Table 4.1).[65] Most of the benefits for local enterprises were of a commercial nature, including assured and subsidized access to raw materials, energy, skilled labour, and increased access to stable sales channels in the state sector. In addition to their regulatory functions, and the provision of professional, technical, and management services (for a fee), these bureaux also allowed Kunshan authorities to play a greater role in provincial and prefectural level decisions regarding planning and policy and, most importantly, to lobby for preferential treatment.[66] In close collaboration with the Economic Cooperation Commission, these bureaux established and cultivated the horizontal linkages described above, while their corporate branches executed the commercial transactions directly on behalf of Kunshan level enterprises or, via the Rural Industry Bureau, for town and village collectives.

Entirely locally financed, these Kunshan based institutional structures emerged to provide a link between local development interests and the hierarchies of the partially reformed command economy structures. It is noteworthy, perhaps even ironic, that the rapid development of rural enterprises in Kunshan outside the command economy was fuelled in part by an equally rapid expansion in the power and intervention of local government. Of course, the local bureaucracy was profoundly more responsive and flexible than the former planned economy structures as it was able to pursue and cultivate opportunities quickly and independently for the benefit of local enterprises. Despite official policies that attempted to separate government administration and the economy, it is clear that the emergence of various institutional structures in Kunshan in fact strengthened and exploited this relationship.

The Economic Cooperation Commission

Perhaps the most interesting of the bureaucratic arrangements devised to encourage and manage these horizontal and vertical linkages, and the resulting transactional activities, was the Kunshan Economic Cooperation Commission (ECC) mentioned above and in Table 4.1.[67] By the mid-1980s local governments in Kunshan realized that rapid industrial growth would not continue unless town and village enterprises could gain more stable access to inputs, markets, investment, and technological and management expertise. While enterprises technically had the freedom to arrange commercial and other linkages, usually through local level purchasing and sales companies, acting on their own they often confronted obstacles. With growing numbers of open markets the sales of output was generally less problematic than the procurement of inputs. As one informant explained:

> town and village enterprises were not part of the state plan so there was always trouble with purchasing materials ... town and village governments did not have adequate access to resources of their own, nor did they have the necessary connections for trade ... information was difficult to obtain and they didn't know where to go for supplies and skilled people.[68]

Thus, in 1984 Kunshan responded to these concerns by establishing the ECC with the goal of providing a conduit to the means of production and sales opportunities for the increasing number of town and village enterprises. Through town offices of the ECC, local enterprises became linked to a complex set of networks and transactional relationships coordinated by 'agents' in the Kunshan level bureaucracy. Most personnel in the ECC had previously worked in local branches of the command economy system such as the Goods and Materials Bureau or the Supply and Sales Office (see Table 4.1). Other employees included representatives from the Kunshan Planning and Economic Commissions who were interested in obtaining information about procurement and sales opportunities for state run and Kunshan level enterprises in order to supplement their planned quotas.[69] Not only were these individuals familiar with the circumstances of local industrial development, they also had intimate knowledge of and connections within the hierarchies of the planned economy.

The specific tasks of the ECC fell into two broad categories. The first and most important included facilitating the exchange of materials by organizing special transactions and the brokering of economic and technological cooperation between town and village enterprises in Kunshan and enterprises and other organizations outside Kunshan. The second category originally included the attraction of capital and other forms of investment and the attraction of technical and management expertise. By 1992 these functions had been largely delegated to the Industrial Trade and Economic Development Corporation and the Labour and Personnel Bureau respectively, while most of the technical exchange and cooperation arrangements were handled through the newly created Economic and Technical Cooperation Office (see Table 4.1).[70]

The dealmaking coordinated by the ECC was innovative and wide ranging. While many of the linkages and contacts were still based upon networks of personal relations, through family, friends, and business or bureau associates, the resulting transactional arrangements had become quite sophisticated. Before the early 1980s, for example, a typical transaction might have involved a state run factory in Shanghai supplying old equipment to a town or village enterprise in exchange for agricultural products. These one-time barter agreements still occurred and usually involved Kunshan providing quantities of rice or edible oil for coal and other materials. However, with the establishment of the ECC in 1984, transactional relationships became more complicated, sometimes involving different types of investment including the sale of local enterprises to outside interests. One example was a bicycle factory in Kunshan that manufactured 70,000 to 80,000 units per year that had been attempting unsuccessfully to develop technical cooperation with the Number Three Bicycle Factory in Shanghai. When the ECC became involved they soon recognized that increasingly discerning consumers were demanding better quality brand-name bicycles than the Kunshan enterprise was able to produce. Against the wishes of the local collective ownership, the enterprise was sold outright to the Shanghai company.[71] The results startled the community. Not only did the sale recoup more than the initial local investment, the Shanghai factory turned around and invested more to improve quality and raise the level of output. By 1992 this rural branch plant of the famous Phoenix brand bicycle company was manufacturing more than 300,000 units per year for the voracious national market. In this example, the community did not control the enterprise, but it benefited enormously from the employment opportunities, increased tax revenues and economic knock-on effects of a highly successful local enterprise. Other famous 'Shanghai-made' products such as shirts and shoes were in fact manufactured in Kunshan through cooperative investment, and technological and management arrangements coordinated by the ECC.[72] While most enterprises remained locally owned and operated, they did acquire a new more flexible and open attitude based on these and other similarly well publicized experiences.

The ECC also cultivated critically important transactional arrangements across hierarchies of the planned economy. These relationships did not follow the conventional vertical patterns of interaction in the state plan. Rather, they tended to intersect where opportunities arose, usually among enterprises at a similar level of the command economy hierarchy, and cutting across the administrative and geographical boundaries, or bureaucratic space, that delineated the flow of goods and materials. In 1992 the ECC brokered access to a stable supply of coal for local enterprises, including a small power station in Qiandeng Town, by arranging a reciprocal investment scheme. Certain local governments and particular enterprises invested more than RMB 10 million in coal production and related facilities in Shaanxi Province, while the local branch of the coal supply bureau in Shaanxi invested in the power station in Qiandeng. Prior to this the power station lost money and the Kunshan enterprises involved experienced difficulties because of the insecure and more expensive supply of coal available outside the state plan. Under the new arrangement, Kunshan gained a stable supply of subsidized coal for local enterprises and the relevant bureau in Shaanxi supplemented its income with an agreed upon proportion of the earnings from the now profitable power station.

Perhaps the most fascinating transactional relations brokered by the ECC involved the exchange of quotas or allocations (*zhi biao*). Although there was usually no direct documented exchange of quotas or allocations *per se*, as with state controlled procurement and sales of key commodities for example, transactions were negotiated as if there were.[73] As one informant explained, 'local quotas utilized in such transactions had to be replaced with quotas of other things'. Through a kind of administrative arbitrage, the ECC might arrange for the relevant bureau to sell a portion of Kunshan's state allocation of subsidized rice to another region in exchange for the opportunity for local enterprises to purchase required inputs. More often, however, the ECC would arrange for town and village enterprises to sell popular consumer goods or industrial products to enterprises and bureaux outside Kunshan in order to secure inputs or sales opportunities for other local enterprises. Coordinating particular exchanges and helping to establish other linkages between enterprises, was also facilitated by providing relevant information regarding available resources and markets.

As has been alluded to throughout this section, the ECC and other local institutional structures also wielded enormous influence over town and village enterprises. These agencies were able to ensure that the activities of local enterprises were compatible with the objectives of the Kunshan government by controlling and manipulating access to preferential transactional relationships, loans and other sources of capital, tax concessions and subsidies and other administratively determined commercial advantages.[74] Chinese companies from outside Kunshan who were interested in establishing an enterprise here, most often approached the ECC to identify potential partners, to help arrange local joint ventures or to negotiate acquisition of suitable enterprises. As was demonstrated earlier, the power and authority of the ECC in facilitating such linkages was utilized to induce the compliance of local enterprises and even local governments. This influence also extended to the large number of enterprises who had managers and technical experts from outside Kunshan. These individuals were invited by the ECC at least twice a year to a working meeting to openly discuss their experiences in Kunshan and to explore ways in which certain problems could be 'solved'.[75]

County level agencies with functions similar to the ECC existed in most advanced regions throughout China, so there was ample scope to facilitate the transactions necessary to support local industrial development in Kunshan. In addition to the increased opportunities for production and sales stimulated by market-like economic reforms, therefore, the ECC and other local institutional structures coordinated access to more stable and subsidized supplies of inputs and to 'assured' or 'contracted' markets for town and village enterprises.[76] Informants reported in 1992 that about 25 per cent of the industrial enterprises in Kunshan (excluding individual enterprises) had initiated ongoing cooperative linkages of some kind with units outside Kunshan.[77] To emphasize the importance of such linkages, such enterprises were responsible for nearly 60 per cent of the GVIO and nearly 75 per cent of net earnings from industry in Kunshan, according to local officials. Most of these enterprises were scattered across the Kunshan countryside, leading the transformation of the rural economy.

Socialist new rural area with Chinese characteristics

This chapter has provided insights into the processes and mechanisms whereby rural communities in Kunshan constructed industrial space by utilizing certain forms of representation. The concept of mega-urbanization introduced in Chapter 2 suggested that the emergence of particular administrative and institutional parameters was a central element of the rural transformation in the lower Yangzi delta. The analysis presented here has revealed how the development imperatives of town and village governments, and the emergence of local administrative and institutional structures, have affected the growth and spatial proliferation of industrial activities in rural Kunshan. These institutional structures embodied a complex web of interactions and interrelationships tied to particular places. Kunshan, town, and village level cadres, who exercised powerful influence through these intensely localized structures, managed and manipulated the transactional networks, frequently creating new ones, in order to maximize community based productive opportunities. This helps to explain the diffuse nature of rural industrial development in Kunshan, and accounts for the lesser importance of external economies and the dynamics of agglomeration proposed in the model of mega-urbanization.

Rural industrialization and the openness and flexibility stimulated by reforms were said to have instilled more 'advanced thoughts' that had broken the parochialism and habits of '1,000 years' of the 'traditional feudal ideas of peasants' (*xiaonong sixiang*).[78] The 'spirit' of this 'new' outlook and its specific outcomes was captured in the expression 'socialist new rural area with Chinese characteristics' (*juyou Zhongguo tese de shehui zhuyi xin nongcun*).[79] The rural transformation this slogan described was, of course, portrayed as superior to the 'basic capitalist ideas' of ownership and economic control.[80] While this pithy phrase rolled very easily off the tongues of local bureaucrats in Kunshan, it only vaguely hinted at the ill-defined complexities of the processes and mechanisms driving the rural transformation. More obvious, was the paradox of local institutional structures, which sought to manipulate and overcome the administrative boundaries and bureaucratic space of the partially reformed command economy, while at the same time constructing their own protected space for local industrial development.

Moreover, by taking advantage of their position to influence crucial linkages in the transactional environment, community governments strengthened their role in local development in Kunshan, rather than separating from the economy as they were obliged according to official policy. This was possible, in part, because conventional neoclassical market mechanisms, such as factor mobility and real prices that would truly reflect cost and scarcity, did not prevail in the Chinese economy.[81] In fact, the intersection of new market-like opportunities and incentives that arose from the reform measures initiated in the late 1970s, and the monolithic structures of the planned economy, were manifested in Kunshan by the emergence of administrative and institutional structures which have assumed many of the features of the old system rather than changing it.[82] While the result has been a flourishing of interactions and inter-relationships, the concomitant downward dispersion of economic and administrative power has deepened the parochialism and balkanization of localities, even as it has empowered them to develop economic linkages with other regions and to determine, and sometimes redefine, the way in which local industrial concerns conducted their exchange relations and other transactional activities.

I would contend, therefore, that the supposedly reformed thoughts of peasants in socialist new rural areas with Chinese characteristics remain in important ways unchanged, and that the rural transformation observed in Kunshan is linked more to the 'Chinese characteristics' side of the expression than to anything else. The impact of these characteristics on the location of industrial enterprises will be discussed in Chapter 6. But first, Chapter 5 will examine several specific case studies to illustrate how underlying processes and mechanisms affected the emergence of specific local outcomes in Kunshan.

Notes

1. ZGXZHC 1990, p. 29; Also see: Appendix 2.
2. Interview notes.
3. Ibid.
4. Ibid.
5. Usually shortened to just town (*zhen*). Hereafter, when referring to the period after 1990 in Kunshan I will use the term 'town'. Until recently there were actually twenty-two towns in Kunshan. Two were administratively merged with nearby towns – Chengnan into Yushan and Dongxi into Chenmu (which later became Jinxi). See: Map 4.1 introduced in the next paragraph.
6. This occurred primarily through the imposition of a 5 per cent construction and maintenance tax as well as other levies and fees.

7. Interview notes.
8. Ibid.; Also see: Appendix 2.
9. Although not specifically discussed in any detail, these organizations were clearly also important. As will become apparent throughout Chapters 4 to 6, several of the most influential individuals interviewed or referred to in the context of local change also held key posts within these organizations.
10. Interview notes.
11. Ibid. Such enterprises were in fact referred to as social welfare factories.
12. The former was originally called the Structural Reform Office (*Tizhi Gaige Bangongshi*) and was established to consider all aspects of economic and political reform. However, after 1989 in Kunshan it became the Economic System Reform Commission (*Jingji Tizhi Gaige Weiyuanhui*). As several local informants pointed out, nobody really spoke officially about political reform, although, by focusing on the economic system political changes would occur 'naturally'.
13. Interview notes; Ho, S. P. S. (1994) *Rural China in Transition: Non-agricultural Development in Rural Jiangsu, 1978–1990.* Oxford: Clarendon, pp. 211–212.
14. Prior to the reforms, cadres were evaluated more on their commitment to political ideology and administrative skills. See: Ho, S. P. S. (1994) op. cit., pp. 212–215; Shue, V. (1988) *The Reach of the State: Sketches of the Chinese Body Politic.* Stanford: Stanford University Press.
15. Hereafter, the term town(ship) and village governments will refer to the theoretically separate, but in practice, overlapping and largely coincidental functions of the CCP, government administration, and economic management. Each of these organizations at the town level supervised their respective village level counterpart.
16. ZGTJNJ 1994, p. 227.
17. These values are consistent with similar figures in Chen, C. L. *et al.* (1994) Rural enterprise growth in a partially reformed Chinese economy. In Findlay, C., Watson, A. and Wu, H. X. (Eds.) *Rural Enterprises in China.* New York: St. Martin's, p. 13; and Ho, S. P. S. (1994) op. cit., pp. 222–223. I have not disaggregated budgetary revenues raised from town enterprises since these funds were not available for local discretionary spending. Most of these revenues were in fact remitted to higher levels of government in lieu of subsistence level state allocations towards local administration and development.
18. Villages in China received no direct budgetary revenues through state allocations. Thus, their spending was financed entirely by locally generated revenues. In this context, community owned enterprises were even more important to village governments than at the town level.
19. Interview notes.
20. The findings presented here are based on interviews with several informants from the Kunshan Rural Industry Bureau and the Yushan Town Industrial Corporation. Interview notes. These findings were confirmed and clarified in discussions with numerous other local officials and enterprise managers.
21. More about the nature of these arrangements will be discussed in the section on the Economic Cooperation Commission below.
22. Informants referred to successes with the processing of local speciality food products in Penglang Town.
23. Although it was not a key issue pursued in discussions with informants, it became clear that individuals in the most important administrative and economic positions were also high ranking members of the local CCP hierarchy.
24. Interview notes; Zhang, P. R. (1993) Diandong geng ming wei Dianshanhu zhen (Diandong changes name to Dianshanhu Town). *KSJJXX*, April 20, p. 1.

25. While such mergers were part of the official policy to improve efficiency and reduce the waste of resouŗces and land, informants emphasized the many complex problems relating to such mergers. These included provisions for redundant labour, old equipment and the need to reconcile local interests, particularly with respect to issues of control and management authority.
26. Interview notes.
27. The persistence of commune and brigade enterprises, in spite of national policies to focus on 'grain first', was discussed in Chapter 3.
28. Interview notes; Byrd, W. A. and Lin, Q. S. (Eds.) (1990) *China's Rural Industry: Structure, Development, and Reform.* Oxford: Oxford University Press, Chapters 4 and 7; Ho, S. P. S. (1994) op. cit., Chapter 6.
29. Others make the same claim. For example see: Tan, K. C. (1993b) Rural–urban segregation in China. *Geography Research Forum* 13, p. 79; Zhang, Z. (1994) Development of rural township enterprises in China: Prospects and problems. *Biennial Conference of the Australian Asian Studies Association*, Perth, 13–16 July, p. 9. Lee, Y. S. (1992) Rural transformation and decentralized urban growth in China. In G. E. Guldin (Ed.) *Urbanizing China.* Westport: Greenwood, pp. 99–101 provides inferential evidence for the link between the ownership of rural enterprises and their locational distribution. However, as Chen, C. L. *et al.* (1994) op. cit., pp. 8–10 has cautioned, the classification of enterprises by type of ownership and control does not always correspond precisely to classification by location. The findings presented here are based on an analysis of the official published statistics, supplemented by data from dozens of interviews and field observations. My intention at this point is simply to establish that enterprises have proliferated into all corners of the Kunshan countryside. More specific evidence regarding the locational characteristics of the enterprises surveyed is presented in Chapter 6.
30. This detailed data for 1996 was the most recent I was able to obtain for Kunshan. Figures presented in this paragraph were calculated from: *KSTJNJ 1991,* p. 67; *KSTJNJ 1996,* p. 115.
31. These findings were consistent with evidence presented in Lee, Y. S. (1992) op. cit., pp. 100–101, who calculated from a sample of 190 small townships in Jiangsu in 1984, that nearly 90 per cent of industrial output from township enterprises was generated by factories within the towns' administrative jurisdictions.
32. *SZTJNJ 1999,* p. 130. Apart from the macro categories of light and heavy industry and a breakdown of ownership for enterprises with gross sales over RMB 5 million, the available data for 1998 did not provide details on the ownership distribution for all enterprises.
33. Calculated from: *ZGTJNJ 1991,* p. 391 and *ZGTJNJ 1997,* p. 411.
34. Calculated from *ZGTJNJ 1990,* p. 391 and *ZGTJNJ 1999,* pp. 410, 413, 421. I say 'at least' here in reference to township and village run enterprises because the gross output of this sector was not reported. I utilized data for gross revenues to approximate gross output. Data from previous years, and for the same year, but for different regions in China, suggests that the former was generally the equivalent of 95 to 100 per cent of the latter.
35. Metal fabrication included metallurgy, forging, metal-work and the primary fabrication of metal components. Machinery included the production of finished machine tools, industrial equipment, electric motors, pumps, etc. Building materials included the production of cement and bricks and other processed materials for construction such as prefabricated concrete components, doors and windows, roofing materials, etc. Other industrial products included semi-processed components for industrial machinery, plastics, packaging materials, paper and most paper products, wire and cable, etc. The

respective proportions from a small number of service enterprises included in the survey data are also presented in Figure 4.1.

36. Interview notes. Sectoral rankings for rural industrial output across *Suxichang* were as follows: Machinery; Textiles; Chemicals; Metal Fabrication; Building Materials. For Suzhou Prefecture the first two were reversed.

37. By far the greatest number of such comments referred to the development of textile factories and the manufacturing of various types of chemicals.

38. Qinghua University Urban–Rural Development Research Group (1995) *Suxichang diqu chengxiang kongjian huanjing fazhan guihua yanjiu* (*Suxichang Area Urban–rural Spatial Environment Development Planning Research*). Beijing: Qinghua University, p. 85.

39. Interview notes. I borrow these terms as they were used by informants. 'Comprehensive' refers to the phenomenon whereby every community wishes to have every kind of industry. What precisely was 'irrational' about regional development will be discussed in the following section, the next chapter, and in the conclusion.

40. Discussed in Chapter 3. See especially: Kwok, R. Y. W. (1992) Urbanization under economic reform. In G. E. Guldin (Ed.) op. cit., p. 73; and Pannell, C. (1992) The role of great cities in China. In G. E. Guldin (Ed.) op. cit., p. 36. This point is elaborated upon in more detail at the end of Chapter 6. There, I provide an analysis of the distribution of markets by product category and the distribution of product categories by market of the enterprises surveyed in Kunshan.

41. Discussed in more detail in Chapter 5.

42. Here I have fused arguments from: Booth, D. (1993) Development research: From Impasse to new agenda. In F. J. Schuurman (Ed.) *Beyond the Impasse: New Directions In Development Theory*. London: Zed, p. 53; and Huang, P. C. C. (1990) *The Peasant Family and Rural Development in the Yangzi Delta, 1350–1988*. Stanford: Stanford University Press, p. 288. As with other elements of the reconceptualization proposed in this study I am not rejecting the conventional arguments. Rather, I merely wish to suggest alternative approaches to cope with the ground level realities.

43. Shue, V. (1988) op. cit., p. 143.

44. Interview notes.

45. Interview notes. Some of the problems associated with this local petty protectionism were severe enough in some cases to be viewed in terms of a regional economic 'warlordism'. See: Marton, A. M. (1995b) At the edge of Shanghai: Linkages and industrial development in rural Kunshan. In M. S. Chen, C. Comtois and L. N. Shyu (Eds.) *East Asia Perspectives*. Montreal: Canadian Asian Studies Association, p. 108.

46. Watson, A. (1992) The management of the rural economy: The institutional parameters. In A. Watson (Ed.) *Economic Reform and Social Change in China*. New York: Routledge, pp. 177–179; Wu, F. L. (1994) Urban process in the face of China's transition to a socialist market economy. *Annual Meeting of the Association of American Geographers*, San Francisco, 29 March–2 April, p. 14.

47. Marton, A. M. (1994) Challenges for metrofitting the lower Yangtze delta. *Western Geography* 4, p. 79.

48. *SHJJ 1949–1982*, p. 961. Referred to as *shangshan xiaxiang* (up to the mountains, down to the countryside) the largest proportion were sent to the northeast (especially Heilongjiang Province), the far west (Xinjiang), and *sanxian* (third front) areas (especially Sichuan Province) to which many strategic and military industries were relocated in the 1950s and 1960s.

49. *SHJJ 1949–1982*, p. 962. Precise figures were extremely difficult to obtain (or do not exist). The available data suggest, however, that by the mid-1980s

only about half of Shanghai's sent down youth had returned. Similarly, many youths sent down from Suzhou came to Kunshan unable to return to the city. Interview notes.

50. Interview notes. Nobody really knew how many Shanghai natives were in Kunshan, but several lifetime residents were convinced that they have been altering local society. References were made in this regard to especially potent socio-cultural stereotypes associated with 'Shanghai wives'.

51. Interview notes.

52. He was in charge of the PLA units that extinguished the enormous Black Dragon Fire in northeast China in 1987 and who turned a tidy profit by harvesting and selling much of the damaged wood.

53. Interview notes.

54. Ibid.

55. One such arrangement was facilitated by my scholarly mentor in Shanghai who had a relative in the coal bureau in Shaanxi Province willing to negotiate a supply deal with contacts we had established in Kunshan during the fieldwork.

56. Interview notes.

57. The new mayor of Kunshan was responsible for a number of initiatives which had a significant local impact, not the least of which was the Special Economic and Technological Development Zone discussed at the end of Chapter 5. His policies were so highly regarded that by 1992 he had become the mayor of Suzhou overseeing all of its six counties.

58. Interview notes.

59. Ibid. I am not referring here to the kind of horizontal linkages that resulted in the expansion of 'cities leading counties' (*shi guan xian*) arrangements initiated in the 1950s mainly to overcome vegetable supply problems.

60. Ibid.

61. Examples included a large electronics enterprise from Jiangxi and a military factory from Guizhou that manufactured refrigerators for local and other domestic markets. Ibid. See note 49 above.

62. As recently as the autumn of 1995, foreign invested companies were locating in Kunshan precisely because of such difficulties. Large investments in Pudong and Shanghai required at least fourteen layers of approval, while in Kunshan the same could be accomplished with fewer than six 'chops'. Moreover, it was faster and more convenient to reach the Shanghai International Airport from just about anywhere in Kunshan than from Pudong and most of downtown Shanghai. Pudong, of course, refers to the area on the east side of the Huangpu River in Shanghai that was designated as a special development zone in 1990.

63. Interview notes.

64. What remained of the Economic Commission concentrated on micro-economic management to facilitate Kunshan's industrial policies and planning, and to provide a link with similar agencies in other regions throughout the administrative hierarchy. Interview notes.

65. The findings presented here are based on interview data from these bureaux.

66. In addition to the commercial benefits already mentioned, such preferential treatment also included consideration for the location of provincial or prefectural level enterprises.

67. Most of the discussion in this section is based on two key interviews with the CCP Policy Research Office and the Economic Cooperation Commission. Interview notes.

68. Ibid.

69. Ibid.

70. Ibid.
71. These were the kinds of arrangements vigorously promoted by the new mayor.
72. Interview notes. Many such products manufactured in Kunshan in fact bore 'Made in Shanghai' labels.
73. Transactions which involved direct exchange of printed coupons were very common among peasants who might fill a state purchasing quota, for example, by sending a family member (often a daughter) into the city to sell products from local rural enterprises, not for cash, but for ration coupons. The coupons would then be used to purchase cheaper subsidized grain in the city, which was shipped back to the farm to be sold to the state to fill the quota. The objective was to free-up peasant labour to concentrate on more profitable non-agricultural activities. Opportunities for such transactions fluctuated with the changing utilization of household rationing.
74. It was through such means, for example, that sizeable private or individual enterprises, which might provide too much competition for town and village collectives, were squeezed to submission or closure.
75. Although not explicitly stated, it was very clear that the 'solutions' involved the Economic Cooperation Commission and other agencies applying the necessary administrative pressures on enterprises to force compliance. This inevitably involved identifying some form of incentive or 'compensation' for the units and individuals concerned.
76. These were terms frequently used by respondents in the enterprise survey questionnaire.
77. Interview notes.
78. Ibid.
79. Ibid.
80. In this context, informants referred specifically to a number of arrangements whereby locally owned enterprises were managed by outsiders, and other situations in which ownership and opportunities for making money were relinquished to outside concerns in amounts exceeding the proportion of their investment.
81. Fan, C. C. (1995) Of belts and ladders: State policy and uneven regional development in post-Mao China. *AAAG* 85 (3); Solinger, D. J. (1989) Capitalist measures with Chinese characteristics. *Problems of Communism* 38 (1), p. 33.
82. This phenomenon is, of course, not unprecedented in the Chinese context. Many of the political, social, and economic structures imposed after Liberation in 1949 were either loosely based on the traditional late imperial forms, or were modified and subverted by local variations in cultural and historical circumstances.

5 Restless landscapes: the local character of spatial change

The detailed case studies in this chapter will highlight some of the ground level realities of the spatial economic transformation that has occurred in Kunshan. The objective is to highlight particular elements which allude first, to the underlying imperatives and forces, largely constructed and negotiated at the community level, which drive local development, and second, to the complex processes and mechanisms which must be captured in a new conceptual framework for understanding mega-urbanization in the lower Yangzi delta. The chapter begins with an examination of the transportation system across Kunshan with particular emphasis on the emergence of a relatively new network of roads. This is followed by a review of the developments in Dianshanhu Town which focuses on the growth and spatial proliferation of town and village industrial enterprises. Included in this section is a discussion of one particular town owned enterprise. The third section is a case study of Tongxin Village. The analysis here reveals how the organization and management of village enterprises was linked to a shift in the structure of village administration and concomitant changes in local agricultural practices. The final section provides an overview of the emergence of specialized development zones throughout Kunshan. It also serves as a means to summarize the spatial implications of issues raised in the context of the other case studies.

Transportation

'Chinese roads make a lasting impression on all who travel over them and the vocabulary of the average traveller is not rich enough to thoroughly relieve the mind of this matter.'[1] These comments from the legendary horticulturist and plant hunter E. H. Wilson spoke of the roads he found in China in 1900. While his dry wit referred to the scarcity and nearly impassable conditions he encountered, the modern traveller might express the same sentiments about roads in Kunshan, but for the opposite reasons. The proliferation of roads and the ubiquitous scenes of upgrading and construction of new roads, were perhaps the most obvious concrete manifestation of the spatial economic transformation in Kunshan. Evolution of the entire transportation network in fact serves as a proxy for the spatial proliferation of non-agricultural activities in the Kunshan countryside. Conventional approaches to understanding the transportation and land-use system focus on the interactions between varying (usually complementary) socio-economic fields. The underlying forces, nearly always analysed within or between urban areas, are most often characterized in terms of distance, journey time or cost.[2] However, this approach tends to overlook other processes within the wider transactional environment. It is these other processes, linked to complex interactions and interrelationships which I have elsewhere labelled 'local realities', which arise and become important for understanding mega-urbanization in the lower Yangzi delta.[3] The objective here is to illustrate the way in which some of these local realities were embodied in the transportation networks in Kunshan.

The emergence of a dense network of roads is perhaps the most revealing.[4] Prior to 1980, Kunshan's 72 kilometres of main roads reached only half of the county's twenty townships. Between 1980 and 1986 vigorous construction efforts connected all the towns via 150 kilometres of main Kunshan level roads (see Map 5.1). By 1989, all these roads had been sealed with asphalt or reinforced concrete at an average width of 7 to 8 metres (see Plate 5.1). In addition to another 84 kilometres of much larger provincial and national highways, including 38 kilometres and a local on–off ramp of the new Nanjing-Shanghai expressway, there were approximately 200 kilometres of town level branch roads by 1993. Averaging 5 to 6 metres in width, such roads were sealed with asphalt or reinforced concrete. As late as 1991 there were seventy-two villages in Kunshan to which vehicles could not drive. By 1997 more than 600 kilometres of roads linked all of Kunshan's then 466 villages to the main network. These are indicated on Map 5.1. These roads ranged from as large as town level roads down to 4 or 5 metre wide packed gravel roads (see Plates 5.1 and 5.2).

The extensive and increasingly dense network of roads emerged in tandem with the dramatic growth and spatial proliferation of non-agricultural activities in Kunshan. This was also reflected in the rapid increases in passenger and freight volumes. The first two columns of Table 5.1 present data on the number of passenger-trips and tonnes of cargo moved along roads in Kunshan between 1980 and 1998. The number of passenger-trips grew from 10,000 in 1980 to over 4.2 million by 1985, when most of the township level roads had been completed. Annual passenger volumes peaked in 1997 at 18.4 million person-trips after which they levelled-off somewhat, reaching 15.55 million in 1998.[5] Cargo volumes transported by road increased by a factor of ten between 1980 and 1991, and by a further ten times to reach 3.84 million tonnes by 1997.[6] It is unclear why the figures for cargo transported in all sectors declined so significantly in 1998 from the year before. Data calculated

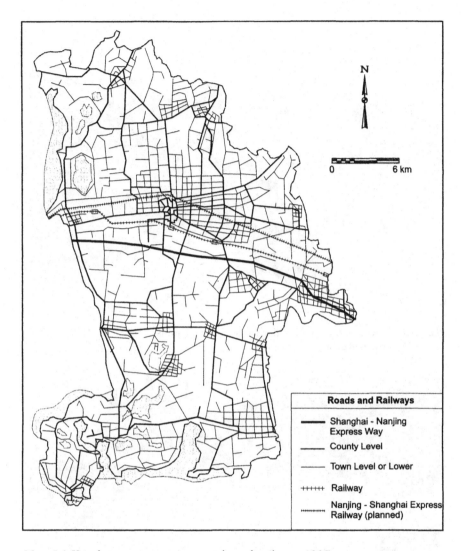

Map 5.1 Kunshan transportation: roads and railway, 1997.

Sources: Adapted from *KSSDMT* (1993); *KSXZ* (1990), unpaginated preface; *SZSJJT* (1992); *SZJTTC* (1992), pp. 28–31; *SZNJ 1998*, Map appendix; Interview notes; Field observations.

from the enterprise survey questionnaire confirms that roads were considered very important to the development of local enterprises. Nearly 80 per cent of the managers surveyed indicated that roads were the most important mode of transportation for their enterprises.

Despite the importance of the road network, extensive field observations, interviews with local informants and careful examination of documentary

Plate 5.1 Town road. A new village road (gravel) joins a town road Chengbei Town, Kunshan.

Plate 5.2 Village road. A new reinforced concrete village road joins a town road Chengbei Town, Kunshan.

Table 5.1 Transportation in Kunshan: passenger and freight volumes, 1980–1998 (selected years) (all figures × 10,000)

	Road		Water		Railway	
	Person-trips	tonnes	Person-trips	tonnes	Person-trips	tonnes
1980	1	4	161	227	59	66
1985	421	9	37	303	90	114
1990	519	40	7	335	83	123
1991	552	36	9	319	89	129
1992	1161	232	7	765	98	148
1993	668	300	6	613	139	142
1994	675	362	1	552	140	139
1995	1445	378	2	717	144	128
1996	1094	380	1	583	118	110
1997	1884	384	–	555	130	99
1998	1555	193	2	440	146	81

Sources: JSSXJJ 1992, pp. 174–184; JSSXJJ 1993, pp. 173–179; JSTJNJ 1991, pp. 422–425; JSTJNJ 1994, p. 313; JSTJNJ 1995, p. 315; JSTJNJ 1996, p. 364; JSTJNJ 1997, p. 391; JSTJNJ 1998, p. 392; JSTJNJ 1999, p. 399; KSXZ (1990), pp. 326–327, 335–336; SZTJNJ 1995, p. 275; SZTJNJ 1996, p. 222; SZTJNJ 1997, p. 212; SZTJNJ 1998, p. 214; SZTJNJ 1999, p. 230–231.

evidence indicates that the economic viability and articulation across administrative boundaries of much of this network was at best weak and irrational. This was most obvious with the village level roads which, like village owned collective industries, have proliferated into the Kunshan countryside. Tongxin Village, for example, near the centre of Kunshan, invested more than RMB 500,000 in 1991–1992 to construct 2 kilometres of a 6 metre wide reinforced concrete road that two years later remained unconnected by undersized or unfinished bridges.[7] Five of the village's six factories and the new village office were located next to or within 100 metres of the nearby town level road, while the village itself had virtually no motorized vehicular traffic except for the odd farm tractor or motorized wheelbarrow. The most apparent function of the road was as a convenient surface to dry and thresh the wheat, rice, and oil seed crops as village residents rode their bicycles to work in village and town factories.

Conversations with village level cadres and Kunshan level transportation officials revealed an 'if we build it, they will come' attitude towards roads. 'Build roads to become rich', or 'small roads equal small fortune, big roads equal big fortune', and other such slogans embodied official policies and deep seated local imperatives for building roads.[8] Even the local gazetteer lists an old Kunshan proverb in this regards: 'a destitute family is not considered bad, but poor roads are extremely bad' (*jia pin busuan pin, lu pin pin sha ren*).[9] Thus, while every village was connected to the larger network, most were also anxious to build and expand their own local roads, Wealthy villages like Tongxin were, in fact, looking for ways to spend their surplus income, and road building was a prominent choice. The dubious economic rationale, and negative effects of such road building, such as the consumption of agricultural land (see Plate 5.1), were offset by perceived gains in terms of easier access to social welfare and educational facilities, potential future uses, and perhaps most significantly, status.[10]

Some of the resulting patterns are apparent in Map 5.1. The desire of every village to be linked directly to a town level road resulted in a fishbone network of village level roads. Across Kunshan in 1993 for example, the roads which connected villages to the larger network crossed town boundaries in only three places, although there were more examples of such cross-boundary roads by 1997.[11] Uneven levels of discretionary revenues and a general lack of coordination across administrative jurisdictions also meant that roads sometimes ended abruptly in fields adjacent to neighbouring villages, or changed from high quality reinforced concrete, to packed gravel, to asphalt all within a few tens of metres. Similar characteristics were also evident among the higher level roads, especially the branch roads between towns. During the initial drive to link towns and villages by road in the early 1980s issues of routeing and the creation of a coordinated and planned network were less important than getting connected to the system. By 1992 Kunshan transportation authorities had become more concerned about building a more efficient network. Their efforts included the development of a system of ring roads that would facilitate traffic flows around and through Kunshan. The objectives were to reroute traffic around the central town of Yushan and to improve key routes which would better serve peripheral parts of Kunshan and provide links to adjacent administrative jurisdictions (see Map 5.1).[12]

Only a small portion of the significant funding required to implement these objectives came through the budgetary allocations of the Transportation Bureau. Road construction in Kunshan was especially costly because of the dense network of canals and waterways. With a bridge required for every 0.7 kilometres of main road on average, bridge building absorbed 70 to 80 per cent of construction costs. In 1993, the 150 kilometres of roads, which formed the core of the network connecting all twenty towns, crossed some 271 bridges. By 1997 the more than 600 kilometres of town and village level roads crossed nearly 5,400 bridges. Construction of the main town level and branch routes was financed mostly by community governments and local enterprises which were required to contribute land, labour, building materials, and cash depending on the degree to which they benefited from the new road. Issues of routeing, links to the existing network, and financing were negotiated between the Transportation Bureau and local concerns. The resulting arrangements usually involved elaborate trade-offs and concessions to bring community governments on side. Of course, the Transportation Bureau utilized its various regulatory and licensing functions to provide 'incentives' for local compliance with Kunshan level initiatives. Chief among these were the rights to develop commercial and other activities adjacent to the new roads.

The Transportation Bureau itself also controlled eleven companies which provided transport services or were in a position to facilitate transport and related business opportunities for local enterprises. Five of these companies, including one that served as a broker for transport services, engaged directly in the movement of passengers and freight. The six other companies pursued a range of activities including ship-building, cable and wire production, vehicle repair, engineering and the supply and sale of road construction materials and equipment. All eleven of these firms also controlled other tertiary services in towns and along roads including shops and restaurants, dance and karaoke clubs, bars and the leasing of retail and commercial property. These latter activities generated half the revenues of these 'transportation' companies. In addition to the funds collected from licensing and other fees, profits from these companies also helped finance the construction of local roads.

In addition to its responsibilities and interests within Kunshan, the Transportation Bureau played an important role in promoting particular linkages with adjacent administrative jurisdictions. Efforts to establish alternative routes through and around Kunshan relied in part upon the cooperation of these other areas. However, disarticulation between roads in Kunshan and other regions, especially Shanghai, was often deeply problematic. Kunshan had been investing in the upgrading of two roads that would improve links to the Shanghai International Airport through Shipu and Dianshanhu Towns in the southeast, and a new road in the southernmost town of Zhouzhuang around the west end of Dianshan Lake into suburban Shanghai (see Map 5.1).

In 1992, the new road in Zhouzhuang ended when it reached the border with Shanghai and the two roads to the airport became very poor on the Shanghai side of the boundary. Transportation officials in Kunshan had been involved in difficult negotiations with Shanghai for many years attempting to convince them of the need to upgrade or build new roads in their jurisdiction. Kunshan officials even claimed that they were willing to finance the necessary construction in Shanghai. It was not until early in 1993 that Shanghai officials had finally acquiesced, but only following a combination of local government pressure on both sides of the boundary, and one particular incident that embarrassed Shanghai into action. One of China's vice-Premiers who had been touring southern Jiangsu was due to visit Shanghai. Kunshan officials persuaded the provincial authorities to deliver the vice-Premier to his Shanghai hosts at one of the places where the road in Kunshan was particularly wide and well built yet of poor quality in Shanghai. By mid-1993 Kunshan officials could boast that it was faster and more convenient to reach the Shanghai International Airport from Kunshan, along the newly improved roads, than from most of downtown Shanghai or anywhere in Pudong. Meanwhile, Zhouzhuang had initiated a new bus service along the new road into Shanghai.[13]

In addition to the increasingly dense network of roads in Kunshan there was an intricate system of canals and waterways. In Chapter 3 I suggested how the long history of convenient transportation and communications along this network helped to explain the spatial proliferation of non-agricultural activities and the underdeveloped hierarchy of settlements. The proliferation of roads largely mirrored the system of canals by providing a contemporary network which enhanced the linkages between many small towns, hundreds of rural communities and larger urban centres. Although most towns and villages have reoriented their commercial, indus-trial, and administrative activities along the new roads, water transport continues to play an important role in local development. Map 5.2 illustrates the system of canals and waterways across Kunshan. In 1993, the network comprised 116 kilometres of first-order trunk lines and 278 kilometres of second-order support lines. Most first-order routes accom-modated vessels between 100 to 200 tonnes gross weight (see Plate 5.3). Second-order routes had a capacity of between 20 to 100 tonnes. Map 5.2 also illustrates the several hundred kilometres of third-order small lines which accommodated vessels up to about 20 tonnes (see Plate 5.4).[14] Although the movement of light goods and passengers on the canals has declined, the transport (and temporary storage) of bulk goods, espe-cially building materials, has steadily increased (see columns 3 and 4 in Table 5.1). Thus, by 1998, ferries transported just under 10,000 passen-gers in Kunshan, down from over 1.6 million in 1980. Meanwhile, freight volumes on canals nearly tripled from 2.27 million tonnes in 1980 to 7.65 million tonnes in 1992, declining somewhat thereafter to 4.40 million tonnes in 1998.

The four railway stations in Kunshan along the Nanjing-Shanghai line have seen steady increases in both passenger and freight volumes since 1980 (see columns five and six in Table 5.1). By 1994, local railway stations handled 1.4 million passengers and about 1.4 million tonnes of cargo, although this latter figure for cargo had declined to 810,000 tonnes by 1998. Exports, including rice, chemicals, machinery, and other equip-ment, accounted for 85 to 90 per cent of railway freight. Most of this traffic was handled at the main station in Yushan, although plans were under way in 1997 to relocate the main cargo facilities to the south end of the new Special Economic and Technological Development Zone just east of Yushan. Map 5.1 also shows the route of the proposed Nanjing-Shanghai express railway line.

Examination of the transportation system in Kunshan highlights in vivid terms the spatial outcomes of the processes and mechanisms which drive local development. It is clear that decisions taken in Kunshan involving transportation investment, like those in other spheres, hinged upon issues at once broader and more specific than those emphasized in the conven-

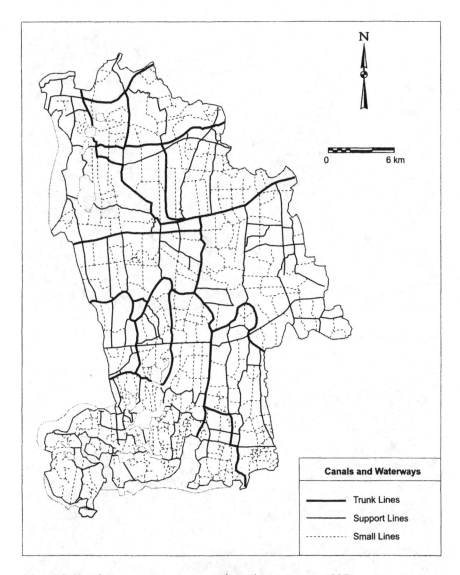

Map 5.2 Kunshan transportation: canals and waterways, 1997.
Sources: Adapted from: *KSXZ* (1990), unpaginated preface; *SHSQT* (1987); *SJNJ 1998*, Map appendix; *SZSDT* (1989); *SZSJTT* (1992); *SZJTTC* (1992), pp. 8, 28–31; *SZNJ 1998*; Map appendix; Interview notes; Field observations.

tional wisdom. Classical transport and land-use studies argue that the key to successful regional development was found in the performance of the transport subsystem, usually measured in terms of transactional costs.[15] The crux of the argument was that there must be traffic, or potential traffic,

Plate 5.3 Main canal. Bacheng Town, Kunshan.

Plate 5.4 Small canal. Penglang Town, Kunshan.

to justify the construction of a transportation network within a given land-use regime. The complementarity of such a system also proposed that introduction of a new transportation network should result in increased traffic and more intensive specific land-uses. However, in Kunshan and elsewhere in the lower Yangzi delta, there was a strong sense in which local imperatives transcended the logic of other factors. At the meso-scale, across county or even town level jurisdictions, this was reflected in the conflict between the demand for roads and the political desire to undertake the necessary steps to build them. Conversely, especially at the village level, the apparent contradiction was between the objectives for building roads and their economic purpose or viability.

However, the transportation network that emerged in Kunshan was an important part of local development, not solely because of its economic impact according to the conventional criteria, but rather as one component and one consequence of the underlying processes and mechanisms within the wider transactional environment. This was also made clear in the way local enterprises responded to the circumstances and conditions of the resulting transactional space.[16] Interestingly, the spatial proliferation of roads in and of itself did not provide commensurate accessibility to adequate levels of transportation services for the large number of spatially scattered community owned enterprises. Thus, of the 2,895 trucks registered in Kunshan in 1993, 2,172 were owned and operated by local enterprises. Only sixty-nine of these vehicles belonged to enterprises that specialized in transportation including those run by the Transportation Bureau, while the remaining 654 trucks were available for hire from individual owners.[17] Local enterprises also operated ninety-two of their own buses, largely for the transportation of industrial labourers. The spatial characteristics of the transportation network in Kunshan, and the movement of passengers and freight it supported, epitomized the complex interactions and interrelationships between the physical environment, the historical circumstances of local social, cultural, and political imperatives, and the patterns and levels of regional economic development in the lower Yangzi delta.

Dianshanhu Town

Located in the southeasternmost corner of Kunshan, Dianshanhu Town exemplifies the patterns and characteristics of rural non-agricultural development across all of Kunshan (see Map 5.3). The town borders Shanghai's suburban county of Qingpu to the east and south and has nearly 25 kilometres of shoreline along Dianshan Lake from which the town takes its name. Living in 8,020 households, the population at the end of 1996 was 26,393, with approximately 4,500 residing in the town seat and the remainder dispersed among the town's twenty-nine rural villages.[18] Table 5.2 summarizes the available data for town and village industrial enterprises

Table 5.2 Town and village industry and agriculture: Dianshanhu Town, Kunshan, 1989–1996

Year	Town and village enterprises (Number)	Enterprise employees (Number)	Industrial output (Million RMB)[a]	Agricultural output (Million RMB)[a]
1989	138	5735	140.9	45.2
1990	127	5115	168.3	49.4
1991	102	5968	232.3	54.7
1992	83	6140	551.2	56.9
1993	81	6840	903.3	53.5
1994	79	5920	965.6	52.9
1995	55	5382	817.2 [b] (584.1)	57.7
1996	57	5325	566.2	60.9

Notes
a 1990 constant values.
b The method of calculating output changed in 1995. The amount shown in brackets and for the subsequent year indicates the total as calculated by the new method.
Sources: Calculated from: *KSTJNJ* (Several years).

and agricultural output in Dianshanhu between 1989 and 1996. Other enterprises outside the town and village levels accounted for less than 1 per cent of total industrial output over the period and have been excluded from the table. In 1989 town and village enterprises employing 5,735 workers generated RMB 140.9 million in output. Of the 138 enterprises, thirty-eight were town level concerns responsible for 54.3 per cent of the total industrial output. Agricultural output in 1989 accounted for about 25 per cent of the GVAIO. Although the number of town and village enterprises steadily decreased to fifty-seven by 1996 due to closings and mergers, the number of employees in such enterprises increased to a peak of 6,849 in 1993 before levelling off again at 5,325 in 1996. Approximately 60 per cent of these workers were employed in town level enterprises over the period. The seventeen town enterprises in 1996 generated 63.7 per cent of the total GVIO that year, while agriculture accounted for less than 10 per cent of the GVAIO. Total industrial output from town and village enterprises grew by an annual average of 33.5 per cent over the seven years to 1996, while the value of the agricultural sector in Dianshanhu saw a comparatively modest 4.5 per cent growth over the same period.

Map 5.3 illustrates the approximate spatial distribution of town and village industrial enterprises across Dianshanhu in 1996 based on the location of village administrations. At least six of the town level enterprises were located some distance from the town seat and are indicated by a 'T' in Map 5.3.[19] In 1992 the average village enterprise generated RMB 1.7 million of output and employed forty-two workers, while the average for town enterprises was RMB 7.6 million and 142 workers respectively.[20] The average value of enterprise output and number of employees for the

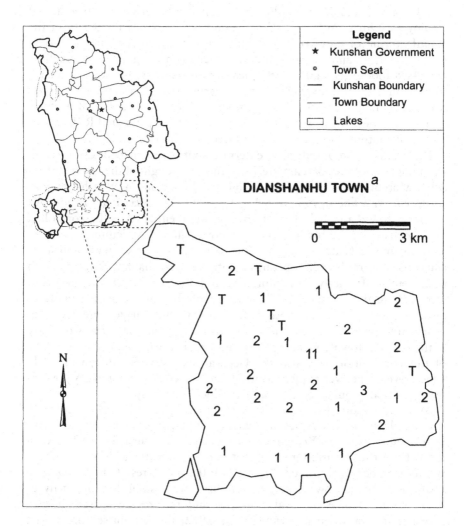

Map 5.3 Location of rural enterprises: Dianshanhu Town, Kunshan, 1996.

Note

a Numerals refer to the number of enterprises and their location. 'T' refers to the town
  level enterprises located outside the town seat.

Sources: Enterprise survey data; Field observations; Interview notes; *KSTJNJ 1996*,
pp. 140–146.

town as a whole were RMB 3.51 million and seventy-three respectively.[21]
Village enterprises ranged in size from tiny chemicals and plastics factories with five to eight employees to one very large packaging materials
manufacturer with 330 workers and several textiles plants with more than
100 employees. Town enterprises included construction materials factories with as few as seventeen workers up to a large cement factory with

715 labourers and four textiles operations with between 250 and 510 employees. Other town and village enterprise activities ranged from the manufacturing of industrial products especially chemicals, metal fabrication, machinery and machine tools, to light consumer products such as processed foods, glass and bottles, leather goods, toys, furniture and electronics. In 1996 the average village enterprise in Dianshanhu produced RMB 6.11 million of output and employed the same number of workers as in 1992. Meanwhile, the average town enterprise generated RMB 25.23 million in output and had 213 employees by the end of 1996.

The proliferation of industrial enterprises into all corners of Dianshanhu was indicative of the spatial patterns common throughout the lower Yangzi delta. Moreover, the wide range of industrial activities in Dianshanhu was consistent with findings for Kunshan and all of the *Suxichang* region. All of these town and village enterprises were either directly controlled or supervised by the town government through the Agriculture, Industry and Commerce General Corporation. Some of the town level industrial enterprises were branch operations of the Dianshanhu Diversification Management (formerly Agricultural Sidelines) Company. Other enterprises were managed as a special sub-category of the town's export management agency. However, most of the town and village enterprises in Dianshanhu were operated under the auspices of the Industrial Company branch of the town's General Corporation. The Chairman of the Board of this corporation was also the General Secretary of the town's CCP, which reveals the overlapping priorities and interests of community government and party bureaucracies, and the local economy.

An examination of one particular town enterprise also reveals some of the underlying characteristics of local industrial development. The Kunshan Dianshanhu Essence (*Xiangjing*) Factory was established in 1981 with funds from the township government and 'contributions' from the initial twenty member work force.[22] Located on 0.65 hectares about a kilometre to the west of the town seat, the enterprise was established primarily to increase the income of local residents and to provide extrabudgetary revenues for the town government. By 1992, the enterprise and related operations employed over 150 workers, virtually all of whom resided in local villages, and 45 per cent of whom were women. The number of employees stabilized at eighty-five to ninety-five workers between 1993 and 1996. Workers and management received training at the enterprise with expertise brought in from Kunshan, Suzhou and Shanghai. Pre-tax earnings in 1991 totalled RMB 1.65 million from a gross output of RMB 5.61 million.[23] Taxes, including local fees and other levies, consumed 58 per cent of earnings, while 30 per cent was turned over directly to the town government, 6 per cent was reinvested in the enterprise, while the remaining 6 per cent was used for worker bonuses. Gross output for 1992 was nearly RMB 8 million. This had grown to RMB 43.5 million by 1996, nearly eight times (in real terms) the 1991 figure. In 1993, the enterprise invested a further RMB 2.5 million to expand the RMB 4.6 million fixed capital base. The first major enterprise expansion prior to that occurred in 1984 when two branch enterprises were created to process inputs. By 1991 these units had been incorporated into the larger enterprise at which time major research and quality control functions were also added. In 1992, the enterprise produced 2,000 tonnes of chemical essence and scents to flavour cigarettes and some food products. The nationally recognized and award winning 'Imperial Crown' brand of essence was exported to more than eighty state run tobacco production facilities that manufactured over 200 brands of cigarettes across twenty-one provinces in China. Most of these sales were contracted through the town's Industrial Company and central government agencies in charge of tobacco production.[24] These 'assured' sales provided the level of stability necessary for the ambitious plans for expansion. Obtaining the more than 400 raw materials required was more problematic. The ECC played an important role brokering access to inputs mostly from Shanghai, Suzhou and Henan. The fact that 70 per cent of output went to factories in Henan clearly influenced access to raw materials from that province.

While the imperatives and rationale for establishing industrial enterprises locally were manifest, field investigations also revealed some of the inherent problems and paradoxes of the rural location of such enterprises. Informants at the essence factory in Dianshanhu indicated that the two most serious disadvantages of its location were lack of adequate transportation and unfavourable local policies.[25] While the railway line in Kunshan was the most important mode of transportation for this enterprise, both for the import of raw materials and the export of finished products, the factory was located 32 kilometres from the cargo facilities in Yushan Town. Only the town of Zhouzhuang and parts of Jinxi in the far southwest of Kunshan were further away from the railway. Unfavourable local policies was a euphemism that usually referred to the fiscal predation and bureaucratic meddling of local governments, or the real or perceived inequalities in the provision of incentives for development.[26] Paradoxically, it was the ease of establishing the enterprise and access to local transportation that were among the most important advantages cited for its location in the first place. These findings were less contradictory than they might seem. They suggest, in fact, that a fundamental shift has occurred away from the priorities of local administrative imperatives which largely determined, and continue to influence, the location and operation of rural enterprises, towards a recognition, especially at the enterprise level, of the need to respond to increasingly important economic considerations. This brief examination of Dianshanhu Town and one of its enterprises has also highlighted aspects of the relationship between local administrative imperatives, the commensurate development of community based institutional structures, and the establishment, location, growth, and operation of rural enterprises.

Tongxin Village

Among the wealthiest communities in Kunshan, Tongxin Village embodied many of the most fundamental local characteristics of the rural transformation that occurred throughout the lower Yangzi delta. The centre of the administrative village was located about 2 kilometres to the northeast of the Chengbei town seat and about 4 kilometres from downtown Yushan. With a population of just over 2,000 in 1991, the village was comprised of 587 households organized into fifteen small groups (*cunmin xiaozu*), which roughly corresponded to the clusters of settlement or natural villages (*zhuang*).[27] The village had an elected seven member village committee (*cunmin weiyuanhui*) responsible for all aspects of community administration. Of the 1,144 strong labour force, more than 90 per cent worked in industrial enterprises in Tongxin, other nearby villages, or in Chengbei or Yushan Towns. In mid-1993, Tongxin village operated six industrial enterprises and an agricultural sideline facility which together employed about 600 workers, half of whom were from the village. Ranked second in Kunshan in 1991, the GVIO of RMB 52.6 million represented 90 per cent of the village's total output and accounted for a local income of production (*guomin shouru*) of RMB 16.3 million that was approximately ten times larger than the average for all of Kunshan's villages. By 1996 Tongxin had a GVIO of RMB 146.31 million (by then a distant RMB 56 million ahead of the second ranked village), although the share of total output from industry had fallen to 84.3 per cent. The per-capita GDP of RMB 34,438 was also by far the highest for all of Kunshan's villages and nearly twice the value for the whole of Kunshan.[28] In terms of agricultural production, with unit area grain yields (mostly rice and wheat) of over 11,000 kilograms per hectare on 113 hectares of arable land (down from 182 in 1991), agricultural productivity in Tongxin was well above the 6,990 kilogram per hectare average for Kunshan.

Recent industrial developments in Tongxin were traced to a set of circumstances which began well before the reform period. Prior to 1970, Tongxin was notorious for its poverty and backwardness. With the mass campaigns of the 'Learning from Dazhai' period in the early 1970s Tongxin was able to improve water control and irrigation which improved rice production to such a level that by 1976 a national meeting about growing rice was held in the village. Though still quite poor, Tongxin village had impressed national officials with its work. Thus, by the end of 1976 the Kunshan Water Conservancy Bureau, that had plans for a facility to electroplate parts for irrigation and pumping equipment, had been 'persuaded' to build the factory in Tongxin. Although it was a very small enterprise with only twelve employees and net earnings of RMB 10,000 to RMB 20,000 from output of RMB 100,000, village leaders immediately recognized its significance. Following early failures, village leaders learned how to capitalize on the success of agricultural reforms in the late 1970s and early 1980s, and to utilize local technical and management expertise, to vigorously promote the development of industrial enterprises. In 1984, for example, a Kunshan native who had retired from a Shanghai weaving factory was invited to provide his expertise for the two newly established textiles and weaving factories in Tongxin. Eventually, the same person also facilitated linkages with textiles concerns in Shanghai which invested old equipment and capital in the electroplating enterprise for the production of textiles related machine tools. By 1992 this enterprise had grown to 305 workers.

The village administration also took full advantage of other opportunities. A young individual entrepreneur who had operated a small hardware factory with only five or six employees turned his factory over to the village in 1986. With his technical aptitude (he also remained manager) and the financial support of the village, the new enterprise was able to successfully develop and market special seals for chemical reaction vessels. By the end of 1991 this factory employed 127 workers, generated RMB 6.6 million in gross output and had net earnings of over RMB 1 million. That same year the young manager was 'absorbed' as a party member – from (capitalist) private entrepreneur to corporate manager of a multi-million RMB company and Communist Party member in five years! Net earnings from the two textiles factories, the electroplating enterprise, the hardware manufacturer and two other industrial enterprises in Tongxin totalled RMB 5.91 million in 1991. Taxes remitted to higher levels of government consumed 35 per cent of these earnings, while 32.5 per cent was reinvested in enterprises, 13 per cent went towards various worker benefits and bonuses, and 19.5 per cent paid for local social welfare and subsidies to agriculture.

These latter expenditures included RMB 500,000 on the village road discussed in the first section of this chapter, RMB 80,000 for a retirement centre, RMB 420,000 for a new primary school, RMB 420,000 to supply running water to every household, approximately RMB 300,000 in each of the five years to 1992 on agriculture, and projects such as a new clinic and simplified roads to all fifteen small village groups. While early investments in industrial development relied on bank loans and contributions from villagers, by mid-1992 the village had a slush fund of RMB 8 million available for new investments. In 1993 some of this money was spent on several new factories located in the wheat and rice fields to the west of the village (see Plates 5.5 and 5.6). By the end of 1996 the GDP of Tongxin's industrial enterprises totalled RMB 52.96 million.

Five of the six established enterprises and the new ones built since 1993, along with the new village office, were located on or within 100 metres of the nearby town level roads. The sixth enterprise (that I was unable to locate despite repeated efforts) was deliberately isolated since it was engaged in 'dirty' and 'polluting' activities. Within the confines of the village's administrative area there were apparent efforts to locate most

Plate 5.5 Fields of canola (April 1992). Tongxin Village, Kunshan (see Plate 4.3).

Plate 5.6 Fields of factories (May 1993). Tongxin Village, Kunshan (see Plate 4.3).

industrial enterprises to take advantage of proximity to the centre of Kunshan and access to the main roads. These natural advantages probably accounted for much of Tongxin's success, although at least two dozen other villages with similar locational advantages did not seem to have benefited to the same degree.[29]

Industrial development in Tongxin instilled a new set of priorities and concerns for the village administration. The name card of the Deputy CCP Secretary of Tongxin indicated that he was also an Assistant Economist and associated with the village Industrial Corporation. Listed on the back of his card were the names of the five key industrial enterprises and their business activities. The divesting of economic (and political) responsibilities away from the centre that occurred during the early stages of the reform period after 1978, resulted in the emergence of new forms of economic organization in Tongxin. These were generally characterized at first by household based individual, cooperative and joint association arrangements which managed relatively small scale non-agricultural activities. By the mid-1980s, along with the rapid growth of local industries, control of the community's economic entities had shifted to a very strong collectively organized and unified style of management based within the village administration. Its authority and power were exercised through the coordination of industrial production, distribution and marketing, tight control over opportunities for employment in local enterprises and the disbursement of funds for economic and social development in the village.

The transformation of the rural economy and commensurate changes in local organizational structures in Tongxin were also reflected in parallel changes that occurred in agricultural production, especially since 1987. While the underlying influence of reforms in the agricultural sector on rural industrialization is well documented, less clear was how the resulting structural shifts in the rural economy affected agriculture. Apart from the obvious impact of having less arable land to cultivate, evidence from Tongxin village and elsewhere in Kunshan, suggests that a fundamental shift was under way in the organization and management of agricultural production. The theoretical implications of this phenomenon for mega-urbanization in the lower Yangzi delta will be introduced at the end of the next chapter, but for now it would be useful to examine what has happened in Tongxin Village.

As in most of the region, crop production in Tongxin rose steadily during the early years of reform up to about 1984. However, the rapid growth of industries in Tongxin that really started to take off in 1985, combined with other factors, led to a decline in crop production, especially rice.[30] By 1987 Tongxin was unable to fill its state purchasing quota. In addition to deep concerns about the loss of farming skills and arable land, these circumstances stimulated important changes in agricultural production in the village. The most obvious of these was the introduction of mechanization and other agricultural technologies after 1987, financed from the proceeds of local industry. In 1985, less than 20 per cent of the crop area was planted by machine. At the end of 1992, except for the harvesting of rice which was still done by hand, all other crop planting and harvesting was done by machine. As a result, in 1991 the village was able to harvest most of the crops before the fields were inundated from that year's devastating floods. Also that year, Tongxin exceeded its 540,000 kilograms rice quota by 266,000 kilograms. Most of the excess rice was sold to the state at 50 per cent above the quota price of RMB 0.54 per kilogram. In 1987, the village established an Agricultural Services Station to coordinate the use of machines, fertilizers and pest control, irrigation and seed varieties.

More importantly, the introduction of these agricultural technologies also required new types of organization and management of farm production to justify the investments. Informants referred to the way in which fields had been 'realigned' and how decisions regarding the use of technologies were becoming increasingly 'coordinated' through the Agricultural Services Station. Moreover, it was clear that efforts were being made in Tongxin to create specialized farming households and larger units managed like agricultural companies by the village. Two related trends were apparent. Individual households contracted with the Agricultural Services Station for access to technology and expertise or, more commonly, households could pay a fee and give-up their fields to specialized farming households under the supervision of the village administration. Of course, households retained access to per-capita allocations of food grains and family vegetable plots, even if their responsibility fields were collectively managed.[31] By the early 1990s experiments with similar processes of readjustment were common across the lower Yangzi delta.[32] Unlike the recent collectivist past, however, this reinvested responsibility for the management of cultivated lands in the village was a grass-roots response to the success of local industrial development and was made possible only by the commensurate transformation of local institutional structures.[33]

Whether or not productivity gains arising from these organizational and technological changes are sufficient to offset the loss of arable land and environmental degradation due to the expansion of settlements and industry, and the proliferation of roads, remains to be seen. Other trends are more clear. Villages and their respective committees (now increasingly elected in China) have in more developed areas like Kunshan largely taken over economic (and political) affairs, and have emerged as the most significant force in the transformation of the rural economy. These village level organizations were even more economically focused than those at the town or county level.

Specialized development zones

While the village played a critical role at the local level, particular projects promoted most often at the town or county level, also had important spatial implications for development in the Kunshan countryside. Most of the 'industrial areas' (*gongye qu*) located in every town and most villages were designated as such in a *de facto* sense following the establishment of industrial enterprises. Furthermore, in most towns investments were made to improve infrastructure to promote specialized industrial areas in or near the town seats. Yet it was quite clear that the location of town and village enterprises across Kunshan was focused neither on particular towns nor on these designated areas. Even one of the many glossy brochures distributed to encourage outside investment promoted all nineteen towns in Kunshan outside the county seat as 'key industrial satellite' towns.[34]

In addition to these industrial areas, there were a number of other special economic and development zones indicative of more deliberate attempts to either build upon or, in most cases, create new localized concentrations of particular land uses. Twenty-eight such special zones in Kunshan are illustrated in Map 5.4 (see also Map 4.1). The central task of these specially designated zones was to enhance local economies of scale by promoting actual or perceived comparative advantages. Except for the Red Flag Industrial Area established prior to the reform period, a further objective was to attract outside investment from elsewhere in China or from overseas.[35] Local governments offered a range of incentives to investors including tax holidays (up to five years), extended leases on land (up to seventy years), regulatory favours, and an expeditious approval process. Town and village enterprises in Kunshan were also encouraged to locate in the new zones, although few did because of the expense associated with leasing land and other opportunity costs. On the other hand, efforts to rehabilitate commercial and market streets in the older sections of towns, in addition to the creation of commercial districts, market areas and residential zones in newer sections, tended to lead to more specialized land uses within the town seats. Moreover, these developments were often successfully balanced with the preservation of historically significant architecture, especially in places like Nangang and Zhouzhuang (see Map 4.1).

Perhaps the most important zone in Kunshan was the Special Economic and Technological Development Zone (*Jingji Jishu Kaifaqu*, or just *Kaifaqu*) established in 1984 on a 6.18 square kilometre parcel just to the east of Yushan Town (see Maps 5.4 and 4.1). By mid-1993 the zone had expanded to 10 square kilometres expanding still further to 20 square kilometres by the end of 1995.[36] In 1990 the Jiangsu provincial government approved the new zone by granting the local administration the authority to approve investments up to $US 30 million. By 1992 China's State Council had recognized the *Kaifaqu* as a national zone – one of only sixteen in China at the time.[37] Ranked fifth in China in terms of output value, the Kunshan zone was unique in that it was completely self-financed by the local government.[38] In the eight years to 1993 more

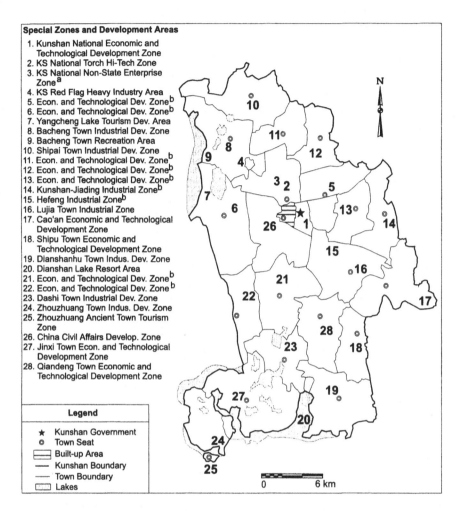

Special Zones and Development Areas

1. Kunshan National Economic and Technological Development Zone
2. KS National Torch Hi-Tech Zone
3. KS National Non-State Enterprise Zone[a]
4. KS Red Flag Heavy Industry Area
5. Econ. and Technological Dev. Zone[b]
6. Econ. and Technological Dev. Zone[b]
7. Yangcheng Lake Tourism Dev. Area
8. Bacheng Town Industrial Dev. Zone
9. Bacheng Town Recreation Area
10. Shipai Town Industrial Dev. Zone
11. Econ. and Technological Dev. Zone[b]
12. Econ. and Technological Dev. Zone[b]
13. Econ. and Technological Dev. Zone[b]
14. Kunshan-Jiading Industrial Zone[b]
15. Hefeng Industrial Zone[b]
16. Lujia Town Industrial Zone
17. Cao'an Economic and Technological Development Zone
18. Shipu Town Economic and Technological Development Zone
19. Dianshanhu Town Indus. Dev. Zone
20. Dianshan Lake Resort Area
21. Econ. and Technological Dev. Zone[b]
22. Econ. and Technological Dev. Zone[b]
23. Dashi Town Industrial Dev. Zone
24. Zhouzhuang Town Indus. Dev. Zone
25. Zhouzhuang Ancient Town Tourism Zone
26. China Civil Affairs Develop. Zone
27. Jinxi Town Econ. and Technological Development Zone
28. Qiandeng Town Economic and Technological Development Zone

Legend

★ Kunshan Government
◎ Town Seat
▭ Built-up Area
— Kunshan Boundary
— Town Boundary
▭ Lakes

Map 5.4   Special development zones: Kunshan, 1997.

Notes
a While this zone is spatially distinct, administratively it is part of the National Torch High Technology Zone.
b These zones are affilliated (*peitao*) with the Kunshan National Economic and Technological Development Zone, although they are spatially distinct and managed by the respective town level bureaucracies.

Sources: Interview notes; Field observations; *JSNJ 1998*, pp. 371–373; *SZNJ 1998*, Map appendix; Zhang, S. C. (1996) *Kunshan Fazhan guiji jishi (A Record of Kunshan's Course of Development)* Nanjing: Jiangsu People's Press.

than RMB 250 million had been expended on infrastructure. At the end of 1992 there were 150 industrial enterprises in the zone with a gross output of RMB 2.3 billion. Of these enterprises, 106 had received some form of foreign investment. There were also 153 tertiary level service enterprises in the *Kaifaqu* with revenues in excess of RMB 500 million in 1992. It was reported in April 1992 that one of Shanghai's vice-Mayors visited Kunshan to investigate successful local strategies for attracting outside investment.[39] By 1996 the number of industrial enterprises in the *Kaifaqu* was down to 132, although their total output had increased to RMB 4.64 billion, just over 20 per cent of the total for all of Kunshan. Meanwhile, by 1997 at least nine other zones affiliated (*peitao*) with the main *Kaifaqu* had been established to take advantage of the same incentives to attract investment. Created, managed and vigorously promoted by the respective town governments, these affiliated zones were spatially distinct from the main *Kaifaqu*, although they 'borrowed' the name of the national level state sanctioned zone to encourage domestic and foreign investment locally (see Map 5.4).

Informants highlighted particular aspects of the development zone that they considered important. Unlike the Red Flag Industrial Area that suffered from its isolation, the *Kaifaqu* was able to take advantage of its proximity to the centre of Yushan by tapping into the town's physical infrastructure. More importantly, the zone had ready access to the town and Kunshan level bureaucratic and management structures. In fact, by 1997 the Kunshan government had relocated most of its offices into a twenty-one storey edifice in the heart of the *Kaifaqu*. Administratively a part of Yushan, which was supposed to manage all town level concerns, investments and the development of enterprises in the zone were supervised by a Kunshan level management committee (see Table 4.1).[40] Enterprises in the *Kaifaqu* were encouraged to establish linkages with other town and village enterprises throughout Kunshan. The electroplating enterprise in Tongxin Village, for example, chrome plated stick-shift components for a factory in the new zone that contracted with a trading firm in Shanghai to supply parts destined for use in Ford pick-up trucks assembled in Japan. Thus, the *Kaifaqu* was seen as a conduit for linking outside investment, especially from Shanghai, with enterprises throughout Kunshan. In addition, many externally invested enterprise partnerships in Kunshan traced their arrival there to failed efforts to negotiate arrangements in Shanghai.[41]

Other special development zones in Kunshan included several town level designated areas which offered similar incentives for industrial development. Lujia and Bingxi Towns for example, established special zones on the peripheries of their administrative regions, but adjacent to the main *Kaifaqu* (see Map 5.4).[42] Although these zones were in more remote parts of the town, they clearly reflected local efforts to build on the advantages of being next to the higher level zone. More common, however, were special zones such as the ones set up in 1992 to the north of the Chengbei town seat, or in Cao'an in the far eastern part of Huaqiao Town (see Map 5.4). These zones were a response to more independent local efforts to take advantage of real or perceived opportunities. Informants in Kunshan reported that industrial output from enterprises located in these special zones, and other designated industrial areas, reached RMB 6.2 billion in 1992 accounting for 54 per cent of the total output for rural industry.[43] They also claimed that about half of the roughly 300 enterprises with foreign investment in 1992, were located in the town or Kunshan level special development zones. However, the planned or desirable direction of developments in these zones revealed a profound lack of specialization. According to one report on the new 7.7 square kilometre special zone in Cao'an, the objective of the area was to 'concentrate' on electronics, textiles, garments, toys, machinery, metal forging, chemicals, light manufacturing, food processing, pharmaceuticals and building materials industries no less![44]

More problematic was the dramatic growth in the number of such zones and their spatial proliferation into productive agricultural lands. Virtually every town in Kunshan, and throughout the lower Yangzi delta, had some sort of a special development zone to attract industry or other non-agricultural activities. Most offered incentives that were illegal at the town level and generally went to great lengths to promote local initiatives. One town in Wujiang to the southwest of Kunshan advertised itself using a delightful corruption of a very famous Chinese proverb: 'Above there is heaven, below there is Hangzhou and Suzhou, but Tongli [Town] is even better!'[45] Local governments in China's booming coastal regions had established more than 1,200 such special development zones covering 7,500 square kilometres of the countryside by mid-1993. By the summer of that same year the central government responded to this 'zone fever' by forcing 1,000 of them to return land with little prospects of development to agriculture, cutting their total area to 1,600 square kilometres.[46] Provincial authorities in Jiangsu also implemented a programme for the strict protection of first and second class grain production lands.[47]

Four other special zones indicated on Map 5.4 were established specifically to promote the development of local tourism. In Bacheng and Dianshanhu Towns in particular, this included the leasing of large tracts of land to developers for villa-type housing and accommodation and other recreational uses such as theme parks and golf courses.[48] Along the south facing shore of Dianshanhu this meant the relocation of four villages including nearly 3,000 people, 852 households, and eleven factories, several of which were subsequently shut down.[49] Evidence from informants and the enterprise survey questionnaire suggested a number of factors which favoured such developments in Dianshanhu Town. Apart from the natural beauty of the lake-front, the new Resort Development Area was promoted as the ideal 'back garden' paradise for Shanghai.[50] In fact, Shanghai and the new international development zones in Pudong in particular, were consistently viewed as positive opportunities for local development. 'Make your money in Pudong – spend it in Kunshan' was a common refrain. Dianshanhu Town was also by far the largest producer of canola in Kunshan.[51] This was considered important since from an engineering and ideological standpoint it was easier to turn some of the 2,200 hectares of canola fields into golf courses than it was to convert rice paddies.

Within the farming sector in Kunshan, the general response to the proliferation of non-agricultural activities was characterized by the dual processes of preservation and specialization. Alluded to in Chapter 4 and above, preservation of farmlands in Kunshan entailed the designation and enforcement of specific agricultural land use targets. It was clear from the large number of special economic zones and the proliferation of non-agricultural activities, however, that the official policy was implemented rather flexibly at the local level. The evolving organization and management of agricultural lands, including specialized agricultural households referred to in the section on Tongxin Village, was complemented by the existence of at least five large state farms in Kunshan that focused on seed production and research (see Map 4.1). There was also evidence from field observations that large plots of agricultural land were being cultivated for specific markets in local food processing and other industrial sectors or for export markets.[52] In addition to changes in the agricultural sector and the emergence of a large number of special development zones and industrial areas in the countryside, there was a growing number of specialized market areas which emerged throughout Kunshan. These included markets in Huaqiao for surplus grains, small commodities, and non-staple foods, a wholesale night market in Zhengyi for aquatic products, a farm products market in Bingxi, and one of China's largest grey-markets for cigarettes.[53]

Taken together, these phenomena suggest that there were conscious efforts undertaken to generate concentrations of particular types of land use and the concomitant agglomeration economies.[54] In practice, however, such efforts remained intensely localized as virtually every administrative jurisdiction endeavoured to construct its own recreational, commercial, and industrial space. The resulting *olla-podrida* of agricultural and non-agricultural activities across Kunshan, albeit largely organized and deliberate at the town and village levels, was confirmed and reiterated in the dense network of roadways and canals highlighted in the first section of this chapter. Some of the specific factors which have directly influenced the location of non-agricultural enterprises in Kunshan will be discussed in the following chapter.

Notes

1. Wilson, E. H. (circa 1920) *If I Were to Make a Garden*, Quoted in: Tozer, E. (1994) On the trail of E. H. Wilson. *Horticulture*, (November), p. 5.

2. Blunden, W. R. and Black, J. A. (1984) *The Land-use/Transport System: Second edition.* Sydney: Permagon.

3. Marton, A. M. (1993) Industrial development and transportation in rural Kunshan: Local reality and regional irrationality. In C. Comtois and B. Q. Fan (Eds.) *Urban Land Use and Transport Systems in China.* Montreal: Centre for Research on Transportation.

4. Unless otherwise indicated, the discussion here is based on lengthy interviews with the Kunshan Transportation Bureau. Interview notes.

5. Based in two competing bus stations in Yushan town (within a block of each other), several specialized passenger transport companies operated nearly 200 buses in Kunshan in 1996. A further 4,000 smaller passenger vehicles (mostly mini-buses and vans) were owned and operated by individuals. *KSTJNJ 1996,* p. 148.

6. Figures for cargo volumes almost certainly underestimated the actual volumes moved. The official totals from the Transportation Bureau were based on reported volumes moved by vehicles owned and operated by the bureau, town and village enterprises, and private vehicles registered in Kunshan – approximately 13,200 vehicles in 1996. *KSTJNJ 1996,* p. 148.

7. Tongxin Village will be discussed in more detail below.

8. Interview notes.

9. *KSXZ* (1990), p. 836. The phrase is more rhythmic in the local dialect: *gabing v'subing, lubing bing saning.*

10. Interview notes.

11. These three roads connected villages otherwise isolated by natural or manmade barriers.

12. I will not discuss the numerous other efforts undertaken to alleviate traffic congestion that went beyond the simple building and readjustment of the physical infrastructure. These included policies to 'rationalize' competition among passenger transport lines, and to limit the number of empty trucks using local roads.

13. Interview notes.

14. *SZJTTC* (1992), p. 8. In fact, there were at least nine levels of canals, but the sources consulted grouped them into three main categories.

15. Blunden, W. R. and Black, J. A. (1984), op. cit.

16. I use the term 'transactional space' here to refer specifically to the physical space across and through which the distribution, transfer, and other movements of commodities, capital, information and people occurred.

17. Interview notes. Although little specific data were available on these individually owned vehicles, anecdotal and observational evidence suggests that they tended to be much smaller. Also, these figures do not include the large number of farm vehicles, especially motorized wheelbarrows, which peasants hired-out during idle farming periods.

18. *KSTJNJ 1996,* p. 31; Interview notes. Only 2,605 people held urban registration (*hukou*) in the town seat.

19. These town enterprises provided their rural addresses in the survey questionnaire, while others were spotted during extensive field observations.

20. The 1992 figures discussed here were based on published projections provided by informants in mid-1992. Interview notes.

21. This figure for output is consistent with the RMB 4 million average calculated from the survey data of enterprises across Kunshan, although the same data also revealed an average of 167 workers per enterprise.

22. The discussion here is based on findings from the survey questionnaire, published information provided by local informants, interviews with local officials, field observations; and: *KSTJNJ 1989,* pp. 330–331; *KSTJNJ 1991,* pp. 250–251; *KSTJNJ 1996,* pp. 216–217.

23. This represents an earnings to output ratio of 29.4 per cent. The average figure for enterprises surveyed across Kunshan was 11.2 per cent. In 1991 revenues from sales totalled 89 per cent of gross output for this enterprise. In 1996 sales were equal to 113 per cent of gross output.

24. Tobacco production across China is tightly controlled by the central government primarily because it was the single largest source of central government revenues.

25. Survey data from enterprises across Kunshan, discussed in more detail in Chapter 6, also revealed that issues of transportation and infrastructure, and unfavourable local policies and administrative interference were the most frequently cited disadvantages of location.

26. According to Byrd, W. A. and Gelb, A. (1990) Why industrialize? The incentives for rural community governments. In W. A. Byrd and Q. S. Lin (Eds.) *China's Rural Industry: Structure, Development, and Reform.* Oxford: Oxford University Press, pp. 377–380, such behaviour was more common in poorer areas. Incentives might include tax concessions and other regulatory 'favours' from local governments.

27. Unless otherwise indicated the discussion in this section is based on interviews with village cadres and local factory managers, numerous field observations, data from the survey questionnaire, and official published statistics. See: *KSTJNJ 1989*, pp. 356–357; 425; *KSTJNJ 1991*, pp. 284–285, 353; *KSTJNJ 1996*, pp. 254–255, 298.

28. *JSTJNJ 1997*, p. 419.

29. This parallels findings described in Chapter 3 which refer to wide variations in levels of development in areas adjacent to large cities.

30. Other factors not specifically related to industrial development included fluctuations in output due to climatic conditions, problems with access to fertilizers and other critical inputs and issues of state set prices and purchasing quotas. Village cadres who were made responsible for filling the shortfall were cursed locally, as in the old days, as 'old landlords' (*lao dizhu*).

31. Informants in Kunshan were sometimes reluctant to discuss many of the details of these 'readjustments'. It turns out that in several villages in Kunshan agricultural land was sometimes sub-contracted or leased to individuals and households who frequently hired farm labour from poorer regions like Anhui Province and Subei to work the fields. Although the hiring of labour for piece rate wages was common and legal, the sub-contracting of agricultural land (in all of its disguised forms) was ideologically extremely sensitive, and technically illegal.

32. *China Daily* (1991b) Rural dream come true, 22 November, p. 3.

33. In a superb study of rural development and peasant households in China, Croll also alludes to a similar conclusion. See: Croll, E. (1994) *From Heaven to Earth: Images and Experiences of Development in China.* London: Routledge, Chapters 2 and 4.

34. Kunshan People's Government (1991) *Kunshan touzi zhinan* (*Kunshan Investment Guide*). Kunshan: Kunshan Printing House, p. 18.

35. The Red Flag Industrial Area was established as a remote location for highly polluting heavy industries.

36. Unless otherwise noted the discussion here is based on several interviews, observations, and Chinese documentary sources. See: Chen, W. (1992) City in Jiangsu attracts more foreign funds. *China Daily*, 17 May, p. III; Chen, W. and Xia, B. L. (1994) Kunshan jiaqiang sanzi qiye guanli (Kunshan strengthens management of 'three capital' enterprises). *Renmin ribao, haiwaiban* (*People's Daily, overseas edition*), 7 December, p. 2; *KSJJXX* (1993) Kunshan kaifaqu queding jinnian gongzuo mubiao (Kunshan clearly sets this

year's work target), 1 January, p. 1; *Shanghai star* (1992) Kunshan leads way for zones, 9 September, p. 9; *Xinhua ribao* (*New China Daily*) (1992) Sheng zhengfu caiqu ruogan zhengce cuoshi jiakuai Nantong, Lianyungang, Kunshan kaifaqu jianshe (Provincial government adopts several policy measures to speed up construction of the Nantong, Lianyungang, Kunshan development zones), 4 April, p. 1; *KSTJNJ* (several years.)

37. Xu, Y. M. and Zhu, Z. Y. (1992) Guowuyuan pizhun Kunshan zifei jinru guojia xulie (State Council approves Kunshan's self-financed development zone at the national level). *KSJJXX*, 15 September, p. 1; *Shanghai Star* (1992) op. cit., p. 9. This status was not the same as the five more famous special economic zones of Shenzhen, Zhuhai, Xiamen, Shantou and Hainan.

38. The first four were Shanghai (Pudong), Guangzhou, Tianjin and Dalian, all of which were located in large cities.

39. *Jiefang ribao* (1992), 4 April.

40. The administrative arrangements were not always so clear in practice. This became obvious when a man who fell through a man-hole cover on a new street in the zone sued for compensation. The town refused to accept responsibility and directed him to the zone's management committee whom the town claimed should pay since they built the road and had the administrative and financial resources to maintain them.

41. In 1995, for example, heavy equipment manufacturer Caterpillar established a dealership in Kunshan. Although not located in the *Kaifaqu*, it was clear that their arrival in Kunshan was a result of better opportunities than in Shanghai. Special thanks to Barbara Forsyth at the Asia Pacific Management Cooperative Programme at Capilano College for providing access to her interview notes.

42. Lujia Town People's Government (1992) *Guoyuo tudi youchang churang qingkuang jieshao* (*Introduction to the Situation of the Leasing of Nationalized Land*). Kunshan: Lujia Town People's Government; *Renmin ribao, haiwaiban* (*People's Daily, Overseas Edition*) (1994) Lujia zhen zhuzhong ruan huanjing jianshe peitao fuwu yinlai gelu keshang (Lujia Town emphasizes a flexible environment developing services to attract business), 9 November, p. 3; Sun, X. M. (1992) Kunshan Jingji Jishu Kaifaqu xingcheng peitao xiaoqu (The Kunshan Special Economic and Technological Development Zone establishes a small zone), *Xinhua ribao*, 14 April, p. 2.

43. In 1991, enterprises in rural industrial areas had a gross output of RMB 3.2 billion accounting for 57 per cent of total rural industrial output. Interview notes. *Shanghai Star* (1992) op. cit., p. 9.

44. *China Daily* (1992) Kunshan launches new special zone, 26 July, p. 4.

45. In Chinese: 'Shangyou tiantan, xiayou Su Hang, Tongli geng jia'. Field observations (23 May, 1993).

46. *China Daily* (1993b) State to strictly control new zones, 17 May, p. 1; *Far Eastern Economic Review* (1993) Zones closed, 26 August, p. 55. For a superb discussion of this phenomenon see: Zweig, D. (1999) *Distortions in the Opening: 'Segmented Deregulation' and Weak Property as Explanations for China's 'Zone Fever' of 1992–1993*. Hong Kong: Hong Kong Institute of Asia-Pacific Studies, The Chinese University of Hong Kong, USC Seminar Series No. 14.

47. *China Daily* (1993a) Protection for land in Jiangsu, 11 May, p. 3.

48. Sixty per cent of all of the land leased in Jiangsu Province between August 1988 and June 1994 was in Kunshan, including 478 parcels totalling 4,054 hectares. These parcels were mostly located in the Bacheng Town Recreation Area, the Dianshanhu Town Resort Development Area, and the Kunshan *Kaifaqu*. See: Map 5.4; Xu, J. P. (1992) Diandong jiang jianzao yige

'Dianshanhu cheng' (Diandong [Dianshanhu] initiates construction of a 'Dianshanhu city'). *KSJJXX*, 28 August, p. 1; Zhou, X. D. (1994) Kunshan tudi churangyun zuo youfang (Kunshan has leased land in the right way). *Renmin ribao, haiwaiban*, 27 June, p. 2.

49. Interview notes; *KSTJNJ 1991*, pp. 306–308.
50. Huang, G. F. (1992) Jian Pudong 'hou huayuan' (Build Pudong's 'back garden'). *Xinhua ribao*, 10 November, p. 2; Ping, R. (1993) Fengjing meili de Diandong Zhen chengwei waishang touzi redian (Picturesque Diandong [Dianshanhu] Town becomes foreign investment hotspot). *KSJJXX*, 15 January, p. 2.
51. *KSTJNJ 1991*, p. 62. In 1991 Dianshanhu grew nearly 5,000 tonnes of oil seeds, nearly twice that of the next largest producer. Sixty per cent of all sown crop acreage in the town was devoted to canola.
52. A large sign over one such field in Lujia Town indicated that it was an 'experimental farm' producing vegetables for a Japanese firm.
53. Located 'near the border with Shanghai' the cigarette market was accorded a degree of legitimacy by authorities in Kunshan who attempted to impose a tax on the revenues it generated.
54. Kunshan People's Government (1992) *Banhao nongcun gongye xiaoqu: Tigao fazhan xiangzhen qiye (Good Management of Rural Industrial Zones will Improve the Development of Rural Enterprises)*. Kunshan: Kunshan People's Government.

6 Linkages and the location of non-agricultural production

Much has been revealed in the previous three chapters about the underlying elements which shaped the patterns and processes of spatial economic transformation in Kunshan and the lower Yangzi delta. The preceding analysis also made frequent reference to the location of rural non-agricultural activities. In this chapter I wish to focus attention more specifically on the linkages between a number of issues introduced below, and the location of non-agricultural production in Kunshan. These linkages arise and become important not just in explaining the locational patterns of rural (mostly industrial) enterprises, but also in terms of providing a deeper understanding of the complex relationships and interdependencies among different factors within the regional space economy.

The first section of this chapter examines the formation and reproduction of capital in Kunshan, both in terms of the sources of local enterprise investment and in the disbursement of net earnings from those enterprises. The second section opens with a detailed comparison of the ownership structure and precise location of the enterprises surveyed in Kunshan. Issues of access to land and the structure of the rural non-agricultural labour force are also discussed. An evaluation of the procurement and marketing characteristics of local enterprises in the third section elaborates in some detail the nature of commercial linkages with other regions. Along with an analysis of enterprise management responses to particular problems, this section also highlights a number of issues regarding the influence of external forces on local development. The chapter concludes with a brief look at how elements of the transactional environment link enterprise location to the pre-modern historical circumstances of place, and pre-reform local sub-cultures of survival.

Investment in local development

Capital formation

Capital formation and financial flows were a key part of the process of non-agricultural development in Kunshan. Numerous studies have explored the major changes to the structure of local finance and investment that have occurred in China during the reforms.[1] Most of this research examines how such changes affected both the mechanisms for savings and investment and the economic environment for investment choices. The purpose of this section, on the other hand, is to focus on the particular characteristics of capital formation in Kunshan which highlight the linkages between investment and the location of non-agricultural activities.

An analysis of the source distribution of investment in the enterprises surveyed serves as our starting point. The most obvious feature of these enterprises was that more than 80 per cent of them were established with funds, and other capital investment, from sources entirely within Kunshan. The respective proportions of enterprises which received some part of their investment from outside Kunshan included: from Shanghai (12.6 per cent); from foreign partners (4.9 per cent); and from else-where in China (1.0 per cent). Of the enterprises with investment from outside Kunshan, 80 per cent were town level partnerships, while the remainder were village level arrangements.[2] The particular sources of capital for the wholly locally invested enterprises is also revealing. Over 77 per cent of these enterprises received a portion of their investment from town or village governments. Meanwhile, the proportion of enter-prises established with funds solely from local governments was 42.9 per cent. Nearly 30 per cent of the locally invested enterprises received all of their initial investment from town or village governments. Coopera-tive investments accounted for 2.4 per cent of locally invested enter-prises and 9.5 per cent utilized entirely borrowed capital. While many enterprises borrowed from local banks, others obtained loans from Rural Credit Cooperatives, local residents, their own workforce, or other enterprises.[3]

Clearly, local non-agricultural development in Kunshan has relied to a large degree on the mobilization of local capital. A crucial source of this capital was the dramatically increased savings deposits of local residents. Growth in rural per-capita incomes, fuelled in the early 1980s by changes in the organization and management of agriculture with the household responsibility system, and 50 to 100 per cent increases in the state purchase prices of key agricultural products, provided the initial basis for increased residential savings. By 1984, along with enhanced local control of farm and sideline production, opportunities for increased earnings from the non-agricultural sector also contributed to greater savings. The first column of Table 6.1 provides figures for residential savings deposits in financial institutions in Kunshan for selected years between 1980 and 1998.[4] These deposits increased by a factor of more than sixteen in the ten years to 1990 and grew by more than nine more times in the eight years to 1998.[5] These savings were by far the greatest single component of deposits in local financial institutions in Kunshan, accounting for an average 54.4 per cent of the nine year period to 1998 (see the second column of Table

Table 6.1 Residential savings and investment in fixed assets in Kunshan, 1980–1998 (selected years) (million RMB)[a]

| | Part A: | | Part B: |
	Residential Savings	Proportion of Total Deposits (%)	Investment in Fixed Assets
1980	39.24	–	17.97
1985	208.02	–	75.17
1990	639.27	56.6	607.58
1991	862.77	56.1	901.26
1992	979.30	45.9	1,405.05
1993	1,359.45	65.7	1,516.99
1994	2,009.20	50.2	4,700.65
1995	3,015.70	52.3	4,498.01
1996	3,988.43	54.0	5,568.01
1997	4,932.87	55.8	5,625.05
1998	5,814.77	53.0	5,798.97

Note
a All figures are current values for the year shown.

Sources: *HDDTNJ 1990*, p. 352; *HDDTNJ 1991*, p. 352; *JSSSN 1949–1989*, pp. 426, 446; *JSSSXJ 1989*, p. 234–235; *JSSXJ 1990*, pp. 304–305; *JSSXJJ 1992*, p. 246; *JSSXJJ 1993*, p. 239; *JSTJNJ 1994*, p. 316; *JSTJNJ 1995*, pp. 318, 348; *JSTJNJ 1996*, pp. 367, 379; *JSTJNJ 1997*, pp. 394, 406; *JSTJNJ 1998*, pp. 395, 407; *JSTJNJ 1999*, pp. 402, 414; *KSTJNJ 1989*, p. 159; *KSTJNJ 1991*, pp. 103, 163; *SZTJNJ 1994*, pp. 162, 256–257; *SZTJNJ 1995*, pp. 74, 324.

6.1). Such deposits became an important source of credit funds for rural non-agricultural development.[6]

Reproduction of capital

Paralleling the growth in residential deposits were changes sanctioned by the State Council, which, by 1984, had considerably enlarged formal credit facilities and which allowed rural enterprise managers and local cadres to seek funds from a range of financial institutions.[7] Part B of Table 6.1 shows the rapid growth in fixed capital investment in Kunshan, largely financed by local borrowing, for selected years between 1980 and 1998. Such investments increased thirty-nine fold between 1980 and 1990 and grew by more than nine more times in the eight years to 1998.[8] Nearly 47 per cent of the total investment in fixed assets in 1991 flowed into the development of local industry, 72 per cent of which was directed to industries located in towns and villages. The remaining 53.1 per cent was split among other productive investments (7.6 per cent, including 2.2 per cent in agriculture and irrigation) and non-productive investments (45.5 per cent, including 7.7 per cent in residential housing).[9] Investment in fixed assets was considered a major means for the social reproduction of fixed capital assets.[10] In 1996 industries in Kunshan absorbed 72.1 per cent of the RMB 5.57 billion in fixed capital investment. Nearly 80 per cent of this industrial investment flowed into town and village level collective and private enterprises. Most of the remainder was invested in the tertiary sector (not including construction). Meanwhile, a relatively tiny proportion (0.8 per cent) of the total was invested in agriculture, although in absolute terms the figure had increased somewhat to RMB 47.2 million in 1996, up from RMB 19.8 million in 1991.[11]

Local control of such investments by rural cadres was exercised through community government management of the profits and other funds of town and village enterprises and the manipulation of the loan portfolios of local banks. Another key element of capital flows in Kunshan was the disbursements of net earnings from rural enterprises. Net earnings was defined for the survey questionnaire as the total value of production less the total value of inputs, including basic labour costs. Local enterprises reinvested 40.4 per cent of their net earnings in enterprise improvement and expansion. A further 19.8 per cent of net earnings were remitted directly to local governments, most of which was available for other investments in local development. A portion of the average 27.1 per cent paid in taxes was also available to town level governments for budgetary expenditures. Officials in Kunshan, bent on promoting pet projects, also leaned on local financial institutions to obtain loans. While lending was supposed to be based on commercial considerations, much of it was in fact politically motivated. Although local branches were directly responsible to higher level banks, local officials, through the CCP, controlled the appointments of the heads of local branches and were thus able to influence local lending priorities.[12]

Rural cadres also channelled capital into new industries and other projects through creative 'grey' market borrowing. State enterprises, county level bureaux and sometimes even local banks often utilized central government subsidies, or money designated for other purposes, to set up special funds for speculative investments (usually in real estate) or for lending at interest rates substantially greater than the official level. Several county and town level officials throughout the lower Yangzi delta referred to such special loans used to finance local projects, especially infrastructure. Interest rates on such loans could reach as high as 25 per cent. The official rates for such lending between 1990 and 1993 averaged between 8 to 11 per cent.[13] Several industrial enterprises in Kunshan also introduced systems of shareholding and other cooperative-type arrangements to raise additional capital and to provide outlets for rural residents flush with savings and who sought alternatives to conventional bank deposits. The Kunshan based Sanshan Textiles Corporation, for example, raised RMB 10 million with a local share issue in March of 1992.[14] In May 1993 the same company raised RMB 100 million with a many-times oversubscribed listing on the Shenzhen stock exchange. The general manager of Sanshan in 1993 was also the CCP General Secretary of the *Kaifaqu* and a vice-Mayor of Kunshan.[15] In a dramatic turn of fortunes in 1998, the company was the first since China's stockmarkets opened in 1990 to be forced to delist from the Shenzhen exchange after recording three straight years of losses.[16]

Other funds for development in Kunshan were raised through a number of local government schemes. Many involved the imposition of arbitrary fees (a growing problem in rural China) such as various levies on local residents, road tolls, and absurdities like mandatory car washes for out-of-province vehicles – especially trucks. One other scheme common throughout the delta and in parts of Guangdong in south China, was the sale of town level urban registration certificates (*chengzhen hukou*). In August 1992, the Kunshan government raised between RMB 150 to RMB 200 million by selling 10,000 urban *hukou* which included all the privileges of living in Kunshan's central town of Yushan. These privileges included access to subsidized social welfare facilities and food, industrial employment and the right to purchase urban commercial housing (also sold by the local government). For Kunshan residents the cost was RMB 15,000, while outsiders were charged RMB 20,000. Informants admitted in May of 1993, however, that this 'urbanization for sale' scheme had degenerated into a fiasco, with urban units like schools and hospitals demanding their share of the proceeds to pay for all kinds of 'costs' associated with the new 'urban' residents.[17]

With fiscal decentralization local governments were under considerable pressure to develop the rural economy. The response of town and village cadres in Kunshan, who emerged as the principal decision makers and entrepreneurs, was to rely primarily upon the local mobilization of capital for investment in non-agricultural activities. Moreover, this self-reliance also meant that the benefits of local investment capital would largely remain within rural communities. Others have emphasized how this self-reliance has led to highly uneven patterns of rural non-agricultural development. Several of the spatial patterns discussed in Chapter 3 highlighted some sense of the disparities within Jiangsu. Combined with large variations in resource endowments and poor factor mobility, '[i]nequalities in fiscal capacity and in the level of economic development are likely to perpetuate and widen'.[18] This is confirmed by the part of the survey in Kunshan which asked respondents to describe why their enterprises were established. With 83.3 per cent of them indicating that the most important reasons related to increasing local government revenues and opportunities for employment and income of local residents, it seems clear that most enterprises would also be located within or near their respective controlling communities. Against this backdrop, was the commonly held view that any industry was good industry. The desire and new opportunities for local residents and cadres to enhance their standard of living and social status of, and within, the community were such that they were very willing to undertake the building of factories, apparently with little regard for the consequences and responsibilities involved. It became clear during the fieldwork that town and village cadres, and ordinary peasants, were anxious to 'absorb' investment that would convert their farmland into factories.[19]

Ownership, land and labour

In the second section of Chapter 4 I suggested that the location of non-agricultural activities was linked in part to the structure of enterprise ownership. The ownership structure and the distribution of gross output by ownership for the enterprises surveyed in Kunshan confirms that non-agricultural enterprises were chiefly located within the spatial jurisdiction of the rural community governments which owned and operated them. Most of the enterprises were owned by towns (47.1 per cent) and villages (44.2 per cent). State run enterprises comprised 6.7 per cent of the total while 'other' enterprises, including a Kunshan level collective and village cooperatives, accounted for the remaining 2.0 per cent. The precise owner-ship designations were, in fact, much more complicated. I have simplified the precise ownership breakdown to emphasize where the respective enter-prises were located. For example, two of the forty-one village enterprises surveyed were joint ventures with foreign and Chinese partners. The remaining thirty-nine were wholly village owned. Similarly, nine of the forty town enterprises were joint venture arrangements, with the remaining thirty-one wholly town owned. In all cases, however, I was able to clarify the precise location of these enterprises by utilizing other data collected in the survey, as well as from interviews and field observations. Meanwhile, the distribution of gross output by ownership shows that 73.0 per cent of the total was attributed to town enterprises, 16.9 per cent was from village enterprises, while state and other enterprises accounted for 8.8 per cent and 1.3 per cent respectively.

This provides a context for Map 6.1 which plots the location and the distribution by date of establishment of the enterprises surveyed. This evidence, perhaps more than any other, confirms the spatial proliferation of rural enterprises into all corners of the Kunshan countryside. Inter-estingly, only two of the seven state enterprises surveyed were located within the urban area of the Kunshan seat in Yushan, while all five of the others were distributed throughout the jurisdictions of four other towns. The third enterprise surveyed in built-up Yushan Town was a Kunshan level collective (see Map 6.1). All village enterprises were located within their villages' administrative boundaries. While a few of the town enterprises were located in or near their town seat, all were located within their towns' administrative jurisdiction. Moreover, 71.2 per cent of the enterprises surveyed were established after the beginning of the reforms in 1978 (see Map 6.1).[20] It seems reasonable to argue at this point that there was a link between ownership and the location of rural non-agricultural activities in Kunshan.

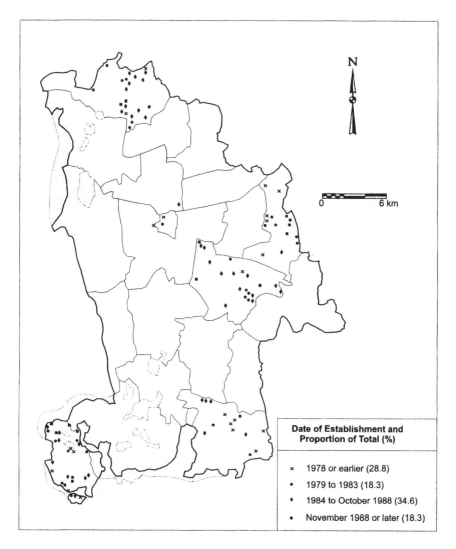

Map 6.1 Kunshan: location of enterprises surveyed.[a]

Note

a Seventy per cent of the enterprises surveyed indicated they were located in a locally designated industrial area.

Source: From the enterprise survey data.

Another key element of the intensely localized administrative impera-tives that played a role in the location of enterprises was access to land. In the China of the early 1990s, there was no free market for land *per se*, although, under certain conditions, land-use rights could be traded.

The state only owned land administratively designated as urban, but it also had the constitutional power to expropriate more land as needed for urban or industrial development.[21] Thus, rural community level governments owned and explicitly controlled virtually all of the land within their jurisdictions. To have located an enterprise outside their administrative boundaries, such as in a special development zone, which might have offered attractive inducements, community governments would, among other things, have incurred costs for leasing land. The cost of land for a locally established town or village owned enterprise, on the other hand, approached zero. While enterprises on average occupied twenty-one *mu* of land, nearly 64 per cent of those surveyed paid nothing for the area they occupied, and almost 85 per cent paid less than 5 per cent of their initial investment towards the cost of land. The survey data also revealed that in most cases the greater part of costs for enterprises which did pay for land was to cover the expense of relocating rural residents. As discussed in the example of Dianshanhu Town in Chapter 5, this sometimes involved the displacement of entire villages. In most cases, however, costs for land included new housing and related infrastructure, compensation paid to residents, and the relocation of ancestral grave sites. With ample farmland nearby it might have seemed easier to build factories there, rather than to relocate residents. However, some informants alluded to the fact that it was administratively less difficult to convert farmland to rural housing, and then to convert already uncultivated land (old housing) into industrial sites.

In addition to access to land, survey respondents also identified other reasons for the particular location of their enterprise. Nearly 42 per cent of the enterprises suggested that proximity to raw materials (5.4 per cent), proximity to Shanghai (15.1 per cent), and access to good transportation and communications (21.1 per cent) were among the most important reasons for their location. Interestingly, only 2.2 per cent of enterprises explicitly indicated that they were located primarily to take advantage of easy access to markets. However, since enterprises were not asked to clarify why proximity to Shanghai was important, it seems reasonable to assume that in many cases it was because of access to the Shanghai market. Also noteworthy is that even though good transportation and communication were highlighted among the most important reasons for enterprise location, as will be discussed below, infrastructure problems were also the most frequently cited disadvantages of enterprise location. The other enterprises cited reasons for their location which were more fundamentally linked to particular local administrative, jurisdictional, or institutional exigencies and opportunities including ease of establishment (22.2 per cent), access to land and labour (22.7 per cent) and to benefit the local community (13.5 per cent).

The issue of labour is worthwhile exploring a little further. In Chapter 3 I discussed how transformation of the rural economy in the lower Yangzi delta led to a shift in the structure of rural employment. Others have focused more specifically on issues of labour productivity and strategies of labour utilization in the Chinese countryside.[22] Here I wish to provide some sense of the link between labour and enterprise location by examining the source distribution of the labour force employed by the enterprises surveyed in Kunshan. Workers from within towns and villages accounted for 91.2 per cent of employment in the respective local enterprises. Only 3.2 per cent of employees came from other parts of Kunshan outside the respective town or village administrative jurisdictions of the enterprise owners, while only another 5.6 per cent came from outside Kunshan. The single largest source of workers from outside Kunshan was Anhui Province immediately to the west of Jiangsu, who comprised 58.5 per cent of the total.

Locally owned and located enterprises employed predominantly local surplus labour which benefited most directly from non-agricultural earnings. Although the provision of employment for local surplus labour was frequently identified as a motivation for the establishment of rural non-agricultural enterprises, other research suggests that there has been a shift away from employment generation *per se*, towards employment levels which reflect the marginal productivity of labour.[23] The 17,159 workers in these enterprises, 57.3 per cent of whom were women, earned an average RMB 188 per month in 1992. The 1,714 managerial, office and sales staff, 32.9 per cent of whom were women, earned an average RMB 220 per month. These were princely sums for rural workers in 1992. Moreover, by employing mostly rural residents, rural enterprises largely avoided the additional costs of having to subsidize housing, food and social welfare as with most state employees. It seems clear that rural enterprises in Kunshan were located in part as a response to pressures to raise the standard of living of rural residents and to avail themselves of a stable, in situ, relatively inexpensive, but generally well educated and skilled industrial workforce. Taken together, the issues of ownership, land and labour exercised a powerful influence over the locational patterns of rural non-agricultural activities.

Enterprise procurement, marketing and management

Procurement, marketing and management activities did not have the same clear link to enterprise location. Like the spatial distribution of rural enterprises, however, these activities were indicative of a variegated, highly dispersed, but very dense network of transactions. As will be demonstrated below, the precise characteristics of these transactions were important elements of the rural transformation. This was especially so in terms of how they were incorporated into, and in turn reshaped, the underlying institutional parameters of regional change in the lower Yangzi delta. Some of the conceptual implications of these complementary phenomena will be introduced at the end of this section and in the fourth and final section of this chapter.

Figure 6.1 charts the distribution of methods for procuring inputs for the enterprises surveyed in Kunshan.[24] Just over 35 per cent of enterprises procured inputs utilizing only one method. The single most important of these was from state enterprises or various bureaux (15.7 per cent), but outside the planned economy (see Part A of Figure 6.1). Only 4.9 per cent of enterprises relied solely on the 'free' market to acquire all inputs. Other methods utilized alone included inputs supplied by the buyer for processing (8.7 per cent), from planned distribution (3.9 per cent), and from town or village enterprises (2.0 per cent). Interestingly, only one of the enterprises which received inputs solely from the planned system was a state enterprise. The others were town or village enterprises. However, most enterprises (64.8 per cent) employed a combination of these methods to procure inputs (see Part B of Figure 6.1). Some of the sub-categories of these combinations are also shown in Part B of Figure 6.1. For example, 59.8 per cent of enterprises obtained some of their inputs from state enterprises, while 43.1 per cent and 42.2 per cent procured a portion of their inputs from the market, or from other rural enterprises respectively.

Similarly, Figure 6.2 illustrates the distribution channels utilized by the enterprises surveyed for the sales of their output. Nearly 52 per cent relied solely on some form of market determined sales (see Part A of Figure 6.2). Various combinations of direct and joint marketing, or fixed sales are also shown for this category. Direct marketing included the sale of output directly to end users either at the factory gate, directly to other

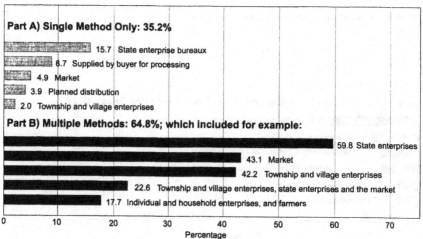

(By proportion of enterprises)

Part A) Single Method Only: 35.2%

15.7 State enterprise bureaux
8.7 Supplied by buyer for processing
4.9 Market
3.9 Planned distribution
2.0 Township and village enterprises

Part B) Multiple Methods: 64.8%; which included for example:

59.8 State enterprises
43.1 Market
42.2 Township and village enterprises
22.6 Township and village enterprises, state enterprises and the market
17.7 Individual and household enterprises, and farmers

Percentage

Figure 6.1 Procurement methods of enterprise inputs in Kunshan.
Source: Calculated from the enterprise survey data.

enterprises or through factory owned retail outlets. Joint marketing included supplying output to retail outlets or commercial (usually wholesale) agents (sometimes including investments to market production) and licensing agreements. Fixed sales were contracted arrangements for the production and supply of specific products to specific customers by agreement. Sales to customers in all these market determined cases might include individuals, other rural enterprises, or marketing agencies, but were always outside the state plan. The remaining 48.2 per cent of enterprises relied on combinations of marketing and other distribution channels which included some type of administratively determined sales. This latter category included planned sales to state enterprises or government bureaux, such as commercial, retail supply or foreign trade agencies, or the processing of raw materials or components that were modified, assembled or repaired for customers. Eighty per cent of these enterprises employed travelling salesmen or other marketing agents, while 50 per cent also negotiated all or part of their sales at trade fairs. Just over 30 per cent also purchased some sort of advertising to promote sales.

These figures for procurement and marketing, combined with the locational patterns of rural enterprises, provide some indication of the intensity and spatial proliferation of transactional activities within and around Kunshan. These activities were supported by rapid growth in communications and information exchange technologies in Kunshan. The number of telephone lines in Kunshan, for example, increased more than fifty-fold from 5,025 in 1987 to 258,523 by 1998. That same year there were

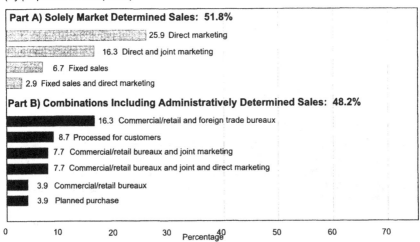

(By proportion of enterprises)

Part A) Solely Market Determined Sales: 51.8%

25.9 Direct marketing
16.3 Direct and joint marketing
6.7 Fixed sales
2.9 Fixed sales and direct marketing

Part B) Combinations Including Administratively Determined Sales: 48.2%

16.3 Commercial/retail and foreign trade bureaux
8.7 Processed for customers
7.7 Commercial/retail bureaux and joint marketing
7.7 Commercial/retail bureaux and joint and direct marketing
3.9 Commercial/retail bureaux
3.9 Planned purchase

0   10   20   30   Percentage 40   50   60   70

Figure 6.2 Distribution channels for sales of enterprise production in Kunshan.
Source: Calculated from the enterprise survey data.

30,200 cellular phone users and 63,738 beeper subscribers, up from 2,000 and 10,000 respectively in 1994.[25]

The spatial patterns of linkages and exchange relationships of rural enterprises in Kunshan also highlight the relative importance of the local and regional transactional networks. Figures 6.3 and 6.4 show the distribution of input procurements and markets for the enterprises surveyed.[26] Exchange relationships with entities in the Shanghai municipal region, while important, need to be considered relative to the importance of transactions with other regions. While procurement of inputs from the rest of China (31.2 per cent – excluding *Sunan*) were comparable to procurements from Shanghai (27.8 per cent), procurements from within Kunshan were also clearly significant (see Figure 6.3). Only 7.3 per cent of inputs came from overseas. That 14.7 per cent of inputs were sourced from within Kunshan, a proportion in the same order of magnitude as the volume of inputs from all of the rest of *Sunan* (19.0 per cent), needs to be considered in the context of the relative size and population of the respective regions. Nearly 14 per cent of the inputs for these enterprises originated in Kunshan, which was less than 5 per cent the population of Shanghai and 1.5 per cent of the population of the rest of *Sunan*.

Details of the sales of output also highlight the relative importance of local markets. The proportions of output exported to Shanghai, the rest

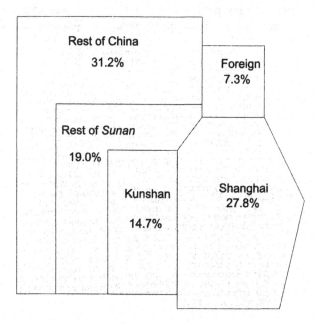

Figure 6.3 Source distribution of the procurement of enterprise inputs in Kunshan.

Source: Calculated from the enterprise survey data.

of China (excluding *Sunan*), and overseas were 31.9 per cent, 29.1 per cent and 23 per cent respectively (see Figure 6.4). Interestingly the proportion of exports to all of the rest of *Sunan* (8.7 per cent) was only slightly larger than that sold locally (8 per cent). More on this latter point below. For now, I wish to emphasize three points which arise from these data. First, in absolute terms, the relative importance of exchange relationships with Shanghai was comparable to that with other regions. Second, compared in per-capita terms or by relative area, Kunshan emerges in its own right as the most significant source of input procurements and markets for the output of local enterprises. Third, Kunshan's exchange relations with the rest of *Sunan* (excluding Shanghai) were only marginally greater than those within Kunshan itself, despite the proximity and size (over 38 million people) of this regional market.

These findings are clarified and expanded in Table 6.2 which shows the distribution of markets by product category and distribution of product categories by market for the enterprises surveyed. Compared horizontally within rows, the figures indicate the relative proportions of total output in each product category sold in each region. Thus, 3.6 per cent of the output value of textiles and garments was sold within Kunshan, 38 per cent was exported to Shanghai, and 1.9 per cent, 39.5 per cent and 17 per cent was exported to the rest of *Sunan*, the rest of China, and overseas respectively. The distribution of markets for chemicals shows a similar profile, although a much larger proportion (33 per cent) was exported overseas. Nearly 58 per cent of building materials were exported to

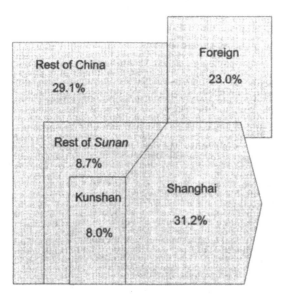

Figure 6.4 Distribution of markets for enterprise production in Kunshan.
Source: Calculated from the enterprise survey data.

Shanghai, only a little over three times the proportion purchased in Kunshan. While no building materials were sold elsewhere in the rest of *Sunan*, nearly 25 per cent of the total was shipped to other places in China (see Table 6.2). The consumer products sector is perhaps the most interesting and revealing. More than 14 per cent of such products manufactured in Kunshan were sold locally, comparable to the proportion exported to all of Shanghai, 6.5 times the output sold to the rest of *Sunan*, and nearly 60 per cent of the value shipped to all of the rest of China. Foreign markets absorbed 44.5 per cent of the output of consumer products made in Kunshan (see Table 6.2).

When compared vertically within each column, the figures in Table 6.2 indicate the relative proportion of total output sold in each region from each product category. Thus, 49.2 per cent of all output sold locally in Kunshan was in the consumer products sector. This proportion represented three-and-a-half to seventy times the value of all local output in each of the other product categories sold in Kunshan by local enterprises.

Table 6.2 Distribution of markets by product category[a] and distribution of product categories by market:[b] Kunshan (%)

	Kunshan	Shanghai	Rest of Sunan	Rest of China	Foreign	
Textiles and	3.6	38.0	1.9	39.5	17.0	(100)
Garments[c]	(9.8)	(26.6)	(4.6)	(29.3)	(15.9)	
Chemicals[d]	4.6	22.6	5.4	34.4	33.0	(100)
	(12.5)	(15.9)	(13.3)	(25.6)	(31.1)	
Building	17.5	57.6	–	24.9	–	(100)
Materials[e]	(13.6)	(11.6)	–	(5.3)	–	
Industrial	6.8	42.9	34.2	16.1	–	(100)
Products[f]	(14.2)	(23.2)	(65.0)	(9.2)	–	
Consumer	14.3	16.1	2.2	22.9	44.5	(100)
Products[g]	(49.2)	(14.4)	(6.9)	(21.6)	(53.0)	
Semi-Processed	0.8	41.9	14.6	42.7	–	(100)
Products[h]	(0.7)	(8.3)	(10.2)	(9.0)	–	
	(100)	(100)	(100)	(100)	(100)	

Notes
a Proportions to be compared horizontally within rows.
b Proportions (in parentheses) to be compared vertically within columns.
c Includes weaving, dyeing and the production of cloth.
d Includes industrial chemicals, pharmaceuticals, paints, dyes, etc.
e Includes cement and bricks, and other materials for construction such as prefabricated concrete components, doors and windows, roofing materials, etc.
f Includes metals and metal fabrication, machinery and other industrial products.
g Includes household items, toys, shoes, processed food and other consumer products.
h Includes the production of semi-processed parts and components under licence or by contract.
Source: Calculated from enterprise survey data.

Only the proportion of total output exported overseas in the consumer products sector (53 per cent), and the proportion of total output sold in the rest of *Sunan* in the industrial products sector (65 per cent) were higher.

Other figures in Table 6.2 are also instructive. The proportions of total output in four of the six product categories exported by Kunshan enterprises to the rest of *Sunan* ranged from zero in the building materials category, to 1.9 per cent, 2.2 per cent and only 5.4 per cent in the textiles and garments, consumer products and chemicals categories respectively. This evidence supports at least two overlapping findings from earlier chapters. First, it is consistent with the fact that the structure of local industrial production across southern Jiangsu was very similar, since only relatively small proportions from most product categories were exported to those areas. Second, these low proportions were also consistent with the presence of a high degree of local protectionism for industries in these sectors.

Taken together, and considered in the context of other findings, the evidence illustrated in Figures 6.3 and 6.4, and Table 6.2 also suggests that the nature of local production activities in Kunshan was apparently not greatly influenced by the patterns of linkages and exchange relationships. This was at least partly attributable to the size and relative immaturity of the fledgling domestic market. Judging by the large number of local agents there were cultivating the domestic markets in China, and the way localities were able to vigorously promote and protect their local interests, it would seem that enterprises in Kunshan were content to influence and take advantage of market opportunities, rather than to respond to external forces by adjusting the structure of local production. It is noteworthy in this context, for example, that a town enterprise in Penglang sewed together workclothes for a Japanese partner which were re-exported to Japan, that a scent factory in relatively remote Dianshanhu Town utilized inputs from central China and exported production to every province, or that two tiny enterprises – one with Thai investment – in a remote village in Shipai Town manufactured nationally recognized brand name candies and frozen snack foods (and their wrappers) for export throughout China.

The key overall point I wish to highlight as a result of this evidence is that the nature of the linkages and exchange relationships of such enterprises in Kunshan did not seem to be a factor in their decisions to locate in rather remote peripheral areas of the countryside (see Map 6.1). This finding is also supported by other evidence from the survey questionnaire where respondents were asked to indicate the greatest disadvantages of the location of their enterprise. Poor transportation and other infrastructure and distance from markets or raw materials together accounted for 61.6 per cent of the disadvantages identified. Local government meddling or 'unfavourable' local policies, and environmental degradation, including the consumption of agricultural land, accounted for approximately 50 per cent each of the remaining 38.4 per cent of problems with enterprise location. Interestingly, at least 44 per cent of the respondents who indicated that access to good transportation and communications was among the most important reasons for enterprise location also said that infrastructure related problems were among the most important disadvantages of their location.

The way in which enterprises dealt with technical and management issues highlights further elements of the intensely localized character of the rural transformation in Kunshan. In nearly 60 per cent of the enterprises, managers relied on the expertise or retraining of workers within the enterprise itself to solve technical and management problems. Other problems were confronted by establishing linkages (13.8 per cent), nearly all of which were with entities outside Kunshan, by attracting expertise from outside Kunshan (18.4 per cent), or by consulting with local governments (3 per cent). Of the 317 senior managers in the enterprises surveyed, 88 per cent were from Kunshan, while all of the remaining 12 per cent (except one manager from Thailand) were from Shanghai. Senior managers from Shanghai worked in 13.5 per cent of the enterprises surveyed.

Among the greatest challenges facing these managers was the provision of adequate levels of training and skills enhancement to maintain the expertise and flexibility of the rural non-agricultural workforce. More than 94 per cent of the enterprises surveyed provided work-related training or study for 5,035 workers, nearly 30 per cent of the total labour force in all enterprises. Just over 60 per cent were apprenticed or studied during work in their respective enterprises. Nearly 25 per cent of these workers received their training in Shanghai or elsewhere in *Sunan,* or benefited from expertise brought in from these areas. Such activities occurred via interrelationships with affiliated enterprises and economic agencies outside Kunshan, including Shanghai 'masters' with various technical or management specializations, and provincial or Shanghai research bodies and tertiary institutions such as the Suzhou Foreign Language Training Institute and the Shanghai Design Institute, a branch of the Suzhou Television University, and Shanghai's Tongji University. On the other hand, more than 75 per cent of employees who received such training, studied in Kunshan under the guidance of local specialists. This heavy reliance on locally based expertise was also reflected in the range of institutional infrastructure in place to support worker training and study. Such infrastructure included the Kunshan Adult Education College and Training Centre, Distance Education Polytechnic, the Economic Commission, staff schools, town level Adult Education Colleges and Training Centres, forty-five regular and vocational middle schools and independently invited local teachers, experts and master technicians and tradesmen.

Taken together, the findings in the preceding three sections highlight a number of issues which need to be accommodated in a new conceptual framework for understanding rural transformation in the lower Yangzi delta and the geography of enterprise location in particular. A common theme to emerge was the focus on local self-reliance in terms of the formation and reproduction of capital, access to land, the availability and training of the industrial workforce, promoting access to inputs and markets, and in dealing with technical and management challenges. Through dense networks of highly localized physical and administrative infrastructure, rural enterprises were linked to a wide array of other places and institutional structures, both within and outside Kunshan.

Moreover, these linkages were not exclusively concentrated nor dependent upon larger urban centres – particularly Shanghai and its population of at least 13 million people within 75 kilometres to the east. Rather, these findings support the contention that it was largely processes and mechanisms other than the conventionally recognized external forces associated with large cities, which played the most significant role in determining the location of rural non-agricultural enterprises and the local characteristics of regional change in the lower Yangzi delta. These other processes and mechanisms were embedded within and influenced by intensely localized administrative and institutional parameters, through which local agents negotiated and managed interactions and interrelationships between places, local industrial production in particular and the wider space economy. These elements were linked together in their mutual constitution as part of the transactional environment conceptualized in Chapter 2 (see Figure 2.2).

Transactional environment

The transactional environment encompassed 'standard' (economic) largely measurable transactional activities and less obvious, but ultimately more important, individual and institutional relationships and interdependencies, which mediated these activities, as manifest and articulated through various transactional networks. The creation of new transactional networks, and the recapturing and modification of former networks, led to the emergence of intensely localized administrative and institutional structures which managed and were in turn influenced by the processes and mechanisms of spatial economic transformation in Kunshan.[27] It was these transactional networks, moreover, which played a fundamental role in determining rural enterprise location in Kunshan. Such an outcome, as was demonstrated earlier, did not preclude new-found concern among enterprise managers about more 'conventional' factors such as transaction and other costs.

In addition, much of the evidence reviewed here, along with that presented in the previous two chapters, also links recent trends in local development to earlier historical circumstances. Reforms initiated in 1978 had, by the early 1980s, instilled not only the new patterns of economic and political relations in the Kunshan countryside, but also reinvigorated some of the older patterns as well. This was reflected perhaps most clearly in the grass-roots readjustment of the relationship between the village and peasant households. In Kunshan, and throughout the lower Yangzi delta, the resulting changes in agriculture and rural non-agricultural organization and output were astonishing. It seems safe to argue now that this had much to do with a recapturing and release of the pre-modern agricultural vitality and production zeal which had been sapped during the collectivist period.[28] This was also associated with a commensurate revitalization of rural markets (*xiangcun jishi*) and the marketing and commercial functions of small towns.[29]

While many of these transactional networks focused on economic linkages, through exchange, investment, labour and management, other networks nested enterprises and their agents within complex webs of economic, political and regulatory security. Usually cultivated through personal relationships, and always embedded in place, these transactional networks institutionalized individual and bureaucratic linkages. Thus, enterprises and their agents also sought to develop any such relationships that would establish them within protective and locally beneficial affiliations. Such activities were deeply rooted in pre-reform sub-cultures of survival. Similar to the late imperial and more recent collectivist past, the greatest challenges confronted by the resulting institutional structures related to the new uncertainties and vicissitudes of the 'socialist market economy'. This included shifting, often traumatic, political 'winds' from the centre, competition from other areas, periodic clampdowns on credit and, somewhat ironically, local government meddling and administrative diktat.[30] The challenges remaining for this study are to more clearly conceptualize the way in which features of these institutional parameters and their transactional environment related to the spatial economic transformation in Kunshan, and to articulate the theoretical and policy implications for mega-urbanization across the entire lower Yangzi delta. These challenges are specifically addressed in the final chapter of this book.

Notes

1. Byrd, W. A. and Lin, Q. S. (Eds.) (1990) *China's Rural Industry: Structure, Development, and Reform.* Oxford: Oxford University Press, Chapters 9 and 10; Deng, Y. T. (1992) Township enterprises and rural finance. *National Workshop on Rural Industrialization in Post-reform China*, Beijing, 19–22 October; Findlay, C., Martin, W. and Watson, A. (1993) *Policy Reform, Economic Growth and China's Agriculture.* Paris: OECD, pp. 32–35; Ho, S. P. S. (1994) *Rural China in Transition: Non-agricultural Development in Rural Jiangsu, 1978–1990.* Oxford: Clarendon, Chapter 7; Mansharan, T. (1992) Credit and financial institutions at the rural level in China – Between plan and market. In E. B. Vermeer (Ed.) *From Peasant to Entrepreneur: Growth and Change in Rural China.* Wageningen: Pudoc; Tam, O. K. (1988) Rural finance in China. *The China Quarterly* 113; Watson, A. (1989) Investment issues in the Chinese countryside. *The Australian Journal of Chinese Affairs* (22); Wong, C.

(1988) Interpreting rural industrial growth in the post-Mao period. *Modern China* 14 (1); Wong, C. P. W. (Ed.) (1997) *Financing Local Government in the People's Republic of China.* New York: Published for the Asian Development Bank by Oxford University Press; Yuan, P. (1994) Capital formation in rural enterprises. In C. Findlay, A. Watson and H. X. Wu (Eds.) *Rural Enterprises in China.* New York: St. Martin's.

2. Unless otherwise stated all figures discussed in this chapter were calculated from the enterprise survey data.

3. Interview notes.

4. These figures do not include enterprise or local government deposits, nor do they include cash and other assets hidden at home by residents. The value of the latter comprised an unknown, but probably significant proportion of total savings.

5. Even if these figures were corrected for inflation the growth rates were substantial.

6. Others have made similar claims. See, for example: Deng, Y. T. (1992) op. cit., pp. 15–17.

7. Kirkby, R. J. R. (1994) Dilemmas of urbanization: Review and prospects. In D. Dwyer (Ed.) *China: The Next Decades.* Essex: Longman, pp. 143–144; Wong, C. (1988) op. cit., p. 11.

8. Though not corrected for inflation, these figures still represent significant growth.

9. Calculated from *KSTJNJ 1991*, pp. 103–107. Small proportions of investment in certain industries were listed as 'non-productive', although they were not consistently disaggregated for all figures. Elsewhere, the official sources provided a value for non-productive fixed capital investment in Kunshan that accounted for 49.5 per cent of the total in 1991.

10. This is elaborated upon in some detail in the official statistical yearbooks. For example, see: *ZGTJNJ 1994*, pp. 183, 186.

11. *KSTJNJ 1996*, p. 49.

12. For a full explanation of how local officials manipulated local lending, see: Lieberthal, K. (1995) *Governing China: From Revolution Through Reform.* New York: Norton, pp. 270–271.

13. Interview notes; *ZGTJNJ 1994*, p. 549.

14. Qian, S. and Zhou, Y. (1992) Jiangsu Kunshan Sanshan Jituan fa gupiao (Jiangsu Kunshan Sanshan Group issues shares). *Jiefang ribao (Liberation Daily)*, 1 April. Interview notes.

15. Interview notes.

16. *Far Eastern Economic Review* (1998) Business briefing, China: Jiangsu Sanshan industry. (1 October, 1998) p. 54.

17. Interview notes.

18. Ho, S. P. S. (1994) op. cit., pp. 235–236; Also see: Byrd, W. A. and Lin, Q. S. (Eds.) (1990) op. cit., Chapter 12; Fan, C. C. (1995) Of belts and ladders: State policy and uneven regional development in post-Mao China. *AAAG* 85 (3).

19. And the sooner the better! Village residents often mistook me and my briefcase full of questionnaires for a foreign investor with a bag of US dollars! 'Please invest here. Use my farmland!' Interview notes.

20. October 1988 corresponded with the implementation of a retrenchment programme which affected many rural enterprises.

21. World Bank (1993a) *China: Urban Land Management in an Emerging Market Economy.* Washington: The World Bank, pp. 41–42.

22. For excellent discussions see: Asian Regional Team for Employment Promotion (1992) *Reabsorption of Surplus Agricultural Labour into the Non-agricultural Sector: A Study of Township Enterprises in China.* New Delhi: International

Labour Organization, pp. 36–40; Wu, H. X. (1994) Rural enterprise contributions to growth and structural change. In C. Findlay, A. Watson and H. X. Wu (Eds.) op. cit., pp. 40, 59–63.

23. Byrd, W. A. and Lin, Q. S. (Eds.) (1990) op. cit., Chapter 11.

24. See Chapter 4 for a discussion of each of these methods. Inputs included energy (except electricity which was usually not listed), semi-processed products or components for modification or assembly, or other raw materials and industrial products such as chemicals.

25. *KSXZ* (1990), p. 353; *SZTJNJ 1995*, p. 279; *SZTJNJ 1999*, p. 234.

26. When designing and testing the survey questionnaire it became clear that it would have been too difficult for respondents to indicate the value of inputs from various sources. Since many inputs were procured through various administratively determined methods, the precise source distribution by value was often unclear, although respondents did know from where their inputs originated. Therefore, the relative proportions of inputs from various sources were estimated based on the rankings and sources of the five most important inputs listed by survey respondents. Admittedly, this was a bit crude, but combined with other components of the analysis it does provide a sense of the source distribution of input procurements. The distribution of markets, on the other hand, was easily determined based on the values listed by survey respondents.

27. This mutual constitution, as I referred to this phenomenon above, is illustrated in Figure 2.2 by the broken arrows from the geography of enterprise and locality elements of the diagram to administrative and institutional parameters.

28. Conceptually 'safe' that is, and ideologically too, if in China.

29. Although fraught with much empirical uncertainty, several studies have made allusions to the number or transaction value of rural markets in China by the mid-1980s as being comparable to levels during the Republican period. See: Fei, X. T. (Ed.) (1986) *Small Towns in China: Functions, Problems and Prospects*. Beijing: New World Press, Chapters 1 and 2; Skinner, G. W. (1985) Rural marketing in China: Revival and reappraisal. In S. Plattner (Ed.) *Markets and Marketing*. Lanham: University Press of America. For other related discussions also see: Findlay, C., Martin, W. and Watson, A. (1993) *Policy Reform, Economic Growth and China's Agriculture*. Paris: OECD, pp. 21–26; Taubmann, W. (1992) The growth of rural towns in China's urban regions. In E. B. Vermeer (Ed.) op. cit., pp. 274–275.

30. Informants frequently utilized terms such as 'threats' or 'battles' with outside 'armies' in this context. This is perhaps attributable to the fact that several senior local cadres were retired or reassigned military officers. Interview notes. Ironic because local governments were, of course, in themselves the leading agents of rural development. This paradox was also discussed at the end of Chapter 4.

7 Mega-urbanization in the lower Yangzi delta: theoretical and policy challenges and responses

In Chapter 1 I suggested that understanding regional development in China could only arise from detailed investigations from within particular landscapes of transformation. The lower Yangzi delta emerged as an especially poignant exemplar of such restless landscapes, epitomizing the key features, prospects, and challenges of spatial economic restructuring in China. Chapters 3–6 have highlighted in considerable detail the nature of the spatial economic restructuring that has occurred in the lower Yangzi delta since the beginning of reforms in 1978 and the key underlying processes and mechanisms which determined the precise character of this transformation.

What then are the theoretical implications of this restructuring in the delta in terms of conceptualizing the forces which drive regional development? Chapter 2 began by justifying deliberations along the three broad theoretical discourses of regional development, the geography of production and urbanization. The objective was to interrogate these frequently disparate debates to highlight elements of each which were relevant for the development of a new conceptual framework for understanding spatial economic restructuring in China's lower Yangzi delta. In the context of preliminary insights into regional transformation in the delta and a review of the pertinent Chinese literature, these discussions culminated at the end of Chapter 2 with three specific assertions:

1   The patterns and underlying processes and mechanisms of regional development in the delta were fundamentally linked to intensely localized characteristics and circumstances within the wider Chinese space economy.
2   Industrialization and the morphology of spatial economic restructuring in the delta were best understood and explained in terms of the complex interactions and interrelationships which constituted the transactional environment.
3   External economies, the dynamics of agglomeration, and the role of large cities and other exogenous forces, while important, were less significant in determining the character of local and regional development in the delta than were endogenous forces.

These assertions have been articulated separately in this book in order to cope methodologically with a number of overlapping concepts and phenomena. Taken together, they were incorporated into an alternative conceptual framework for understanding rural transformation and mega-urbanization proposed at the end of Chapter 2.

This framework provided a checklist of the important elements of regional development in the lower Yangzi delta which informed the inquiry along five intersecting modes of analysis. The first was a survey of the pre-reform historical geography of the region which highlighted local sub-cultures of political and economic survival. The second concentrated on an exploration of spatial economic restructuring characterized primarily by the growth and spatial proliferation of non-agricultural activities and employment within highly productive and densely populated agricultural regions. The third, and perhaps most important mode of analysis, examined in some detail the administrative and institutional parameters to show how they were linked to intensely localized exigencies and opportunities for development. The fourth briefly considered the growth of population in areas defined as urban which revealed the apparent capacity to rapidly industrialize without transferring large numbers of people into big cities. While some effort was also made to examine the movement of labour in this context, this part of the analysis was limited by the lack of adequate data.[1] The fifth focused on the morphological aspects of regional development in the lower Yangzi delta by investigating the patterns and underlying processes and mechanisms of industrialization, and the specific factors which influenced the location of enterprises.

Industrialization and industrial location in the delta, in fact, provided the rubric which framed and informed the major findings from each of these modes of analysis which are summarized in the next section. This establishes the context for several refinements of the conceptual framework introduced in the second section of this chapter which reviews the theoretical implications of this study. The final section of this concluding chapter, will introduce a planning and management agenda for the lower Yangzi delta.

Negotiating and managing the regional transformation: institutional parameters and rural agglomeration

Underlying my review of the theoretical debates about regional development, industrial location and urbanization in Chapter 2, was the assumption that organizational forms of production systems were linked to spatial relations which were themselves embedded in the regional geography of place. This assumption not only informed the analyses undertaken in this study, it also helped to highlight the conceptual reformulations necessary to understand and explain the patterns and processes of regional transformation in the lower Yangzi delta. It turns out, moreover, that engaging such theoretical problems in the context of a detailed empirical analysis yields far more in terms of a meaningful conceptual framework than merely interrogating such issues in the abstract.

As Massey, in her second edition of *Spatial Divisions of Labour* has recapitulated, the foundation of such a method of conceptualizing was to acknowledge the uniqueness of place, and to emphasize the analysis of 'connections', interrelationships, and interdependencies to reveal 'causal structures' which underlie local specificities of regional change.[2] This justifies the particular approach of this study which explored regional transformation in the lower Yangzi delta from a 'rural' perspective. It was in these restless landscapes of the Chinese countryside where the development of 'market socialism' had its deepest and perhaps most lasting impression.[3] What also makes this perspective so important and interesting is the focus on the intersection of processes and mechanisms which 'influence/ encourage/restrain/ mould the operation of each other', in what Massey calls 'axes of articulation'.[4] Some will fret about what they perceive as the inherent indeterminacy of this approach when, in fact, what we are faced with is profound complexity. Methodologically, this approach enables the researcher to grapple with this complexity and to propose relevant generalizations. Furthermore, if we are to move beyond merely understanding mega-urbanization in the lower Yangzi delta, to intervene in it, then an appreciation of the specificities of its local character is essential.[5]

The field investigations, and subsequent analysis of spatial economic restructuring in Kunshan and the lower Yangzi delta, unearthed key interactions and interrelationships, embedded within administrative and institutional parameters, which constituted fundamental elements of the region's transactional environment. The resulting 'causal relations' which linked locality to the geography of enterprises in the delta, were captured in Figure 2.2 which is repeated in revised form in the next section.[6] These linkages became the analytical focus in response to initial findings which suggested, among other things, that regional development here was more complex than merely in terms of its relationship to, and purported dependence upon, urban centred external (global) forces. An examination of the way in which local organizational structures were constituted, for example, revealed more about the construction of industrial space in places like Kunshan than emphasizing a dominant role for nearby cities, particularly Shanghai. Undertaking the analysis in this way, elaborated upon the nature of the transactional networks within the local and regional space economies, and the linkages through which local agents negotiated and managed them.

The resulting administrative and institutional structures, most frequently defined and embedded within locality and place, and their articulation and emergent effects, both determined the patterns and processes of local economic transformation, as well as the role of place within the wider space economy. By invoking this line of argument I am deeply cognizant of the debates revolving around agency and structure, and in the danger of conceptualizing locality itself as agent.[7] Nevertheless, this does not weaken my intention to highlight the relationships between locale and institutional structures by focusing on the transactional activities and networks of local agents which determined local and regional patterns of development.

Some might prefer to characterize this perspective in terms of the political geometry of power relations or to emphasize the way social relations of production constructed social space and production systems.[8] However, these approaches inevitably tend to reduce the relevance of locale merely to that of a 'meeting place' of intersecting, usually externally determined layers of agency, interests, and social relations.[9] The approach advocated in this study paid a great deal more attention to the constellation of circumstances uncovered in the Chinese countryside which elevated locales and places there to a more fundamental role in the production of industrial space. This is consistent with the gist of my first assertion above which emphasized the critical links between locality (and less explicitly, place) to the patterns, processes and mechanisms of regional development in the delta. Analysis of the relevant processes and mechanisms, moreover, highlights the potential for dealing with the policy challenges of mega-urbanization across the entire lower Yangzi delta through small scale local economic and 'administrative' strategies. More about these strategies later, but first a conceptual elaboration of the underlying processes and mechanisms.

This study has identified four broad phases of spatial economic restructuring in the lower Yangzi delta. The first two referred to the pre-modern and post-Liberation periods up to the beginning of the most recent reforms in 1978. The former was generally characterized by the emergence of small agricultural land holdings, community and household level control and management of water conservancy, the proliferation of agricultural sidelines, handicrafts, and other off-farm activities into the countryside, and the development of many small towns. The latter phase was generally characterized by the collectivization of agriculture, severe restrictions and rigorous enforcement of the movement of people, the urbanization or prohibition of most non-agricultural activities in the countryside, and the communization of virtually all aspects of rural economic and social life.

The third phase, beginning with the introduction of reforms in 1978, saw the dismantling of certain collective structures particularly in agriculture and the reemergence of household level economic decision-making in the countryside. Combined with the devolution of financial and administrative responsibilities away from the centre, this led to a substantial diversification and restructuring of the rural economy. The two most obvious features were the spatial proliferation of non-agricultural activities in the countryside, and the emergence of institutional structures linked to the evolving relationship between local governments, community development and a partially reformed command economy. These findings highlight the linkages between industrialization and spatial economic restructuring in the delta and the interactions and interrelationships which constituted the transactional environment.

By the late 1980s and early 1990s, a subtle, but important shift in the character of this transformation began to emerge. This fourth phase, most evident in well-off regions of the delta such as Kunshan, was distinguished by the reinvesting of certain economic responsibilities back into community administrations, especially at the village level. Of course, the organization and function of these local administrations has altered since the beginning of reforms. This shift of responsibilities was reflected in changes to the organization and management of economic activities and in the spatial structure of agricultural and non-agricultural production systems emphasized and promoted by local governments.

The patterns and trends of this phase of regional transformation I will now characterize as rural agglomeration. The term comes from my translation of the Chinese words *nongcun juluo*. Found in only one rather obscure Chinese publication, precisely what these words referred to was unclear.[10] They arose throughout this particular Chinese study in the context of efforts to conceptualize rural industrial development and phenomena associated with urban transition in southern Jiangsu. I have appropriated the term in translation – rural agglomeration – to refer here to the elements which characterized this fourth phase of spatial economic restructuring in the lower Yangzi delta.

Some of these elements were linked to the circumstances and local sub-cultures of earlier periods referred to in my assertion about the critical role of locality. Others emerged as a response to more conventional concerns with the rationalization of economic activity generally characterized by attempts, within intensely localized priorities, to encourage the concentration of agricultural and non-agricultural land uses. This most often occurred through the establishment and promotion of specialized industrial, commercial, or recreational development zones, the merging of farmland into specialized agricultural operations, and the location of industrial enterprises to take advantage of the real or perceived benefits of local administrative or physical infrastructure. In some cases, industrial enterprises were also located in as remote a location as possible to 'hide' their 'backwardness' and deleterious environmental impact. However, with notable exceptions such as the Kunshan level *Kaifaqu*, the processes and mechanisms which determined and executed such imperatives remained highly focused on the relevant local administrative jurisdiction. Thus, while villages and towns may have chosen to locate non-agricultural activities based on more conventional economic criteria, this generally occurred only within their administrative boundaries. Similar outcomes were also revealed in the patterns of roads within and between villages, towns, and county level and higher jurisdictions. These findings are consistent with the emphasis on local or endogenous forces proposed above.

It is the administrative and institutional parameters of this rural agglomeration through which particular contemporary patterns and processes were also linked to earlier circumstances. The downward dispersion of administrative and economic power away from the centre since the beginning of reforms, and the emergence of local organizational structures, parallels particular patterns of the late imperial period. A key feature of these patterns was the centrifugal tendencies of administrative jurisdictions which affected development across the wider lower Yangzi delta region.

Two examples not previously discussed help to illustrate this point. Wuxi County to the east of Kunshan for many years resisted the opportunity to be elevated to county level 'city' status despite the fact that it by far exceeded all the official economic criteria.[11] The problem was that the administrative seat of the county was located within the boundary of Wuxi City proper, which was itself the administrative seat of the three county level units under its prefectural level jurisdiction. Wuxi County officials were deeply concerned that the control and benefits of the county economy, China's richest, would be lost to the Wuxi City administration if the county level city seat remained within the city proper. It was not until the autumn of 1995, after Wuxi County had invested enormous sums of money to develop a new administrative seat in Dongting Town just seven kilometres to the west of Wuxi City, but outside its administrative jurisdiction, that the county was elevated to city status and renamed Xishan. Wuxi City proper was compensated for the loss of the county seat by the transfer of nineteen villages from the county to the newly expanded city region.

This fragmentation and coalescing of administrative and economic power away from big cities into the adjacent countryside was an important part of rural agglomeration. Thus, while some commentators have referred to conventional notions of agglomeration in the *Suxichang* region, this evidence demonstrates that the opposite trend is more apparent, especially at the meso-scale.[12] This finding not only confirms the relative importance of local forces, it also reveals the critical role of administrative and institutional parameters at the core of the transactional environment proposed above.

This latter point is reinforced by the second example which relates to the development of a number of sizeable port and transshipment facilities in several locations along the south bank of the Yangzi River and along major waterways of inland regions in *Suxichang*. Representatives from each of these ventures claimed their facilities would provide competitive services to customers within wildly overlapping catchment areas across the delta, usually including most of Shanghai![13] In practice they could only 'guarantee' that enterprises and agencies within their own administrative jurisdictions would utilize the facilities, even if it was more sensible for them to direct their business to other ports or alternative infrastructure.

The bureaucratic intervention implied by such developments was reflected in the emergence of administrative and institutional structures through which local governments and their agents profoundly mediated the transactional environment.

One particularly interesting consequence of these emerging structures was the grass-roots shift towards the unified organization and management of agricultural production seen, for example, in Tongxin Village. It is significant, perhaps even ironic, that many of the central goals of collectivist agriculture prior to 1978, were being implemented by the mid-1990s by village governments in cooperation with rural households. It seems that this element of rural agglomeration began with a return to a version of the pre-modern structures of agricultural production. More importantly this most recent 'readjustment' (*tiao zheng*) in the organizational and spatial structure of agricultural production could only have occurred with a commensurate transformation in local administrative and institutional structures.

Patterns of industrial location in the lower Yangzi delta also emerged in response to the same administrative and institutional structures linked to the restructuring of the rural economy and local growth machine politics. Industrial space in the countryside was constructed through processes and mechanisms of growth, rather than through the efficient allocation of enterprises across the economic landscape. Industrialization itself, largely depended upon the capacity of local actors to negotiate and manage access to the means of production and markets. Under such conditions, decisions about the precise location of enterprises were in most cases not subject to the economic logic of conventional factors. That is, industries in the delta produced economic space without being 'held hostage' to pre-existing spatial distributions of supply and demand.[14] Moreover, while the efforts to create access to inputs and markets were operationalized via intensely localized administrative and institutional structures, this did not necessarily translate into the formation of dense industrial clusters, or even in the building-up or expansion of urban centres, although this was a frequently stated regional development objective.

That is not to say that these phenomena were absent in the wider space economy. However, transactional activities and their networks, while spatially dispersed, remained heavily focused on the development of 'rural' locales. Thus, industrialization and the location of enterprises were functionally situated within their administrative and institutional parameters, which were themselves deeply embedded within their territorial milieu.[15] While this attachment to local interests and place resulted in greater flexibility and responsiveness, it also meant that the most fundamental exigencies and opportunities which stimulated and sustained industrialization were largely immobile.

Taken together these findings, which I have characterized generally as rural agglomeration, verify the three assertions made at the beginning of this chapter. It is now important, after having elaborated in some considerable detail upon the numerous elements of spatial economic restructuring, to step back and reassess how all these components fit into the big picture of regional development in the lower Yangzi delta. The theoretical implications of this reassessment have already been alluded to in the preceding analyses, in terms of the critical interactions and interrelationships highlighted in the mega-urbanization framework, and in reporting the precise spatial outcomes observed in the field. The next section will articulate and clarify the nature of these theoretical implications.

Theoretical implications: urban transition or regional resilience?

In Chapter 2 I argued for a theoretical 'middle ground' which included several overlapping elements. The first emphasized the need to redefine the conditions and processes underlying the emergence of 'new' regions of economic activity and was less concerned with the distinction between urban and rural. Spatial economic restructuring in the lower Yangzi delta was largely centred within regions neither clearly urban nor rural. McGee, in his *desakota* formulation, has recognized the uniqueness and significance of such zones in the context of large 'extended metropolitan regions' in Asia. While *desakota* necessarily challenged conventional views about urban transition, it remained a largely heuristic device to help explain the empirical circumstances of 'Asian' urbanization.[16] This study of the lower Yangzi delta has built upon the insights of this perspective through a detailed analysis of the underlying forces driving transformation in the regional space economy. It has done so by invoking two further elements of the middle ground proposed in Chapter 2. The first was a 'middle level' industrial geography which incorporated the broader theories of location and the production of industrial space within a framework that accommodated local experiences and circumstances. The second of these elements privileged local level forces through a detailed examination of their articulation with, not subordination to, exogenous (usually urban centred) influences. The objective was to develop a conceptual framework that elaborated upon the complex interactions and interrelationships between economic development and the form, nature and organization of production in the lower Yangzi delta. The framework which emerged also served to uncover, and then suggested methodologies to evaluate, the critical linkages between the underlying processes and mechanisms and the specific spatial consequences of regional economic transformation in the delta.

The fundamental elements of this middle ground are reiterated in a revised conceptual framework of rural agglomeration and mega-urbanization illustrated in Figure 7.1. Included are several small, but important changes to the original figure illustrated at the end of Chapter 2 which highlight

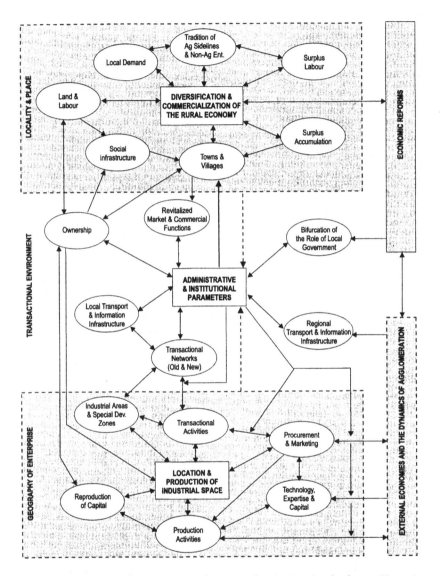

Figure 7.1 Rural agglomeration and mega-urbanization in the lower Yangzi delta.

Note Ag= Agricultural

particular relationships clarified in the analysis and findings in the preceding four chapters. The top part of the diagram is re-labelled 'locality *and place*' in order to emphasize the historical, economic, and socio-political subcultures that defined place. In addition to the explicit recognition of the tradition of agricultural sidelines and non-agricultural activities, these other circumstances which determined the character of place need to be understood in order to appreciate local and regional development. Within this component of the conceptual framework I have added 'labour' to the issue of land. This is to be distinguished from 'surplus labour' in which processes related to the diversification of the rural economy have released labour from agriculture. Rather, labour is emphasized here, with land, in this new subcomponent of locality and place, to indicate its importance with respect to the location of industrial enterprises as discussed in Chapter 6. Clarification of this linkage also requires highlighting more strongly the relationship between ownership and local administrative and institutional parameters. This mutual interdependence is captured in Figure 7.1 with a new bi-directional arrow between the two. Taken together, the issues of ownership, land, and labour, as they were manifested within intensely localized administrative and institutional structures, are shown as directly affecting the location of industrial activity.

Two further changes to the conceptual framework more clearly indicate the linkages between the local formation and reproduction of capital and the location of industrial enterprises. Capital formation for non-agricultural investment in the lower Yangzi delta, largely based upon local surplus accumulation (see the top part of Figure 7.1), was most often organized by town and village governments who, through their corporate-like organizations, were the primary owners and operators of industrial enterprises. Hence, the new bi-directional arrow between the 'towns and villages' sub-component in the top of the diagram and 'ownership'. As was demonstrated in Chapter 6, the local reproduction of capital occurred primarily through two methods. The first included returns on investments in production activities, and the second included community government manipulation of the loan portfolios of local banks or of funds managed through the still persistent, though partially reformed command economy structures. This second method is expressed in Figure 7.1 with a new bi-directional linkage between 'ownership' and 'administrative and institutional parameters'. Thus, the formation and reproduction of capital were associated not only with local surplus accumulation and production activities, but also with the location and production of industrial space. This linkage is indicated with another new bi-directional arrow between the 'reproduction of capital' sub-component and the 'location and production of industrial space' at the bottom of Figure 7.1.

Also in the bottom part of the diagram, I have re-labelled the geography of enterprise sub-component of 'industrial organizations' to refer specifically to the 'industrial areas and special development zones' discussed in Chapter 5. While the creation and promotion of such zones were linked to the desire to encourage conventional external economies and local comparative advantage, their precise locations and functions remained profoundly mediated by intensely localized administrative and institutional structures.

The final clarification to the conceptual framework highlights the impact these evolving administrative and institutional structures had on the organization and management of the agricultural sector referred to in the previous section and discussed in Chapter 5. I have, therefore, added a new arrow from 'administrative and institutional parameters', in the centre of the diagram, to 'towns and villages' and indirectly to the changes which occurred in the rural economy illustrated in the top of Figure 7.1. This linkage was a result of the mutual interdependencies among evolving administrative and institutional structures which mediated the local geography of industrial production, and which in turn affected those structures in such a way (captured in the dotted arrow from the geography of enterprise to administrative and institutional parameters) to provide the grass-roots organizational desire and wherewithal to effect 'readjustment' in agricultural production.

What then, are the theoretical implications of rural agglomeration and mega-urbanization in the lower Yangzi delta? The alternative conceptualization proposed here begins by situating the most important factors and outcomes of regional transformation in the Chinese countryside. It does so by linking the location and production of industrial space, through a highly transactional environment, characterized primarily by intensely localized administrative and institutional parameters, to the diversification and commercialization of the rural economy. This approach emphasizes the underlying dynamics of the interactions and interrelationships as they affected and were affected by spatial economic restructuring in the delta. The resulting theoretical framework allows the observer to conceptually and methodologically grapple with the emergence of large, densely populated areas of mixed, highly productive agriculture and rapidly proliferating non-agricultural activities. It is significant, for example, that the Kunshan economy was especially good at generating wealth through a particular combination of agricultural and industrial production.

While linkages with large cities were clearly important for places like Kunshan, it was the emergence of a spatially dispersed, but highly integrated and dense transactional environment which contributed to the *in situ* stabilization or resilience of local production systems. Deeply rooted in locality and place, it was this transactional environment and its largely self-generated transactions of growth which propelled spatial economic restructuring in the Kunshan countryside. Furthermore, these rapidly restructuring regions, with a previously distant presence in the hierarchy of non-agricultural production systems (at least during the more recent collectivist past), have by many measures equalled or exceeded long established industrial centres. Can the Kunshan countryside continue to be considered 'rural'? Is all or part of Kunshan 'urban'? In the context of the conceptual framework proposed here, these distinctions are less important than understanding the processes and mechanisms which have affected the emergence of such highly productive mixed agricultural and non-agricultural regions. Moreover, by rejecting this rural–urban dichotomy the conceptual framework can accommodate spatial patterns and morphologies which conform clearly to neither.

It also provides the necessary opportunity to challenge conventional views of the role of large cities in regional development. While mega-urbanization in the lower Yangzi delta included forces linked to the presence of large cities and other external economies (see the bottom right of Figure 7.1), their influence on the local geography of enterprises was conceptualized as ancillary to the dominant local forces of transformation which I have associated with rural agglomeration. Thus, while linkages between Kunshan, large cities, and other regions were important in terms of the magnitude of transactional activities, these external relations apparently did not significantly influence the spatial patterns of local development.

Such an approach also cautions against the narrow view of spatial economic restructuring in the delta as merely the penetration of urban interests and urban land uses into agricultural regions. In fact, there is some evidence to suggest that particular outcomes of rural agglomeration have stimulated limited industrial reforms in nearby cities. Informants in Kunshan, for example, recounted a famous story, *Li Xiangnan Jincheng*, about a peasant guerrilla during the Anti-Japanese War who entered cities to harass the occupying forces.[17] The metaphor referred to the way industrial products from Kunshan were able to compete with, and force changes in, the quantity and quality of urban industrial output.[18] Less obvious, but perhaps more important, were the organizational and management changes in large, mostly state run urban industries, as they were forced to respond to the growing bureaucratic entrepreneurialism of town and village industries, in addition to other challenges. These linkages are illustrated in the arrows from 'production activities' and 'procurement and marketing' to 'external economies and the dynamics of agglomeration' in the bottom right of Figure 7.1.

The notion of rural agglomeration is also intended to capture the paradox of economic development as it was linked to the expanding power and influence of local governments to promote growth, and the rising appreciation of, and localized attempts to respond to, these external economies and the dynamics of conventional agglomeration. Yet the evidence strongly suggests that the underlying processes and mechanisms driving regional economic restructuring in the lower Yangzi delta will likely persist for some time. While the resulting patterns of agricultural and non-agricultural development will likely deepen, their fundamental character will remain essentially unchanged. It is possible to make this assertion with some certainty since the concepts of rural agglomeration and mega-urbanization recognize and accommodate intensely localized and deeply embedded place-based features of this restructuring which will not easily change under the current circumstances.

On the other hand, is there a point in the regional transformation at which agglomerative tendencies will take over? Is the spatial economic restructuring observed in the lower Yangzi delta merely a transitional phase preceding the growth of large urban agglomerations? Ignoring for the moment the issue of whether or not this would be a desirable outcome, the alternative framework I am proposing does clearly indicate the linkages and interrelationships which would need to be modified or displaced in favour of alternative interdependencies before a transition to more conventional urban forms might emerge. At their most basic level the necessary conditions would need to include changes or elimination of the influence of administrative and institutional structures which have profoundly mediated the local geography of enterprises. This might involve the revamping of ownership and property rights to allow for free market transfers of land and capital, meaningful tax measures to redistribute the benefits of economic development, or banking and financial reforms which entrenched commercial, rather than politically motivated decision making. Such changes imply the decoupling of administrative and institutional parameters from territory which might adversely affect the underlying processes and mechanisms driving economic development in the first place. A similar outcome might also emerge in any case as a consequence of severe environmental degradation and the haphazard consumption of arable land by non-agricultural development.

Conventional processes and patterns of urbanization may also occur as a result of the strengthening of external economies and enhancing the dynamics of agglomeration through further economic reforms. The nature of the product structure and the distribution of external markets reviewed in Chapters 4 and 6 become important in this context. Will endogenous factors in Kunshan continue to dominate the character of local development if there was a shift in the type of commodities it produced and to whom they were sold? If Kunshan were, for example, to increase exports of consumer products to Shanghai or foreign markets, issues such as efficiency and quality, technology and capital inputs, and product cycles might be expected to exercise greater influence over key interactions and interrelationships which determine the local geography of production. Increased access and exposure to the global economy including, among other things, a freer domestic market-place that reflected true prices, would more directly affect the transactional and production activities of enterprises, perhaps stimulating greater economies of scale and other efficiencies. However, without commensurate adjustments elsewhere in the system, such changes might, conversely, stimulate even greater administrative interference to protect and promote local enterprises.

Of course, there is a multiplicity of alternatives and possible outcomes which may be explored. In all cases rural agglomeration and mega-urbanization as conceived here provide a conceptual framework that illustrates the complex interactions and interrelationships underlying spatial economic restructuring in the lower Yangzi delta. Moreover, it suggests methodologies to investigate how changes which affect these linkages (introduced or otherwise) might also affect the processes and mechanisms which determine specific patterns of local and regional development. The implications of this conceptual and analytical emphasis on local specificities for policy formation and strategic planning are introduced in the final section of this book.

Planning and management agenda: Chinese solutions for Chinese problems

Stressed throughout this book was a theoretical and methodological reorientation towards the critical dimensions of locality and place as they determined the character of local and regional change in the lower Yangzi delta. I have not advocated however, focusing solely upon local specificities and differences. In Chapter 2 I rejected the often tortuous post-modern struggle with the representation (and reproduction) of endless contingency and uniqueness. Moreover, the critical dimensions of spatial economic restructuring in the delta, while largely rooted and defined by locality and place, were not confined to small scale disaggregated units. Confronting the challenges for planning and management of the lower Yangzi delta mega-urban region requires that we perceive these dimensions not just in terms of their particularities, but also in terms of their conjectural nature and articulation across the wider space economy.

Many development practitioners have expressed dismay at their collective inability to adequately contend with the planning and policy challenges posed by mega-urban regions in China and the rest of Asia.[19] This brings us to the fourth element of the middle ground introduced at the end of Chapter 2 which aimed to bridge theory and practice by providing a meaningful conceptual and analytical framework as the basis for developing relevant planning and policy strategies. Based on the major findings and theoretical reformulations of this study, this section will introduce three broad sets of priorities which frame an agenda for the planning and management of the lower Yangzi delta mega-urban region. The first revolves around issues of spatial relations between varying socio-economic fields.[20] The second addresses administrative and institutional structures which influence decision making and control. The third set of priorities is concerned with information needs, data gathering, and monitoring.

If regional transformation is reconceptualized as a function of interactions and interrelationships over space, the formation of planning policies must recognize and respond to the specificities of intensely localized processes and mechanisms which underlie these linkages and their constituent transactional networks. The functional relationships among the many actors within and between socio-economic fields in the lower Yangzi delta were more complex, for example, than the general extension of urban influence over the hinterland. Yet the assumptions implicit in most responses to the spatial economic restructuring in such regions underlines how economic actors in large cities were seen to provide the impetus for change, or how transformation in the countryside was supposedly determined by proximity to urban metropolis.[21] Growth profiles and development scenarios based on these assumptions envisaged industrial relocation from urban core into the surrounding countryside, and the filling-up of rural areas which previously contained only insignificant levels of non-agricultural activity.[22]

The resulting planning and management agendas, usually prepared in urban ivory towers, ignored or overlooked critical elements of mega-urbanization in the lower Yangzi delta. The importance and persistence of highly productive farming, especially of staple food commodities, and its juxtaposition with the growth and proliferation of non-agricultural activities was a common example. Calls for the development of transportation including arterial routes between major centres, the exploitation of pre-existing networks, and increased flexibility in transportation modes were another example.[23] Noble and arguably necessary objectives, they were reflected in the recently completed Nanjing-Shanghai Expressway and other bridge, highway, railway, and port development projects. However, by focusing on these high profile and costly transportation mega-projects, attention was drawn away from critically important local level practical realities. Regional integration and planning of transportation infrastructure in the delta were, for example, in constant conflict with the objectives of community governments who spoke passionately about local initiatives, but generally lacked a broader regional perspective.

Therefore, planning and management strategies in the lower Yangzi delta must hinge upon issues at once broader and more specific than those most frequently emphasized. This requires a fundamental reorientation of the way in which such regions are conceptualized. Several Chinese studies have attempted to provide a conceptual and analytical middle ground by invoking notions of rural–urban symbiosis (*chengxiang yitihua*) or 'unity' (*xietiao chengxiang guanxi*).[24] While much of this work refers to the conventional distinction between 'urban' and 'rural', it has also refocused attention on the interactions and interrelationships which link various socio-economic fields as they construct revitalized intervening regions of economic activity. Some Chinese planners have responded by generating development scenarios which emphasize the (re-)emergence of such regions and their important morphological characteristics. Referred to as 'clustered mix-use ecologic communities' (*zutuan shiduoyong shengtai shequ*) this perspective evokes the processes and mechanisms highlighted in rural agglomeration.[25]

Implications for the planning and management agenda for the lower Yangzi delta mega-urban region are manifest. Many local and regional development practitioners in China were deeply critical of official policies embedded in the slogans 'leave the land, but not the countryside; enter the factory, but not the city' (*litu bulixiang; jinchang bujincheng*) which tended to obscure the need to create well planned integrated regions by breaking down rural–urban, interregional, and local barriers. The steady development of agriculture could be ensured, for example, only through the continuous 'restructuring' of 'business circles' in the countryside by allowing peasants to 'leave the land *in order to* leave the countryside' (*litu yilixiang*) and to 'enter the factory *and* enter the city' (*jinchang youjincheng*).[26] This would help reduce the tension between competing land-uses in a more 'unified' spatial structure of agriculture and industry. The basic element of this approach would involve the development of central towns 'positioned' in such a way as to 'gather the functions' of the regional economy. This would include serving as the 'global company' (*huanqiu gongsi*) for exchange relationships, as centres of culture and social welfare, capital, technology and information, and as the markets for labour.

The underlying objective would not be recentralization or large scale urbanization, but rather to promote the integration of a restructuring countryside with big cities by strengthening the functions of appropriately positioned smaller central towns. This necessarily includes the development and improvement of tertiary services to enhance the circulation of capital, technology, information and labour, and the efficient exchange of goods to encourage enterprises in places like Dianshanhu Town in Kunshan to relocate from the periphery into the town seat. Establishing well serviced and appropriately situated special development zones in some towns, and at the county level, would help to stimulate more coordinated, less haphazard land uses. Such strategies also conform to some of the contours of the pre-modern period during which vibrant economic exchange between rural and urban sectors was channelled through small market towns and larger county level towns.[27]

Some have envisaged similar planning objectives which sought to manage the regional transformation in other parts of Asia by developing smaller centres.[28] However, the resulting implementation strategies which emerged from these plans focused on the need for institutional changes which included increasing decentralization of decision making and control. Circumstances in the lower Yangzi delta suggest, on the other hand, the need for a more coordinated set of policies which coopt, or at least accommodate, exceedingly powerful and divergent local interests into a more meaningful regional plan. Planning is one thing, as it turns out, and implementation quite another. Or as one key informant remarked whimsically '*fu guihua, qiong kaifa*' (planning is rich, but development is poor). This brings us to the second set of priorities which help shape the planning and management agenda for the delta.

Perhaps the greatest challenge for planning and policy formation in the lower Yangzi delta mega-urban region relates to issues of management, decision making and control. Once again a fundamental reorientation of perspective is required. For example, the key findings of this study contradict the suggestion that the forces which have stimulated spatial economic restructuring in such regions transcended political boundaries, administrative areas and ideology.[29] In fact, the problem facing planners is the way in which territorially based local administrations are able to manage their economies as discrete, autonomous entities. The prominent role of community governments in this context was to utilize administrative rather than economic means to vigorously promote their own local interests against regional or national interests. The problems which arose were a result of conditions I would characterize as 'all carrots and no sticks'. While the reforms have stimulated the emergence of new exigencies and opportunities within an increasingly intense transactional environment, this has not been matched by the development of appropriate administrative and institutional structures. The planning and management agenda for the delta needs to include administrative and institutional changes that would encourage the development of more open transactional relationships across administrative boundaries. This can only occur by introducing mechanisms to ensure that local governments see their role as providing incentives, services and an appropriate regulatory environment, to develop production rationally and in a sustainable manner, rather than 'bolstering' their own socio-economic and political power through bureaucratic intervention.[30]

Reducing the interference of local governments in the economy could occur through restructuring and adjustment of administrative boundaries and the authority of local governments.[31] Such changes must confront particular administrative phenomena such as the centrifugal tendencies of local governments which pull economic power away from established centres. Contrary to those who have suggested that the 'centrality' of an 'urban place' in China is strengthened following reclassification to higher administrative status, evidence from Wuxi described above, and from Kunshan, have demonstrated how such administrative changes were rather more complex.[32] After Kunshan's elevation to 'city' status, for example, all of its twenty townships also achieved greater administrative and economic power by reclassification as designated towns. Perhaps the strengthening of county level administrations does not have to result in a commensurate upgrading of lower level bureaucracies.

Another approach to institutional reform would focus specifically on the need for some sort of administrative authority at the scale of the mega-urban region, perhaps including sectoral sub-components. These might function initially as business organizations within government bureaux to coordinate and plan across the entire region. Objectives would include balancing and redistributing earnings as necessary, the introduction of more unhindered competition to encourage local comparative advantages, and mechanisms to prevent duplication and waste.[33] These objectives would not be realized in the case of the lower Yangzi delta through increased decentralization of decision making and control.[34] Instead, the priorities for administrative and institutional changes would include increasing the participation of local authorities in regional level (lower Yangzi delta) decision making. The regional administrative and institutional amalgamation this suggests could be achieved through the creation of new alliances and networks. Through a kind of 'opportunistic local incrementalism' these networks would be negotiated and balanced, for the benefit of regional planning and management of the delta, based on various financial and socio-political incentives.[35]

There is historical precedent in the lower Yangzi delta for the grass-roots coordination of community level action for regional benefit. Enlightened local officials during late imperial times, occasionally with the encouragement and support of the state, drew upon pre-existing community organizations to respond to the issues of water control and management across large parts of the delta.[36] As in the past, however, implementing the administrative and institutional changes necessary to address contemporary planning and management challenges in the delta requires bridging the deep divisions of local interests and power.

Finally, the planning and management agenda for the lower Yangzi delta must also address the issues of information needs, data gathering, and monitoring. The intensity of the transactional environment, multiplicity of apparently incompatible land uses and concerns about environmental degradation require the development of new systems of monitoring, data collection and dissemination. Data collection in China generally occurs regularly, rapidly and at a small enough scale to help identify areas of change. The problems are with accuracy and availability.[37] Although the accuracy and dissemination of official statistics has improved, there is a need to re-examine the framework within which it occurs. Data gathering necessarily relies upon a highly decentralized system of reporting, but which is subject to the vested interests of community and even enterprise level bureaucrats. Differing sets of books were often maintained, if at all, depending on the intended audience: Statistics Bureau; Tax Bureau; etc.

Data collection and monitoring must remain sensitive to the ambiguities of a highly mixed land-use system since this was a central and persistent feature of the lower Yangzi delta. However, it is also essential for all the various levels of government and their reporting agencies to identify and utilize the same consistently defined demographic and economic indicators and to implement standardized methods of monitoring and reporting procedures across the entire region. Moreover, there needs to be a much greater level of transparency in these methods and procedures, and all of the resulting information must be made freely available. Overcoming the pervasive reluctance or inability to share information will allow researchers to presage alternative development scenarios wherein careful monitoring would indicate the most likely patterns to emerge. By highlighting significant trends, potential problems and areas of opportunity, planning and management practitioners, and commercial interests in the delta could anticipate, lobby for, and coordinate more effective responses.

However, it is also important to accept that the location of production and the functions of rural communities and central places across space rarely result from deliberate design. The emphasis therefore, must be upon seeking an understanding of the processes and mechanisms which underlie the patterns observed or sought after, what establishes these processes and mechanisms, and what stabilizes and reproduces them. The theoretical and methodological reformulations outlined in this book have provided a conceptual and analytical framework to help explain, predict and manage the complexities of spatial economic restructuring in the lower Yangzi delta. Crucial to understanding these restless landscapes was an exploration of the character of locality and place. Ultimately, general conclusions about processes of spatial economic transformation observed in China, and the planning and policy formation that results, must rest upon detailed analyses of local social, political, and economic change.

Notes

1. That is not to say that labour markets and urban formation were unimportant in the context of this study. Rather, the gathering of appropriate data was not a high priority given the analytical focus on other elements of the regional transformation.
2. Massey, D. (1995) *Spatial Divisions of Labour: Social Structures and the Geography of Production, Second Edition.* London: Macmillan, pp. 316, 319.
3. This statement is not made without some considerable evidence and thought. See: Blecher, M. (1995) Collectivism, contractualism and crisis in the Chinese countryside. In R. Benewick and P. Wingrone (Eds.) *China in the 1990s.* London: Macmillan, p. 105; Joseph, W. A. (1994) Introduction: Toward the post-Deng era. In W. A. Joseph (Ed.) *China Briefing, 1994.* Boulder: Westview, p. 3; Marton, A. M. (1995c) Mega-urbanization in southern Jiangsu: Enterprise location and the reconstitution of local space. *Chinese Environment and Development* 6 (1 and 2), pp. 11–12; Zweig, D. (1987) From village to city: Reforming urban-rural relations in China. *International Regional Science Review* 11 (1), p. 57. Others contend, unreasonably in my view, that the impact of China's Special Economic Zones is more significant (from an anonymous reviewer of the article by Marton cited above).
4. Massey, D. (1995) op. cit., pp. 316–320. In Chapter 6 I referred to this as 'mutual constitution'. I continue to search for an appropriate term to capture the essence of this phenomenon: whereby *a* influences *b*, which because it is influenced by *a*, itself in turn influences *a*. 'Complementarity' perhaps?
5. This view is inspired and supported by Massey, D. (1995) op. cit., p. 325.
6. I have borrowed the term 'causal relations' as it is used by Massey, D. (1995) op. cit., p. 323. For example, she emphasizes the fluidity, relational nature, and fundamental processes of mutual interaction in her '*combination* of layers' analysis, which fundamentally contradicts the geological metaphor so often invoked (emphasis in the original, p. 321). Also see my earlier discussion of Massey in Chapter 2.
7. See: Cox, K. and Mair, A. (1991) From localized social structures to localities as agents. *Environment and planning A* 23 (2); Marsden, T. *et al.* (1993) *Constructing the Countryside.* London: UCL Press, pp. 135–146.
8. Cox, K. and Mair, A. (1991) op. cit.; Massey, D. (1991) A global sense of place. *Marxism Today* (June); Massey, D. (1995) op. cit.

9. See Chapter 2. Massey, D. (1991) op. cit.; Massey, D. (1995) op. cit., p. 338. Massey's conceptualization of place and locality as most frequently embedded in spatial structures, for example, is fundamentally contrary to the perspective I am proposing here. However, in fairness to Massey and others, such conceptualizations arose from analyses of capitalist, non-Asian, advanced economy contexts in which they may arguably be more applicable.

10. Nanjing Normal University, Department of Geography (1990) *Jiangnan nongcun juluo yu chengshihua yanjiu: Sunan fada diqu nongcun chengzhenhua tujing tantao* (*Jiangnan Rural-agglomeration and Urbanization Research: Methods of Inquiry into Southern Jiangsu Rural Urbanization*). Nanjing: Nanjing Normal University, Department of Geography, pp. 11–12, 60–62.

11. The findings presented here are based on several interviews and discussions with several visiting Chinese scholars at the *Reinterpreting Contemporary Urban Development Theory on Mega-urban Regions in the Asia Pacific Context Workshop* (1995) Vancouver, December 13–15.

12. Ibid. Similar phenomena were also occurring in Wu County around Suzhou City and Wujin County surrounding Changzhou City.

13. Interview notes.

14. Storper, M. and Walker, R. (1989) *The Capitalist Imperative: Territory, Technology, and Industrial Growth*. New York: Basil Blackwell, p. 70.

15. Territorial milieu refers here to the spatial networks of relationships over a particular area through which actors exercise a high degree of implicit or explicit control.

16. Some have criticized McGee for the failure of the extended metropolis model, and its constituent *desakota* formulation, to move beyond a descriptive level. For example, see: Chan, K. Y. (1993) Review of Ginsburg, N. S., Koppel, B. and McGee, T. G. (Eds.) 'The extended metropolis: Settlement transition in Asia'. *Urban Geography* 14 (2).

17. Interview notes.

18. Others have made the same claim. See: Findlay, C., Watson, A. and Wu, H. X. (1994) Rural enterprises in China: Overview, issues and prospects. In C. Findlay, A. Watson and H. X. Wu (Eds.) *Rural Enterprises in China*. New York: St. Martin's, p. 187; Zweig, D. (1987) op. cit., pp. 56–57.

19. This was the general consensus of planners who participated in the *Reinterpreting Contemporary Urban Development Theory on Mega-urban Regions in the Asia Pacific Context Workshop* (1995) op. cit. See also: Chreod Ltd. (1996) The Yangtze delta megalopolis. *International Conference on Towards a Sustainable Future*, Qinghua University, Beijing, 26 April, p. 13.

20. In the context of mega-urbanization and rural agglomeration, I am now less inclined to use terms such as 'urban' and 'rural'. Thus, I refer here to 'socio-economic fields' to include regions, spatially and conceptually, between the two, and which are difficult to define as either.

21. McGee, T. G. (1991a) The emergence of 'desakota' regions in Asia: Expanding a hypothesis. In N. Ginsburg, B. Koppel and T. G. McGee (Eds.) *The Extended Metropolis: Settlement Transition in Asia*. Honolulu: University of Hawaii Press. The same point is reiterated in more sophisticated terms in McGee, T. G. (1995a) Metrofitting the emerging mega-urban regions of ASEAN: An overview. In T. G. McGee and I. M. Robinson (Eds.) *The Mega-urban Regions of Southeast Asia*. Vancouver: UBC Press, pp. 16–20 where the dynamics of mega-urbanization are analysed as processes of *urbanization* and the transactional revolution, *urbanization* and globalization, and *urbanization* and structural change (emphasis added).

22. Chreod Ltd. (1996) op. cit., pp. 4, 6–10.

23. Ibid., p. 4; McGee, T. G. (1995a) op. cit., pp. 23–24.

24. Zhang, Y. L. (1989) Woguo chengxiang guanxi de lishi kaocha (Historical overview of urban–rural relations in China). *Zhongguo nongcun jingji (Chinese Rural Economy)* (10), p. 8 (second part of a study which appeared in two issues).

25. Qinghua University Urban–Rural Development Research Group (1995) *Suxichang diqu chengxiang kongjian huanjing fazhan guihua yanjiu (Suxichang Area Urban–rural Spatial Environment Development Planning Research)*. Beijing: Qinghua University, pp. 57–58.

26. The discussion here is based on: Zhang, S. C. (1991) Fazhan zhongxin zhen de jidian kanfa (Several views on developing central towns). *Jiangsu minzheng (Jiangsu Civil Administration)* (24), p. 41; Zhang, S. C. (1996) *Kunshan fazhan guiji jishi (A Record of Kunshan's Course of Development)*. Nanjing: Jiangsu People's Press; and several interviews with the above author.

27. Large county level towns in the contemporary context of the lower Yangzi delta refers here to places like the Kunshan seat of Yushan with populations between about 50,000 to 100,000 people.

28. Douglass, M. (1995b) Global interdependence and urbanization: Planning for the Bangkok mega-urban region. In T. G. McGee and I. M. Robinson (Eds.) op. cit., pp. 71–74 proposes the concept of a 'regional network' to capture the dynamics and opportunities of spatial restructuring in the Bangkok mega-urban region. Similarly Robinson, I. M. (1995) Emerging spatial patterns in ASEAN mega-urban regions: Alternative strategies. In T. G. McGee and I. M. Robinson (Eds.) op. cit., pp. 78–79, 85 calls for decentralization in the form of polycentred or multinucleated spatial forms.

29. Ginsburg, N. (1991) Preface. In N. Ginsburg, B. Koppel and T. G. McGee (Eds.) op. cit., p. xvii.

30. Watson, A. (1992) The management of the rural economy: The institutional parameters. In A. Watson (Ed.) *Economic Reform and Social Change in China*. New York: Routledge, p. 182.

31. Chen, C. K. and Deng, Z. Q. (1993) Xingzheng quhua chezhou jingji fazhan de yanjiu (A study of administrative divisions impeding economic development). *Dili xuebao (Acta Geographica Sinica)* 48 (4); Fan, J. (1993) Dui woguo guoti guihua jige zhuyao wenti de chongxin renshi (Rethinking some principal problems of China's territorial planning). *Dili yanjiu (Geographical Research)* 12 (1); Liu, J. D. (1992) Woguo xingzheng quhua de gaige (Reform of China's administrative divisions). *Kexue (Science)* 44 (4). Zhang, G. X. (1993) Jiji wentuo de tuijin chengxiang jiehe buxingzheng quhua gaige (Vigorously and appropriately promote urban rural integration and reform of administrative divisions). *Chengshi wenti (Urban problems)* (5). Currently, Chinese research into such administrative divisions reform is considered very sensitive. Research teams were in fact advised by central and provincial authorities to treat the investigations as a secret to avoid stirring any unwanted political ramifications.

32. Tan, K. C. (1993a) China's small town urbanization program: Criticism and rethinking. *Geojournal* 29 (2), p. 161.

33. Liu, J. D. *et al.* (1992) Rationalizing coastal development: A proposal to coordinate planning and management of Shanghai ports. *International Conference on Urban Land Use and Transport Systems*, Shanghai, June 8–12.

34. McGee, T. G. and Robinson, I. M. (1995) ASEAN mega-urbanization: A synthesis. In T. G. McGee and I. M. Robinson (Eds.) op. cit., p. 354.

35. The term is borrowed from R. J. R. Kirkby as he used it during the Reinterpreting contemporary urban development theory on mega-urban regions in the Asia Pacific context workshop (1995) op. cit.

36. Huang, P. C. C. (1990) *The Peasant Family and Rural Development in the Yangzi Delta, 1350–1988.* Stanford: Stanford University Press, p. 38.
37. See: Appendix 1.

Appendix 1
Notes on Chinese statistical sources

This appendix introduces some of the problems associated with the use of official Chinese statistical sources. While China's demographic, social, and economic statistics are abundant and fairly reliable by developing country standards, there are still a number of pitfalls which add to the difficulty of using Chinese data. Some of the specific definitional and other issues relating to such difficulties are discussed throughout the book as they arise. The objective here is to highlight the other main problems confronted in the analysis and to explain how they were addressed. I will not attempt to provide a comprehensive and detailed survey of all the complications that exist with the use of Chinese statistics.[1] Rather, I will only elaborate briefly on four specific issues as they relate to the analysis undertaken in this study: certain definitions not explained in the text; discrepancies between sources of the official statistics; geographical comparability; and the comparison of indices of value over time.

Frequently quoted figures in this book relate to gross values of output. Output refers specifically to the total value of production (of society) (*shehui zong chanzhi*) in what used to be called the material products sectors. These included industry, agriculture, construction, transportation, postal and telecommunications services, commerce, wholesale, retail, storage of goods, supply and distribution and food services. After 1992 national level and most provincial and sub-provincial statistical yearbooks no longer reported gross output in sectors other than industry, agriculture and sometimes construction. Industry, the main focus of this study, is defined in the statistical sources to include the extraction of natural resources, the processing of farm and sideline products, the manufacturing of industrial and consumer products, and the repairing of industrial products such as machine tools, machinery and means of transportation. Output does not refer to income or profitability. It does, however, provide the best sense of the level of economic activity occurring in particular regions and sectors.

Gross domestic product (*guonei shengchan zongzhi*), on the other hand, is defined as the total value of all products and services produced by all resident units in a particular region, including all sectors, less the total value of inputs of non-fixed assets, materials and services. Gross domestic product differs from income, which usually includes value added in most sectors, as defined in the official statistics, and is referred to variously as national income (*guomin shouru*) or national income of production (*guomin shouru shengchan'e*). Meanwhile, the statistical sources have adopted three broad categories for output and gross domestic product. These are not specifically referred to in the book, but were sometimes used to make certain calculations and are, therefore, worth mentioning here. Primary production (*di yi chanye*) included only agriculture. Industry as described above, was categorized as part of secondary production (*di er chanye*) along with construction. Tertiary production (*di san chanye*) included all other sectors not in the first two.

Discrepancies and inconsistencies in the official Chinese data played havoc with the analysis. I often found figures in the statistical yearbooks, for example, which were inconsistent with those published in earlier or subsequent volumes for the same region, or which did not correspond to data in other sources for the same year. Sometimes, published figures also differed from those provided by informants. In other cases the precise meaning of certain figures, especially for larger scale aggregated data, was somewhat unclear. I was able to identify the most likely values by consulting a range of additional published sources and by discussing the discrepancies with informants and research collaborators. Thus, several of the maps and tables throughout this study, and other findings presented in the text, were based on an analysis of data compiled from several over-lapping sources. Map 3.8 in Chapter 3, for example, includes a reference to a Wuxi statistical yearbook which also contained county level data for the entire province of Jiangsu and which was used to cross-check figures from the other sources. Such methods for ensuring the reliability of these data were very time consuming and were often deeply frustrating.

Moreover, the level of accuracy of the official statistics remained highly uncertain. Some have suggested, for example, that figures for various types of rural industries appear to seriously underestimate actual values of output, levels of employment and even the number of enterprises.[2] Others, including the Chinese State Statistical Bureau itself, have also suggested that there is widespread reporting of false figures for a range of statistics by local authorities.[3] Considered in the context of a variety of other sources, however, analysis of the official published data can provide a reasonably good sense of actual conditions.

At various points in this book, and in some detail in Appendix 2, I discuss the sometimes confusing terminology and shifting boundaries of China's administrative divisions. Statistics are tabulated in most cases according to these administrative divisions. Straightforward use of data series becomes problematic and misleading without compensating for these changing circumstances. The statistical sources themselves provide only vague indications that the coverage of particular data series have changed.

The administrative divisions of the city of Shanghai as of the end of 1998, for example, in no way resemble the Shanghai of 1991, which were also very different from the divisions in 1985. Therefore, time series data illustrated for Shanghai in several maps and charts had to be corrected for the fact that several former suburban counties were amalgamated into the new city districts. Thus, data utilized from earlier sources had to be corrected for this discrepancy. While the official classifications of Kunshan and most county level units in southern Jiangsu may have changed, the administrative boundaries remained relatively constant making comparisons over time less problematic. However, there were some notable exceptions, some of which are discussed in the text.

There were other spatial idiosyncrasies in the official statistics which also needed to be resolved or acknowledged as part of the analysis. In Appendix 2 I discuss the difficulties of reconciling the actual extent of urban built-up areas and the administrative boundaries of the urban districts. A further and related clarification is also necessary regarding the data presented for the various city districts illustrated in several maps in the text. These administratively 'urban' areas also included official resident populations and land uses that were in fact still classified as 'rural' and agricultural. In terms of population, for example, in 1993 prior to the most recent administrative boundary changes, 14.6 per cent of Shanghai's urban population of nearly 9.5 million was statistically considered rural. Similarly, 15.3 per cent of Nanjing's 2.6 million people and 16.3 per cent of Suzhou's 872,600 people were statistically tabulated as rural (see Appendix 2).[4]

The legal status of individuals in China is still determined through a national system of registration (*hukou*), although it is gradually becoming less associated with the actual place of residence. Most of these officially rural residents in such city districts could, by most standards, be considered urban, even though they were not so designated in the published statistics. Thus, data plotted for rural labour and rural incomes in the city districts illustrated in Maps 3.4 and 3.5, for example, should not be considered significant since they applied only to a relatively small area and a minority of the local population. On their own and across the wider region of Jiangsu and Shanghai, these idiosyncrasies may not be all that important. Taken together, multiplied by their frequency, and considered at smaller sub-regional scales, they become more significant.

In addition to addressing geographical comparability in time series data, similar efforts were also made to ensure that the relevant statistics were also compared in constant value terms as well. In all but a few instances, clearly noted in the text where such comparable values proved elusive, all temporal data are compared in constant values. In most cases I was able to calculate values from the implied deflators provided for comparative statistics in the official sources. Some have suggested that the deflators for industrial output, particularly in rural areas, probably seriously underestimates the true level of inflation.[5] In a few cases, particularly in the most recent statistical yearbooks, annual year on year growth rates for several key indices, compared in constant value terms, were already calculated and tabulated.

In the case of Map 3.8, which required comparison of 1985 and 1991 industrial output data, I calculated comparable values using a more complicated method. Industrial output data by county level units for Jiangsu and Shanghai were available in 1980 constant values. Similar data for later years appeared only in current values. However, the 1992 yearbooks for Jiangsu and Shanghai provided data for one year (1990) in which figures for industrial output were given in 1980 and 1990 constant values. Using the Jiangsu and Shanghai level implied deflators for the 1990s data, and corrected to the 1980 constant value, I was able to calculate 1991 industrial output values in 1980 constant values to compare with the 1985 data. The sources cited on the figure refer to all the specific pages consulted to make these calculations. Admittedly, this method of correcting the data was a bit crude since it did not account for regional variations in the levels of inflation. However, it was an improvement over the alternative of comparing data in current values which would have greatly exaggerated the actual levels of growth. Moreover, since the spatial patterns revealed were contiguous, internally consistent, and no less than startling, it was reasonable to consider them significant in my view (see Map 3.8).

In more general terms, by highlighting some of the limitations to the official statistical sources and by explaining the efforts undertaken in this study to achieve some degree of consistency, it is hoped that the analysis of such data will be made somewhat more informative.

Notes

1. There are numerous studies which provide excellent overviews and analysis of various types of Chinese statistical sources. For example, see: Naughton, B. (1995) *Growing out of the Plan: Chinese Economic Reform, 1978–1993.* Cambridge: Cambridge University Press, pp. 327–339 (Statistical appendix); Odgaard, O. (1992) *Private Enterprises in China: Impact on Agriculture and Social Stratification.* Aldershot: Avebury, pp. 234–250 (Appendix 1: Statistics on private rural enterprises).
2. Odgaard, O. (1992) op. cit., p. 237.
3. *Far Eastern Economic Review* (1994) China; True: Numbers lie. 22 September, p. 87.
4. *HDDTNJ 1994*, pp. 15–151.
5. Naughton, B. (1995) op. cit., pp. 329–330.

Appendix 2
Structure of Chinese administrative divisions

Throughout this study I have made reference to various types of administrative divisions. The objective of this appendix is to provide some further clarification of these administrative divisions and the related nomenclature, particularly as they apply to Jiangsu Province and Shanghai. I do not intend to undertake an exhaustive analysis of the changing structure of Chinese administrative divisions, nor will I focus on the details of how specific designations were determined and applied.[1] As was demonstrated in the book, the official criteria were frequently disregarded or distorted in response to local imperatives with particular implications for territorial and spatial economic patterns. Furthermore, like most administrative divisions elsewhere, such designations in China were only vaguely related to concepts of urban and rural. In any case, I wish to explain the meaning of the terms as I have used them in the book and the specific spatial extent to which they referred, especially as illustrated in Maps 1.1, 3.1, and 4.1.

Currently, China's administrative system is divided into five levels: provincial, prefectural, county, township and village. The two provincial level (*shengji*) administrative units in this study were Jiangsu Province (*sheng*) and Shanghai Municipality (*shi*). Their authority and jurisdiction were sanctioned directly by the central government. In most instances, these areas were referred to in the text simply as Jiangsu and Shanghai. All subsequent administrative designations fall under these provincial level units.

Next in the hierarchy were the prefectural level (*diji*) administrative units. In Jiangsu there were thirteen such units which together comprised the entire 102,600 square kilometres of the province as illustrated in Map 3.1.[2] According to the Chinese nomenclature, these areas were referred to as prefectural level municipalities or cities (*diji shi*). To help avoid confusion I have referred to them in the text as prefectures. Corresponding to each prefecture is a city (also *shi*) from which the prefecture takes its name, and which serves as the seat of the prefectural government. In the case of Nanjing, this city is also the seat of the provincial government (the capital), while in other cases prefectural seats sometimes also included the government seat for a lower level surrounding county level unit. These prefectural seats were subdivided into city districts (*shixia qu*) of which there were forty-four across the thirteen prefectures in Jiangsu in 1998. These city districts were further subdivided into 206 neighbourhood offices (*jiedao banshichu*). Each prefecture also included between three to eight county level units. Therefore, unless otherwise qualified, when the name of a prefecture appears in the text I am referring to the entire administrative unit including the county level units and the city districts. For example, Wuxi refers to Wuxi City, as defined by its five city districts, and its three county level units, including one which was (until the end of 1995) also called Wuxi. It was not unusual for many of the areas designated as city districts to include large tracts of countryside.

County level (*xianji*) units constituted the next layer in the administrative hierarchy. Such units in Jiangsu generally fell into two categories. The first was the regular county (*xian*) units of which there were thirty-three in 1998. These were administered directly by prefectural units. The second was county level cities or municipalities (*xianji shi*) which essentially had the same administrative status as prefectural seats, particularly in terms of their relationship to the provincial government. There were thirty-one of these in 1998 for a total of sixty-four county level units in all of Jiangsu. Elevation to county level city status brought certain benefits. These are described in some detail in the text for the case of Kunshan. Such regions, though referred to as cities or municipalities, in most cases also included vast areas of countryside.

The region of Shanghai Municipality deserves special consideration here. In 1991 it included twelve city districts and nine suburban counties (*jiaoxian*). Although several of these counties easily qualified for reclassification as county level cities, since they were administered directly by a provincial level municipality they could not be so designated. These divisions have since undergone radical restructuring to accommodate the rapidly expanding power and territorial influence of the central city in general, and the special focus on development of the Pudong New Area east of the old city centre in particular. By the end of 1997, Shanghai had absorbed and reorganized four former suburban counties entirely as new city districts for a total of fifteen. This represented a near quadrupling in the administrative area of city districts to 2,643 square kilometres over the previous five years to account for more than 40 per cent of the 6,341 square kilometres of the entire municipality, leaving only five suburban counties. Similar, though less dramatic administrative restructuring, has also occurred in Jiangsu. By the end of 1997 all counties south of the Yangzi River in Jiangsu had been elevated to county level city status.

Fourth in the administrative hierarchy were the township level (*xiangji*) units. Broadly classified as townships (*xiang*) or designated towns (*jianzhi zhen* or just *zhen*) they each had their own government which reported to their respective county level or in some cases city district units. The actual areas of administrative jurisdiction for townships and designated towns (or just towns) included the built-up township centres and the surrounding countryside wherein up to several dozen villages were located. The 684 towns and 1,594 townships in Jiangsu and Shanghai in 1991 constituted the lowest level of the central government administrative hierarchy. Like county level city status, reclassification as a designated town brought new privileges. These are also discussed in the text. By the end of 1998, the number of designated towns in Jiangsu and Shanghai had grown to 1,220, with a commensurate decline in the number of townships. Also at this administrative level were a number of other designations, based on particular criteria, used to describe various settlements. These ranged from rural market towns (*jizhen*) and small towns (*xiao chengzhen*) to small cities (*xiao chengshi*) which usually included county seats (*xian cheng* or *xianshu zhen*) and sometimes larger designated towns. These various classifications had little to do with whether these settlements were truly urban. Of the twenty designated towns in Kunshan, for example, some former townships, others only rural market towns, all but two included built-up settlements of perhaps 2,000 to 6,000 people in 1996. However, for most of the 450,000 residents of the Kunshan countryside, the nearest truly urban place was Yushan, the county seat, with perhaps 75,000 people (see Figure 4.1).[3]

The fifth level of the administrative system was comprised of village (*cun*) based units. Villages and their respective areas in Jiangsu and Shanghai, were controlled by 37,966 village committees (*cunmin weiyuanhui*) in 1998. Under the supervision of township level governments, these locally elected grass-roots committees were responsible for every aspect of village administration. Similarly, there were also 9,397 residents' committees (*jumin weiyuanhui*) across Jiangsu and Shanghai in 1998 which managed local affairs in city districts and the built-up residential areas of towns and small cities. Residents' committees are to be distinguished from the much smaller number and less grass-roots structure of urban neighbourhood offices. There were only 625 resident's committees in Jiangsu and Shanghai in 1991. In Kunshan in 1997 there were 463 village committees, no neighbourhood offices, 128 residents' committees, and 4,765 village small groups (*cunmin xiaozu*).[4] These latter groups roughly corresponded to the sub-village clusters of households sometimes called natural villages (*zhuang*).

Finally, I would like to review the multiple meanings of one Chinese term to highlight the sometimes confusing character of administrative divisions in China and the nomenclature which has emerged to designate its particular components. Perusal of any political or administrative map of China reveals that the Chinese character *shi*, meaning city or municipality, is used to designate no fewer than five distinct types of administrative units. It can refer to the provincial level municipal region of Shanghai *shi*, including the city proper and its suburban counties. Shanghai *shi* can also refer specifically to the core group of city districts. It is further used to designate prefectural level municipalities such as Suzhou *shi*, including their county level units and the respective prefectural seats, from which the prefecture takes its name, and whose city districts are also called *shi*. Several county level administrative units such as Kunshan are also known as *shi*, and are referred to as municipalities or cities in the literature, official statistics and by local officials and ordinary residents.

This very brief introduction only hints at the spatial and bureaucratic complexities of China's administrative divisions. Added to this, moreover, is the fact that most of the precise territorial boundaries which embody this structure are still either unclear, not legally defined, or are subject to sometimes violent disputes. Informants and some local publications in Kunshan referred to an administrative area for the jurisdiction some 56.4 square kilometres larger than that listed in the official provincial and prefectural statistics. Apparently, most of the discrepancy lay along the boundary with Shanghai, especially in the convoluted littoral region in the south of Kunshan, where the precise control of land has immense implications for who would benefit from local development. Currently, there are more than 1,000 unresolved provincial level boundary disputes in China, involving 20 per cent of the total length of such boundaries and some 140,000 square kilometres of land. These figures do not include the enormous number of sub-provincial boundary disputes.[5]

Complexities indeed!

Notes

1. For a more comprehensive discussion see the references cited in Note 65 at the end of Chapter 3. Also see: Wang, X. Y. (1993) The development of China's small towns. In G. Guldin and A. Southall (Eds.) *Urban Anthropology in China*. Leiden: Brill, pp. 151–153.
2. Unless otherwise noted all the figures provided for Jiangsu and Shanghai are based on: *JSTJNJ 1992*, pp. 7, 10; *JSTJNJ 1995*, p. 5; *JSTJNJ 1998*, pp. 16, 18; *SHTJNJ 1992*, pp. 13, 15; *JSTJNJ 1999*, p. 20; *SHTJNJ 1995*, pp. 17, 19; *SHTJNJ 1998*, pp. 2, 4, 5.
3. See the discussions at the end of Chapter 3 regarding the size of small towns and levels of urbanization in Kunshan and China.
4. *SJTJNJ 1995*, p. 15; *SJTJNJ 1998*, p. 14; *JSTJNJ 1999*, p. 20.
5. Liang, C. (1996) PRC marks boundaries to prevent disputes. *China Daily*, 10 April, p. 3.

Glossary of Chinese terms

baogan daohu Production responsibility system: sometimes *baochan daohu*. Refers to the shift in the organization and management of agricultural production to rural households which was initiated in the early part of the reform period. This phenomenon is generally associated with the beginning of the most important economic changes in rural China and with significant increases in the yields of grains and other agricultural products.

Changjiang Literally 'Long River': Yangzi (Yangtze) River, China's largest and third longest in the world.

chengshi Literally 'walled' city: refers to urban (areas) most often with city districts. Combined with the suffix '*hua*' to mean urbanization.

chengxiang yitihua Urban–rural integration or symbiosis: a term which attempts to capture the 'ecological' nature of the relationships between the countryside and smaller cities and towns embedded in relatively productive agricultural regions (see *xietiao chengxiang guanxi* below).

cun Village: usually with its own distinct administrative area and a locally (now increasingly democratically) elected village head. Most also have a village people's committee (*cunmin weiyuanhui*).

cunmin xiaozu Village small group: still identified in the county level statistics. Roughly equivalent to the natural village clusters or *zhuang* (see below).

geti Individual: used to be combined frequently with '*hu*' for household to refer to individual entrepreneurs. Now most often listed with the term *qiye* in the official statistics to refer to individual enterprises (see *qiye* below).

gongye Industry: industrial production; see Appendix 1.

gongye (xiao) qu Industrial (small) area or zone: most often locally designated and spatially distinct (usually with a wall around it).

guanxi Literally connections or relations: referring to a complex array of personal contacts and mutually reinforcing interactions, relationships, obligations and favours between individuals which usually arise from their particular working functions, power and privileges.

hengxiang lianxi Horizontal linkages: used to refer to more commercially based individual and institutional relationships which crossed regions and administrative hierarchies (see *guanxi* above and *zhongxiang lianxi* below).

hezuo cooperative: usually in reference to domestic and sino–foreign (joint venture) enterprises

hukou Household registration: a formal system of household based administrative, statistical and legal designations; now breaking down, but formally used to strictly control migration through a system of urban food and basic commodities subsidies and access to other urban based privileges (see *nongye renkou* below).

jianzhi zhen Formerly a township (*xiang*) that has been administratively 'elevated' to a designated town (see *xiang* and *zhen* below).

Jingji jishu kaifaqu Economic and technological development zone, often abbreviated to just *kaifaqu.*

jiti Collective: often combined with *qiye* to refer to collective enterprises; most often associated with rural town(ship) and village industrial enterprises, although there is an increasingly important urban collective sector as well (see *qiye* below).

jituan Group: refers to the phenomenon of enterprises amalgamating either to absorb loss making concerns and/or to improve economies of scale and other efficiencies

jizhen Market town: usually associated with the periodic agricultural and commodity markets of traditional China.

kaifaqu See *Jingji jishu kaifaqu* above.

lianhu Joint household: usually combined with *qiye* to refer to a particular type of household based enterprise (see *qiye* below).

litu bulixiang, jinchang bujincheng 'Leave the land but not the countryside, enter the factory but not the city': one of many slogans meant to capture the essence of the process of rural transformation; associated with rural industrialization (*xiangzhen gongyehua*)

neibu Literally 'internal': usually refers to documents and other materials meant only for internal or domestic circulation in China, and most often only among the politically well connected few

nongcun usually used to refer to rural (areas): sometimes village (see *cun* above).

nongcun juluo Rural agglomeration: in the original Chinese it refers to a sense of combining or a disbursed amalgamation of phenomenon in rural areas over space.

nongye Agriculture (production).

nongye renkou Administratively, statistically and legally defined rural (sometimes peasant) population: now increasingly less associated with actual place of residence. With the prefix '*fei*' to refer to non-agricultural population (usually, though not always living in urban districts urban) (see *hukou* above).

qiye Enterprise: combined with any number of locational and/or ownership designations to connote an enterprise (often, though not always, industrial).

Renmin gongshe People's commune: disbanded in most areas of China by 1984, it corresponded to the most important unit of production in the pre-reform collectivist period. The re-emergence of township administrations and their respective territories are most closely associated with these former units of economic and social organization.

shang you zhengce, xia you jice 'Above there is policy, below there is strategy' (or sometimes countermeasures [*duice*]): refers to the attitude and response of local authorities in China to central directives which are frequently reinterpreted and distorted at the local level to take advantage of perceived loopholes, and sometimes as a pragmatic means of ensuring political and economic survival.

shenchan dadui Production brigade: sub-unit of the commune disbanded with the larger organization in most of China in 1984; roughly equivalent to the current administrative villages (*cun*) of perhaps two to four hundred households (see *Renmin gongshe* above).

shenchan xiaodui Production team: sub-unit of the production brigade. In the lower Yangzi delta it was roughly the same as the natural village (*zhuang*) of between thirty to fifty households (see *zhuang* and *Renmin gong she* above).

shenchan xiaozu Production small group: sub-unit of the production team; comprised of one to a few households (see *Renmin gong she* above).

sheng Province.

shi City: municipality; prefecture; national level municipality; county level city (municipality) (see Appendix 2).

siying Private: thus, *siying qiye*, refers to private enterprise (see *qiye* above).

Subei Northern Jiangsu Province: a combination of the '*su*' in Jiangsu and '*bei*' meaning north; usually, though not always, associated with the poorer part of Jiangsu. The term does also carry a certain sense of economic and cultural backwardness

Sunan Southern Jiangsu Province: as above except that '*nan*' is the word for south; usually the area of Jiangsu Province south of the Yangzi River. The term as it is used in Chinese always invokes the sense of an economically prosperous and culturally advanced region.

Suxichang Taken from the '*Su*' in Suzhou, the '*xi*' in Wuxi, and the '*chang*' in Changzhou to refer to the most developed part of southern Jiangsu Province. Used in China the term evokes perceptions similar to *Sunan* above.

tiao zheng Readjustment: usually in reference to changes in the organization and management of agricultural production which have arisen as a result of transformations in other sectors.

xian County.

xian cheng County city: a smaller city sometimes with 'urban' administrative districts.

xianji shi County level city (municipality): formerly a county (*xian*) that has been 'elevated' to city status (see Appendix 2).

xianshu zhen County-led town: usually a larger town at the county level that often, though not always, serves as the county seat.

xiang Township (or non-designated town): also frequently used to refer to the countryside or rural areas.

xiangcun Township-village: used most often to refer to rural (areas) (see *nongcun* above).

xiangzhen qiye Township-town enterprise: used to refer to rural (or non-urban) usually industrial enterprises (see *qiye* above).

xietiao chengxiang guanxi Unity (of) urban–rural linkages: similar to *chengxiang yitihua* above but with less emphasis on the 'wholeness' than on the linkages themselves.

zhen Town or (administratively) designated town: see *jianji zhen* above (see Appendix 2).

zhongxiang lianxi Vertical linkages: connections and relationships (personal and institutional) which tended to follow conventional bureaucratic hierarchies. Usually associated with the planned economy structures (see *hengxiang lianxi* above).

zhuang (Natural) village; 'organic' clusters of rural households very common in southern Jiangsu.

Bibliography

Allen, J., Massey, D., and Cochrane, A. (1998) *Rethinking the Region*. London: Routledge.

American Rural Small-Scale Industry Delegation (1977) *Rural Small-scale Industry in the People's Republic of China*. Berkeley: University of California Press.

Archer, K. (1993) Regions as social organisms: The Lamarckian characteristics of Vidal de la Blache's regional geography. *AAAG 83* (3), pp. 498–514.

Asian Regional Team for Employment Promotion (1992) *Reabsorption of Surplus Agricultural Labour into the Non-agricultural Sector: A Study of Township Enterprises in China*. New Delhi: International Labour Organization.

Bai, D. M. (1981) Weixing cheng nengqi kongzhi shiqu guimo de zuoyong ma? (Are satellite towns a useful means of controlling the population in urban districts?). *Jianzhu xuebao (Architectural Journal)* (4), pp. 24–27.

Baker, J. and Pedersen, P. O. (Eds.) (1992) *The Rural–urban Interface in Africa: Expansion and Adaption*. Uppsala: The Scandinavian Institute of African Studies.

Bell, L. S. (1992) Farming, sericulture, and peasant rationality in Wuxi County in the early twentieth century. In T. G. Rawski and L. M. Li (Eds.) *Chinese History in Economic Perspective*. Berkeley: University of California Press, pp. 207–242.

Bird, J., Curtis, B., Putnam, T. and Robertson, G. (Eds.) (1993) *Mapping the Futures: Local Cultures, Global Change*. London: Routledge.

Blecher, M. (1995) Collectivism, contractualism and crisis in the Chinese countryside. In R. Benewick and P. Wingrove (Eds.) *China in the 1990s*. London: Macmillan, pp. 105–119.

Blunden, W. R. and Black, J. A. (1984) *The Land-use/Transport System: Second Edition*. Sydney: Pergamon.

Booth, D. (1985) Marxism and development sociology: Interpreting the impasse. *World Development* 13 (7), pp. 761–787.

—— (1993) Development research: From impasse to new agenda. In F. J. Schuurman (Ed.) *Beyond the Impasse: New Directions in Development Theory*. London: Zed, pp. 49–76.

Brown, L. A. (1988) Reflections on third world development: Ground level reality, exogenous forces, and conventional paradigms. *Economic Geography* 64 (3), pp. 255–278.

Butimer, A. (1995) Review of 'Vidal de La Blache: 1845–1918. Un Génie de la Géographie'. *AAAG 85* (2), pp. 406–408.

Byrd, W. A. and Gelb, A. (1990) Why industrialize? The incentives for rural community governments. In W. A. Byrd and Q. S. Lin (Eds.) *China's Rural*

Industry: Structure, Development, and Reform. Oxford: Oxford University Press, pp. 358–387.

Byrd, W. A. and Lin, Q. S. (Eds.) (1990) *China's Rural Industry: Structure, Development, and Reform.* Oxford: Oxford University Press.

Byrd, W. A. and Lin, Q. S. (1990) China's rural industry: An introduction. In W. A. Byrd and Q. S. Lin (Eds.) *China's Rural Industry: Structure, Development, and Reform.* Oxford: Oxford University Press, pp. 3–18.

Cai, Q. M., Zhao, P. S. and Jiang, M. K. (1991) Butong fazhan jieduan xiangzhen qiye yu nongye neizai guanxi chutan (Exploration of the internal relationship between rural enterprises and agriculture at different developing periods). *JSJJTT* (2), pp. 39–43.

Chambers, R. (1983) *Rural Development: Putting the Last First.* Harlow: Longman.

Chan, K. W. (1987) Further information about China's urban population statistics: Old and new. *The China Quarterly* 109, pp. 104–109.

—— (1988) Rural–urban migration in China, 1950–1982: Estimates and analysis. *Urban Geography* 9 (1), pp. 53–84.

—— (1994a) *Cities with Invisible Walls: Reinterpreting Urbanization in Post-1949 China.* Hong Kong: Oxford University Press

—— (1994b) Urbanization and rural urban migration in China since 1982: A new baseline. *Modern China* 20 (3), pp. 243–281.

Chan, K. W. and Xu, X. Q. (1985) Urban population growth and urbanization in China since 1949: Reconstructing a baseline. *The China Quarterly* 104, pp. 583–616.

Chan, K. Y. (1993) Review of Ginsburg, N. S., Koppel, B. and McGee, T. G. (Eds.) 'The extended metropolis: Settlement transition in Asia'. *Urban Geography* 14 (2), pp. 205–208.

Chen, C. K. and Deng, Z. Q. (1993) Xingzheng quhua chezhou jingji fazhan de yanjiu (A study of administrative divisions impeding economic development). *Dili xuebao (Acta Geographica Sinica)* 48 (4), pp. 329–336.

Chen, C. L., Findlay, C., Watson, A. and Zhang, X. H. (1994) Rural enterprise growth in a partially reformed Chinese economy. In C. Findlay, A. Watson and H. X. Wu (Eds.) *Rural Enterprises in China.* New York: St. Martin's, pp. 4–23.

Chen, J. Y. and Hu, B. L. (1991) Chengshihua renkou yu laodongli wenti yanjiu (Urbanization, population and labour force research problems). In B.C. Zhang, J. Y. Chen and Y. X. Zhou (Eds.) *Zhongguo chengshihua daolu hongguan yanjiu (Macro-research on China's Road to Urbanization).* Harbin: Heilongjiang People's Press, pp. 88–115.

Chen, W. (1992) City in Jiangsu attracts more foreign funds. *China Daily*, May 17, p. III.

Chen, W. and Xia, B. L. (1994) Kunshan jiaqiang sanzi qiye guanli (Kunshan strengthens management of 'three capital' enterprises). *Renmin ribao, haiwaiban (People's daily,* overseas edition). 7 December, p. 2.

China daily (1991a) Kunshan races on fast track. 27 October, p. 4.

—— (1991b) Rural dream come true. 22 November, p. 3.

—— (1992) Kunshan launches new special zone. 26 July, p. 4.

—— (1993a) Protection for land in Jiangsu. 11 May, p. 3.

—— (1993b) State to strictly control new zones. 17 May, p. 1.

Chreod Ltd. (1996) The Yangtze delta megalopolis. *International Conference on Towards a Sustainable Future*, Qinghua University, Beijing, 26 April.

Cohn, W. (1950) *Chinese Painting*. London: Phaidon.

Corbridge, S. (1982) Urban bias, rural bias, and industrialization: An appraisal of the works of Michael Lipton and Terry Byres. In J. Harris (Ed.) *Rural development: Theories of Peasant Economy and Agrarian Change*. London: Hutchinson.

—— (1986) *Capitalist World Development: A Critique of Radical Development Geography*. London: Macmillan.

—— (1989) Marxism, post-Marxism, and the geography of development. In R. Peet and N. Thrift (Eds.) *New Models in Geography: The Political-economy Perspective*. London: Unwin, pp. 224–254.

—— (1990) Development studies. *PIHG* 14 (3), pp. 391–403.

—— (1991) Third world development. *PIHG* 15 (3), pp. 311–321.

—— (1993) Marxisms, modernities, and moralities: Development praxis and the claims of distant strangers. *Environment and Planning D: Society and Space* 11, pp. 449–472.

Cox, K. and Mair, A. (1991) From localized social structures to localities as agents. *Environment and Planning A* 23 (2), pp. 197–213.

Croll, E. (1994) *From Heaven to Earth: Images and Experience of Development in China*. London: Routledge.

Cronon, W. (1991) *Nature's Metropolis: Chicago and the Great West*. New York: Norton.

Deng, Y. T. (1992) Township enterprises and rural finance. *National Workshop on Rural Industrialization in Post-reform China*. Beijing, 19–22 October.

Dicken, P. and Thrift, N. (1992) The organization of production and the production of organization: Why business enterprises matter in the study of geographical industrialization. *TIBG* 17, pp. 279–291.

Dong, Z. B. (1961) *Qingming Shanghe Tu (Qingming Festival by the River)*. Taibei: National Taiwan University.

Douglass, M. (1995a) Viewpoint; Bringing culture in: Locality and global capitalism in East Asia. *Third World Planning Review* 17 (3), pp. iii–ix.

—— (1995b) Global interdependence and urbanization: Planning for the Bangkok mega-urban region. In T. G. McGee and I. M. Robinson (Eds.) *The Mega-urban Regions of Southeast Asia*. Vancouver: UBC Press, pp. 45–77.

Duan, X. M. (1993) Nongcun gaige he fazhan mianlinde xin wenti (Facing the new problems of rural reform and development) *ZGNCJJ* (8), pp. 16–21.

Edwards, M. (1989) The irrelevance of development studies. *Third World Quarterly* 11 (1), pp. 116–136.

—— (1993) How relevant is development studies? In F. J. Schuurman (Ed.) *Beyond the Impasse: New Directions in Development Theory*. London: Zed, pp. 77–92.

Entrikin, J. N. (1994) Place and region. *PIHG* 18 (2), pp. 227–233.

Escobar, A. (1984–85) Discourse and power in development: Michel Foucault and the relevance of his work to the third world. *Alternatives* 10, pp. 377–400.

Ettlinger, N. (1994) The localization of development in comparative perspective. *Economic Geography* 70 (2), pp. 144–166.

Fan, C. C. (1995) Of belts and ladders: State policy and uneven regional development in post-Mao China. *AAAG* 85 (3), pp. 421–449.

Fan, J. (1993) Dui woguo guoti guihua jige zhuyao wenti de chongxin renshi (Rethinking some principal problems of China's territorial planning). *Dili yanjiu (Geographical Research)* 12 (1), pp. 56–63.

Far Eastern Economic Review (1993) Zones closed. 26 August, p. 55.

—— (1994) China; True: Numbers lie. 22 September, p. 87.

—— (1998) China: Jiangsu Sanshan industry. 1 October, p. 54.

Fei, H. P. (1993a) Qiye yu quyu jingji xietiao fazhan yanjiu (Research on coordinating enterprises and regional economic development). *JJDL* 13 (3), pp. 23–29.

—— (1993b) Duochang qiye kongjian yanhua moshi yanjiu (Study of the models of the spatial evolution of multi-plant enterprises). *DLKX* 13 (4), pp. 322–330.

Fei, X. T. (1939) *Peasant Life in China*. London: Routledge.

—— (1984) Xiao chengzhen da wenti (Small towns, a big issue). *Liaowang (Outlook)*. January, pp. 16–30.

—— (Ed.) (1986) *Small Towns in China: Functions, Problems and Prospects*. Beijing: New World Press.

Feng, Y. F. (1983) Fazhan xiao chengshi shi woguo chengshihua weiyi zhengque de daolu ma? (Is the development of small cities China's only correct road to urbanization?). *JJDL* 3 (2), pp. 136–140.

Findlay, C., Martin, W. and Watson, A. (1993) *Policy Reform, Economic Growth and China's Agriculture*. Paris: OECD.

Findlay, C., Watson, A. and Wu, H. X. (1994) Rural enterprises in China: Overview, issues and prospects. In C. Findlay, A. Watson and H. X. Wu (Eds.) *Rural Enterprises in China*. New York: St. Martin's, pp. 173–190.

Forbes, D. and Thrift, N. (Eds.) (1987) *The Socialist Third World: Urban Development and Regional Planning*. Oxford: Blackwell.

Funnell, D. C. (1988) Urban-rural linkages: Research themes and directions. *Geografiska Annaler* 70B (2), pp. 267–274.

Gao, A. M. (1992) Jiangsu sets its growth strategy. *China Daily*, 26 March, p. 4.

Geertz, C. (1963) *Agricultural Involution: The Process of Ecological Change in Indonesia*. Berkeley: University of California Press.

Geographical Society of China (Ed.) (1990) *Recent Development of Geographical Science in China*. Beijing: Science Press.

Gilbert, A. (1988) The new regional geography in English and French-speaking countries. *PIHG* 12 (2), pp. 208–228.

Giles, H. A. (1918) *History of Chinese Pictorial Art*. London: Bernard.

Ginsburg, N. (1991) Preface. In N. Ginsburg, B. Koppel and T. G. McGee (Eds.) *The Extended Metropolis: Settlement Transition in Asia*. Honolulu: University of Hawaii Press, pp. xiii-xviii.

Goldstein, S. (1990) Urbanization in China, 1982–1987. *Population and Development Review* 16 (4), pp. 673–701.

Gong, F. X. (1992) *Zhongguo qinggongye jingji wenti tansuo (Exploring the problem of China's Light Industrial Economy)*. Beijing: Economic Science Press.

Gregory, D. (1981) Alfred Weber and location theory. In D. R. Stoddart (Ed.) *Geography, Ideology and Social Concern*. Oxford: Basil Blackwell, pp. 165–185.

—— (1989) Areal differentiation and post-modern human geography. In D. Gregory and R. Walford (Eds.) *Horizons in Human Geography*. London: Macmillan, pp. 67–96.

Gu, C. L., Chen, T., Ding, J. H. and Yu, W. (1993) Zhongguo dachengshi bianyuanqu texing yanjiu (Study of the special characteristics of the fringes of China's mega-cities). *DLXB* 48 (4), pp. 317–328.

Gu, C. L. and Chen, Z. G. (1994) Zhongguo dadushi kongjian zengzhang xingtai (Metropolitan spatial growth patterns in China). *CSGH* 18 (6), pp. 45–50, 19, 63.

Harvey, D. (1985) *The Urbanization of Capital: Studies in the History and Theory of Capitalist Urbanization*. Oxford: Basil Blackwell.

He, B. S. [Ho, S. P. S.] (1991) *Jiangsu nongcun feinonghua fazhan yanjiu (Research on Rural Non-agricultural Development in Jiangsu)*. Shanghai: Shanghai People's Publisher.

Ho, S. P. S. (1994) *Rural China in Transition: Non-agricultural Development in Rural Jiangsu, 1978–1990*. Oxford: Clarendon.

Hou, C. M. (1963) Economic dualism: The case of China, 1840–1937. *Journal of Economic History* 23 (3), pp. 277–297.

Hu, B. L. (1991) Industrial guidance in the urbanization process. Asian Institute of Technology, Bangkok. Unpublished manuscript.

Hu, H. Y. (1947) A geographical sketch of Kiangsu Province. *Geographical Review* 37 (4), pp. 609–617.

Hu, X. W. (1994) Jiaqiang duiquyu he chengshi fazhan de guihua yu tiaokong (Strengthening the planning and readjustment of urban and regional development). *CSGH* 18 (2), pp. 1–5, 62.

Huadong diqu tongji nianjian (East China Area Statistical Yearbook) (Several years). Beijing: State Statistical Publishers.

Huang, G. F. (1992) Jian Pudong 'hou huayuan' (Build Pudong's 'back garden'). *Xinhua ribao*. 10 November, p. 2.

Huang, M. D. (1991) Xiandai qiye zuzhi de quwei xuanze jiqi kongjian yingxiang (Organization of location choice of modern enterprises and their spatial influence). *JJDL* 11 (4), pp. 7–11.

—— (1993) *Chengzhen tixi de jiegou yu yanhua: Lilun fenxi yu shizheng yanjiu* (The Structure and Evolution of Urban Systems: Theoretical Analysis and Case Study). Unpublished Ph.D. dissertation: East China Normal University, Shanghai.

Huang, P. C. C. (1985) *The Peasant Economy and Social Change in North China*. Stanford: Stanford University Press.

—— (1990) *The Peasant Family and Rural Development in the Yangzi Delta, 1350–1988*. Stanford: Stanford University Press.

Human Geography Research Office (1990) *Jiangnan xiangcun chengshihua bijiao yu fazhan yanjiu (Comparative and Development Research of Rural Urbanization in Southern Jiangsu)*. Nanjing: Nanjing Normal University, Department of Geography.

Jacobs, J. (1984) *Cities and the Wealth of Nations: Principles of Economic Life*. New York: Random.

Jiangsu nianjian (Jiangsu Almanac) (Several years). Nanjing: Jiangsu Almanac Publishers.

Jiangsu sheng shixian jingji 1989 (Jiangsu Province City and County Economy 1989). Beijing: State Statistical Publishers.

Jiangsu sheng shixian jingji 1990 (Jiangsu Province City and County Economy 1990). Beijing: State Statistical Publishers.

Jiangsu shixian jingji 1992 (Jiangsu City and County Economy 1992). Beijing: State Statistical Publishers.

Jiangsu shixian jingji 1993 (Jiangsu City and County Economy 1993). Beijing: State Statistical Publishers.

Jiangsu sishinian 1949–1989 (Jiangsu Forty Years 1949–1989). Beijing: State Statistical Publishers.

Jiangsu tongji nianjian (Jiangsu Statistical Yearbook) (Several years). Beijing: State Statistical Publishers.

Jiangsu xiangzhen qiye nianjian (Jiangsu Rural Enterprises Almanac) (Several years). Nanjing: Jiangsu Almanac Publishers.

Jiefang ribao (1992), April 4.

Johnson, L. C. (1993) Preface. In L. C. Johnson (Ed.) *Cities of Jiangnan in Late Imperial China*. Albany: State University of New York Press, pp. ix-xiii.

Joseph, W. A. (1994) Introduction: Toward the post-Deng era. *China Briefing, 1994*. Boulder: Westview, pp. 1–6.

Kirkby, R. J. R. (1985) *Urbanization in China: Town and Country in a Developing Economy 1949–2000 AD*. London: Routledge.

—— (1994) Dilemmas of urbanization: Review and prospects. In D. Dwyer (Ed.) *China: The Next Decades*. Essex: Longman, pp. 128–155.

Koppel, B. (1991) The rural–urban dichotomy re-examined: Beyond the ersatz debate? In N. Ginsburg, B. Koppel and T. G. McGee (Eds.) *The Extended Metropolis: Settlement Transition in Asia*. Honolulu: University of Hawaii Press, pp. 47–70.

Kunshan dianhua haobu 1996 (Kunshan Telephone Directory 1996). Kunshan: Post and Telecommunications Bureau.

Kunshan jingji xinxi (Kunshan Economic Information) (1993) Kunshan kaifaqu queding jinnian gongzuo mubiao (Kunshan clearly sets this year's work target). 1 January, p. 1.

Kunshan People's Government (1991) *Kunshan touzi zhinan (Kunshan Investment Guide)*. Kunshan: Kunshan Printing House.

—— (1992) *Banhao nongcun gongye xiaoqu: Tigao fazhan xiangzhen qiye (Good Management of Rural Industrial Zones will Improve the Development of Rural Enterprises)*. Kunshan: Kunshan People's Government.

Kunshanshi dinming tu (1993) *(Kunshan Municipality Place Names Map)*. Kunshan: Kunshan Place Names Office.

Kunshan tongji nianjian (Kunshan Statistical Yearbook) (Several years). Kunshan: Kunshan Statistical Publishers.

Kunshan xianzhi (1990) *(Kunshan County Gazetteer)*. Shanghai: Shanghai People's Publishers.

Kwok, R. Y. W. (1992) Urbanization under economic reform. In G. E. Guldin (Ed.) *Urbanizing China*. Westport: Greenwood, pp. 65–85.

Lee, Y. S. (1989) Small towns and China's urbanization level. *The China Quarterly* 120, pp. 771–786.

—— (1991) Rural non-agricultural development in an extended metropolitan region: The case of southern Jiangsu. In N. Ginsburg, B. Koppel and T. G. McGee (Eds.) *The Extended Metropolis: Settlement Transition in Asia*. Honolulu: University of Hawaii Press, pp. 137–156.

—— (1992) Rural transformation and decentralized urban growth in China. In G. E. Guldin (Ed.) *Urbanizing China*. Westport: Greenwood, pp. 89–118.

Leung, C. K. (1993) Personal contacts, subcontracting linkages, and development in the Hong Kong–Zhujiang delta region. *AAAG* 83 (2), pp. 272–302.

Li, B. R. (1983) Woguo chengzhenhua daolu wenti de taolun (A discussion of China's road to urbanization). *CSGH* 6 (2), pp. 27–28/26.

Li, C. (1974) *The Travel Diaries of Hsu Hsia-K'o*. Hong Kong: Chinese University of Hong Kong.

Li, M. B. (1983) Woguo chengzhen fazhan de zhanwang (China's urban development and prospects). *Chengxiang jianshe (Urban–rural Construction)* 12 (1), pp. 16–18.

Li, M. H. (1994) Woguo renkou qianyi de liuxiang (China's migration flow). *Renkou yanjiu (Population Research)* 18 (3), pp. 48–51.

Li, W. Y. (1986) Developing regional industrial systems in the Chinese People's Republic. In F. E. I. Hamilton (Ed.) *Industrialization in Developing and Peripheral Regions*. London: Croom Helm, pp. 335–351.

—— (1990) Recent development of industrial geography in China. In Geographical Society of China (Ed.) *Recent Development of Geographical Science in China*. Beijing: Science Press, pp. 197–203.

Li, X. J. (1991) Guanyu gongsi dili yanjiu de jige wenti (Some problems in the research of firm geography). *JJDL* 11 (3), pp. 42–46.

—— (1993) Chanye lianxi yu nongcun gongyehua de qiye fenxi (Analysis of industrial linkages and rural industrialization enterprises). *JJDL* 13 (2), pp. 35–40.

Liang, C. (1996) PRC marks boundaries to prevent disputes. *China Daily*, 10 April, p. 3.

Liang, R. C. (1989) Gongye de dengji leixing jiqi jiegou tezheng de tantao (Inquiry into the categories and structural features of industrial areas). *DLXB* 44 (1), pp. 56–67.

—— (1992) Lun gongyequ de xingcheng yu fazhan (On the formation and development of industrial regions). *DLKX* 12 (4), pp. 336–343.

Lieberthal, K. (1995) *Governing China: From Revolution Through Reform*. New York: Norton.

Lin, F. R., Wang, Z. D. and Tang, Q. L. (1992) Guanyu nongye quyu zonghe kaifa ruogan lilun wenti de tantao (Inquiry into certain theoretical issues of the comprehensive development of rural areas). *JJDL* 12 (3), pp. 34–38.

Lin, J. B. (1993) Guanyu kaifaqu de jige wenti (On the problems of development zones). *JJDL* 13 (2), pp. 1–4.

Lipton, M. (1977) *Why Poor People Stay Poor: A Study of Urban Bias in World Development*. London: Temple.

Liscombe, K. M. (1993) *Learning from Mount Hua: A Chinese Physician's Illustrated Travel Record and Painting Theory*. Cambridge: Cambridge University Press.

Little, D. (1989) *Understanding Peasant China: Case Studies in the Philosophy of Social Science*. New Haven: Yale University Press.

Liu, D. H. and Ma, M. (1991) Renwen dilixue yuqi duiguotu guihua lilun yanjiu de gongxian ji fazhan wenti (Theoretical research contributions of human geography to the problems of development of territorial planning). *JJDL* 11 (4), pp. 16–23.

Liu, J. D. (1992) Woguo xingzheng quhua de gaige (Reform of China's administrative divisions). *Kexue (Science)* 44 (4), pp. 46–50.

Liu, J. D., Tang, J. Z., Shu, Q. and Zhang, M. (1992) Rationalizing coastal development: A proposal to coordinate planning and management of Shanghai ports. *International Conference on Urban Land Use and Transport Systems*, Shanghai, June 8–12.

Liu, Y. L. (1969) *Qingming Shanghe Tu zhi zonghe yanjiu (Qingming Festival by the River Comprehensive Research)*. Taibei: Haitian.

Loehr, M. (1980) *The Great Painters of China*. New York: Harper Row.

Lovering, J. (1990) Fordism's unknown successor: A comment on Scott's theory of flexible accumulation and the re-emergence of regional economies. *IJURR* 14 (1), pp. 159–174.

—— (1991) Theorizing postfordism: Why contingency matters (a further response to Scott). *IJURR* 15 (2), pp. 298–301.

Lu, D. (1992) *Zhongguo gongye jingji de gaige yu fazhan (China's Industrial Economic Reform and Development)*. Beijing: Economic Management Press.

Lu, D. D. (1990) *Zhongguo gongye buju de lilun yu shijian (China's Industrial Distribution: Theory and Practice)*. Beijing: Science Press.

—— (1991) Woguo gongye buju yanjiu qude quanmian zhongda jinzhan (Seeking overall significant progress in China's industrial location research). *JJDL* 11 (2), p. 78.

Lujia Town People's Government (1992) *Guoyuo tudi youchang churang qingkuang jieshao (Introduction to the Situation of the Leasing of Nationalized Land)*. Kunshan: Lujia Town People's Government.

McGee, T. G. (1991a) The emergence of 'desakota' regions in Asia: Expanding a hypothesis. In N. Ginsburg, B. Koppel and T. G. McGee (Eds.) *The Extended Metropolis: Settlement Transition in Asia*. Honolulu: University of Hawaii Press, pp. 3–25.

—— (1991b) Presidential address: Eurocentrism in geography – The case of Asian urbanization. *The Canadian Geographer* 35 (4), pp. 332–344.

—— (1995a) Metrofitting the emerging mega-urban regions of ASEAN: An overview. In T. G. McGee and I. M. Robinson (Eds.) *The Mega-urban Regions of Southeast Asia*. Vancouver: UBC Press, pp. 3–26.

—— (1995b) Geography and development: Crisis commitment and renewal. *Cahiers de géographie du Québec* 39 (108), pp. 527–536.

McGee, T. G. and Robinson, I. M. (1995) ASEAN mega-urbanization: A synthesis. In T. G. McGee and I. M. Robinson (Eds.) *The Mega-urban Regions of Southeast Asia*. Vancouver, UBC Press, pp. 343–355.

Ma, L. J. C. and Cui, G. H. (1987) Administrative changes and urban population in China. *AAAG* 77 (3), pp. 373–395.

Ma, Q. Y. (1983) Woguo chengzhenhua de tedian ji fazhan qushi de chubu fensan (A preliminary analysis of the characteristics and development trends of China's urbanization). *JJDL* 3 (2), pp. 126–131.

Manoharan, T. (1992) Credit and financial institutions at the rural level in China – Between plan and market. In E. B. Vermeer (Ed.) *From Peasant to Entrepreneur: Growth and Change in Rural China*. Wageningen: Pudoc, pp. 183–215.

Marmé, M. (1993) Heaven on earth: The rise of Suzhou, 1127–1550. In L. C. Johnson (Ed.) *Cities of Jiangnan in Late Imperial China*. Albany: State University of New York Press, pp. 16–45.

Marsden, T., Murdoch, J., Lowe, P. and Munton, R. (1993) *Constructing the Countryside*. London: UCL Press.

Martin, R. (1993) Classics in human geography revisited: 'Spatial divisions of labour', commentary I. *PIHG* 17 (1), pp. 69–70.

Marton, A. M. (1993) Industrial development and transportation in rural Kunshan: Local reality and regional irrationality. In C. Comtois and B. Q. Fan (Eds.) *Urban Land Use and Transport Systems in China*. Montreal: Centre for Research on Transportation, pp. 460–478.

—— (1994) Challenges for metrofitting the lower Yangtze delta. *Western Geography* 4, pp. 62–83.

—— (1995a) Review of 'The East Asian miracle: Economic growth and public policy'. *Environment and Planning A* 27 (4), pp. 667–668.

—— (1995b) At the edge of Shanghai: Linkages and industrial development in rural Kunshan. In M. S. Chen, C. Comtois, and L. N. Shyu, (Eds.) *East Asia Perspectives*. Montreal: Canadian Asian Studies Association, pp. 101–111.

—— (1995c) Mega-urbanization in southern Jiangsu: Enterprise location and the reconstitution of local space. *Chinese Environment and Development* 6 (1 and 2), pp. 9–42.

Massey, D. (1973) Towards a critique of industrial location theory. *Antipode 5* (1), pp. 33–39.

—— (1979) In what sense a regional problem? *Regional Studies* 13 (2), pp. 233–243.

—— (1984) *Spatial Divisions of Labour: Social Structures and the Geography of Production*. New York: Methuen.

—— (1991) A global sense of place. *Marxism Today* (June), pp. 24–29.

—— (1993a) Classics in human geography revisited: 'Spatial divisions of labour', author's response. *PIHG* 17 (1), pp. 71–72.

—— (1993b) Questions of locality. *Geography* 78 (2), pp. 142–149.

—— (1994) *Space, Place and Gender*. Cambridge: Polity.

—— (1995) *Spatial Divisions of Labour: Social Structures and the Geography of Production, Second Edition*. London: Macmillan.

—— (1999) Space-time, 'science' and the relationship between physical geography and human geography. *TIBG* 24 (3), pp. 261–276.

Miao, C. H. (1994) Quyu chengxiang gongye de xietiao fazhan zhanlue (Strategies for coordinating the regional development of urban and rural industries). *JJDL* 14 (2), pp. 46–50.

Mote, F. W. (1973) A millennium of Chinese urban history: Form, time, and space concepts in Soochow. *Rice University Studies* 59 (4), pp. 35–65.

Murphey, R. (1977) *The Outsiders*. Ann Arbor: University of Michigan Press.

Murphy, A. B. (1991) Regions as social constructs: The gap between theory and practice. *PIHG* 15 (1), pp. 22–35.

Murray, P. and Szelenyi, I. (1984) The city in transition to socialism. *IJURR* 8 (1), pp. 90–107.

Nanjing Normal University, Department of Geography (1990) *Jiangnan nongcun juluo yu chengshihua yanjiu: Sunan fada diqu nongcun chengzhenhua tujing tantao (Jiangnan Rural-agglomeration and Urbanization Research: Methods of Inquiry into Southern Jiangsu Rural Urbanization)*. Nanjing: Nanjing Normal University, Department of Geography.

The National Population Census Office (1991) *Zhongguo disici renkou pucha de zhuyao shuju (Major Figures of the Fourth Population Census of China)*. Beijing: State Statistical Publishers.

Naughton, B. (1995) *Growing out of the Plan: Chinese Economic Reform, 1978–1993*. Cambridge: Cambridge University Press.

Ning, Y. M. and Yan, Z. M. (1993) Woguo zhongxin chengshi de bupingheng fazhan ji kongjian kuosande yanjiu (The uneven development and spatial diffusion of China's central cities). *DLXB* 48 (2), pp. 97–104.

Odgaard, O. (1992) *Private Enterprises in China: Impact on Agriculture and Social Stratification*. Aldershot: Avebury.

O hUallachain, B. (1993) Industrial geography. *PIHG* 17 (4), pp. 548–555.

Pang, X. M. (1992) An analysis of the role of cooperations [sic] between urban and rural industries in the development of rural industry in China. *The Journal of Chinese Geography* 3 (1), pp. 1–16.

Pannell, C. W. (1980) Geography. In L. A. Orleans (Ed.) *Science in Contemporary China*. Stanford: Stanford University Press.

—— (1990) China's urban geography. *PIHG* 14 (2), pp. 214–236.

—— (1992) The role of great cities in China. In G. E. Guldin (Ed.) *Urbanizing China*. Westport: Greenwood, pp. 11–39.

Pannell, C. W. and Veeck, G. (1989) Zhujiang delta and Sunan: A comparative analysis of regional urban systems and their development. *Asian Geographer* 8 (1 and 2), pp. 133–149.

—— (1991) China's urbanization in an Asian context: Forces for metropolitanization. In N. Ginsburg, B. Koppel and T. G. McGee (Eds.) *The Extended Metropolis: Settlement Transition in Asia*. Honolulu: University of Hawaii Press, pp. 113–135.

Peet, R. (1993) Reason, space, modernity: The future of development geography. *Association of American Geographers Annual Meeting*, Atlanta, 6–10 April.

—— (1994) Review of 'Beyond the impasse: New directions in development theory'. *AAAG* 84 (2), pp. 339–342.

Peet, R. and Watts, M. (1993) Introduction: Development theory and environment in an age of market triumphalism. *Economic Geography* 69 (3), pp. 227–253.

Peng, Q. (1993) Chanye jiegou de chengzhang yu jingjiqu de kuozhang (Development of industrial structure and the expansion of economic regions). *DLYJ* 12 (1), pp. 79–86.

Phelps, N. A. (1992) External economies, agglomeration and flexible accumulation. *TIBG* 17 (1), pp. 35–46.

Ping, L. (1993) Fengjing meili de Diandong Zhen chengwei waisheng touzi redian (Picturesque Diandong [Dianshanhu] Town becomes foreign investment hotspot). *KSJJXX*, 15 January, p. 2.

Potter, R. B. and Unwin, T. (Eds.) (1989) *The Geography of Urban–rural Interaction in Developing Countries*. London: Routledge.

Post, K. and Wright, P. (1989) *Socialism and Underdevelopment*. London: Routledge.

Pred, A. R. (1966) *The spatial dynamics of US urban industrial growth, 1860–1914*. Cambridge: MIT Press.

Preston, D. (1975) Rural–urban and inter-settlement interaction: Theory and analytical structure. *Area* 7 (3), pp. 171–174.

Pudup, M. B. (1988) Arguments within regional geography. *PIHG* 12 (3), pp. 369–390.

—— (1992) Industrialization after (de)industrialization: A review essay. *Urban Geography* 13 (2), pp. 187–200.

Qian, S. and Zhou, Y. (1992) Jiangsu Kunshan Sanshan Jituan fa gupiao (Jiangsu Kunshan Sanshan Group issues shares). *Jiefang ribao (Liberation Daily)*, 1 April, p. 4.

Qinghua University Urban-Rural Development Research Group (1995) *Suxichang diqu chengxiang kongjian huanjing fazhan guihua yanjiu (Suxichang Area Urban–rural Spatial Environment Development Planning Research)*. Beijing: Qinghua University.

Rees, J. (1989) Regional development and policy. *PIHG* 13 (4), pp. 577–588.

—— (1992) Regional development and policy under turbulence. *PIHG* 16 (2) pp. 223–231.

Reinterpreting Contemporary Urban Development Theory on Mega-urban Regions in the Asia Pacific Context Workshop (1995), University of British Columbia, Vancouver, 13–15 December.

Renmin ribao, haiwaiban (*People's Daily*, overseas edition) (1994) Lujia Zhen zhuzhong ruan huanjing jianshe peitao fuwu yinlai gelu keshang (Lujia Town emphasizes a flexible environment developing services to attract business). 9 November, p. 3.

Robinson, I. M. (1995) Emerging spatial patterns in ASEAN mega-urban regions: Alternative strategies. In T. G. McGee and I. M. Robinson (Eds.) *The Mega-urban Regions of Southeast Asia*. Vancouver: UBC Press, pp. 78–108.

Rondinelli, D. A. (1983) *Secondary Cities in Developing Countries: Policies for Diffusing Urbanization*. Beverly Hills: Sage.

—— (1985) *Applied Methods of Regional Analysis: The Spatial Dimensions of Development Policy*. Boulder: Westview.

Rowe, W. T. (1993) Introduction. In L. C. Johnson (Ed.) *Cities of Jiangnan in Late Imperial China*. Albany: State University of New York Press, pp. 1–15.

Sayer, A. (1985) Industry and space: a sympathetic critique of radical research. *Environment and Planning D: Society and Space* 3, pp. 3–29.

Sayer, A. (1989) Post-fordism in question. *IJURR* 13 (4), pp. 666–695.

Sayer, A. and Walker, R. (1992) *The New Social Economy: Reworking the Division of Labour*. Cambridge: Blackwell.

Schuurman, F. J. (Ed.) (1993a) *Beyond the Impasse: New Directions in Development Theory*. London: Zed.

—— (1993b) Introduction: Development theory in the 1990s. In F. J. Schuurman (Ed.) *Beyond the Impasse: New Directions in Development Theory*. London: Zed, pp. 1–48.

Scott, A. J. (1986) Industrialization and urbanization: A geographical agenda. *AAAG* 76 (1), pp. 25–37.

—— (1987) *Industrial Organization and Location: Division of Labour, the Firm, and Spatial Process*. Department of Geography, UCLA.

—— (1988a) Flexible production systems and regional development. *IJURR* 12 (2), pp. 171–186.

—— (1988b) *Metropolis: From the Division of Labour to Urban Form*. Berkeley: University of California Press.

—— (1991a) Flexible production systems: Analytical tasks and theoretical horizons – A reply to Lovering. *IJURR* 15 (1), pp. 130–134.

—— (1991b) A further rejoinder to Lovering. *IJURR* 15 (2), p. 302.

Shanghai jiaoqu tongji ziliao huibian 1990 (*Shanghai Suburban Statistical Information Compilation 1990*). Shanghai: State Statistical Publishers.

Shanghai jingji 1949–1982 (*Shanghai Economy 1949–1982*). Shanghai: Shanghai Academy of Social Sciences.

Shanghai nianjian (*Shanghai Almanac*) (1998) Shanghai: Shanghai Yearbook Publishing House.

Shanghai shi jiaoqu gongye qiye daquan (*Complete Listing of Shanghai's Suburban Industrial Enterprises*) (1988). Shanghai: State Statistical Publishers.

Shanghai shi quantu (*Shanghai Map*) (1987). Shanghai: China Map Publishers.

Shanghai Star (1992) Kunshan leads way for zones. 9 September, p. 9.

Shanghai tongji nianjian (*Shanghai Statistical Yearbook*) (Several years). Shanghai: People's Publisher.

She, Z. X. (Ed.) (1991) *Taihu liuyu ziran ziyuan ditu ji* (*Lake Tai basin Natural Resources Atlas*). Beijing: Science Press.

Shen, D. Q. (1988) Changjiang liuyu kaifa de zhengtixing, jieduanxing yu leixingxing (The periodicity, typicality and overall development of the Yangzi River valley). In Y. F. Si (Ed.) *Zhongguo Kexueyuan Nanjing Dili yu Hupo Yanjiusuo jikan* (*Memoirs of the Chinese Academy of Sciences Nanjing Institute of Geography and Limnology*), vol. 5. Nanjing: People's Press, pp. 93–102.

Shen, D. Q. and Cui, G. H. (1990) Urban geography and urban planning. In Geographical Society of China (Ed.) *Recent Development of Geographical Science in China*. Beijing: Science Press, pp. 204–213.

Shen, X. P. (1987) Shilun gongyequ gongye qiye chengzu buju de jingji xiaoguo he zuijia guimo de queding (Discussion of the economic effect of the location of industrial enterprises and the determination of optimum size). *DLXB* 42 (1), pp. 51–61.

Shi, Q. W. and Wu, W. (1992) Gongye buju: Zai buju lun (Industrial location and relocation theory). *JJDL* 12 (2), pp. 44–48.

Shi, Y. S. (1992) Xiangcun dilixue fazhan de huigu yu zhanwang (Development of rural geography: Retrospect and prospect). *DLXB* 47 (1), pp. 80–88.

Shih, J. C. (1992) *Chinese Rural Society in Transition: A Case Study of the Lake Tai Area, 1368–1800*. Berkeley: Institute of East Asian Studies.

Shuai, J. P. (1993) Woguo xiangzhen qiye fada diqu de fazhan dui nongyequ weide yinxiang (Influence of China's flourishing rural enterprise development on agricultural areas). *DLYJ* 12 (3), pp. 64–71.

Shue, V. (1988) *The Reach of the State: Sketches of the Chinese Body Politic*. Stanford: Stanford University Press.

Sidaway, J. D. and Simon, D. (1990) Spatial policies and uneven development in the 'Marxist-Leninist' states of the third world. In D. Simon (Ed.) *Third World Regional Development: A Reappraisal*. London: Paul Chapman, pp. 24–38.

Sigurdson, J. (1977) *Rural Industrialization in China*. Cambridge: Council on East Asian Studies, Harvard University.

Skinner, G. W. (1977) Regional urbanization in nineteenth-century China. In G. W. Skinner (Ed.) *The City in Late Imperial China*. Stanford: Stanford University Press, pp. 211–249.

—— (1985) Rural marketing in China: Revival and reappraisal. In S. Plattner (Ed.) *Markets and Marketing*. Lanham: University Press of America, pp. 7–47.

Smith, N. (1989) Uneven development and location theory: Towards a synthesis. In R. Peet and N. Thrift (Eds.) *New Models in Geography: The Political Economy Perspective*. London: Unwin, pp. 142–163.

Solinger, D. J. (1989) Capitalist measures with Chinese characteristics. *Problems of Communism* 38 (1), pp. 19–33.

Special Zones Office of the State Council (1991) *Zhongguo yanhai chengshi jingji jishu kaifaqu* (*China's Coastal Municipal Economic and Technological Development Zones*). Beijing: State Council.

State Statistics Bureau (1999) *Zhonghua Renmin Gongheguo: 1998 guomin jingji he shehui fazhan tongji gongbao* (*People's Republic of China: 1998 Economic and Social Development Statistical Communiqué*) (26 February 1999). Online. Available HTTP: http://www.stats.gov.cn/gb/gb98c.html (21 October 1999).

Stohr, W. B. and Taylor, D. R. F. (Eds.) (1981) *Development from Above or Below? The Dialectics of Regional Planning in Developing Countries*. Chichester: Wiley.

Storper, M. (1987) The new industrial geography, 1985–1986. *Urban Geography* 8 (6), pp. 585–598.

Storper, M. and Scott, A. J. (Eds.) (1992) *Pathways to Industrialization and Regional Development.* London: Routledge.

Storper, M. and Walker, R. (1989) *The Capitalist Imperative: Territory, Technology, and Industrial Growth.* New York: Basil Blackwell.

Strassberg, R. E. (1994) *Inscribed Landscapes: Travel Writing from Imperial China.* Berkeley: University of California Press.

Sui, Y. Z. (1992) Chengxiang ronghe xitong de SD dongtai guotu guihua chutan (Study of the SD territorial planning for the city-countryside fusion system). *JJDL* 12 (4), pp. 26–29.

Sun, X. M. (1992) Kunshan Jingji Jishu Kaifaqu xingcheng peitao xiaoqu (The Kunshan Special Economic and Technological Development Zone establishes a small zone). *Xinhua ribao.* 4 April, p. 2.

Sun, Y. S. and Lin, Y. Z. (1988) Nongcun chengzhenhua de guochengji qileixing (Processes and types of rural urbanization). *JJDL* 8 (1), pp. 31–35.

Suzhou nianjian (Suzhou Almanac) (Several years). Shanghai: Xingjie Tushu Publishers

Suzhou shi ditu (Suzhou Map) (1991). Suzhou: China Map Publishers.

Suzhou shi jiaotong tu (Suzhou Transportation Map) (1992). Suzhou: Suzhou Transportation Bureau.

Suzhou shi jiaotong tuce (Suzhou Transportation Atlas) (1992). Suzhou: Suzhou Transportation Bureau.

Suzhou tongji nianjian (Suzhou Statistical Yearbook) (Several years). Beijing: State Statistical Publishers.

Tam, O. K. (1988) Rural finance in China. *The China Quarterly* 113, pp. 60–76.

Tan, K. C. (1993a) China's small town urbanization program: Criticism and rethinking. *Geojournal* 29 (2), pp. 155–162.

—— (1993b) Rural–urban segregation in China. *Geography Research Forum* 13, pp. 71–83.

Taubmann, W. (1992) The growth of rural towns in China's urban regions. In E. B. Vermeer (Ed.) *From Peasant to Entrepreneur: Growth and Change in Rural China.* Wageningen: Pudoc, pp. 273–291.

Taylor, P. J. (1999) Places, spaces and Macy's: Place-space tensions in the political geography of modernities. *PIHG* 23 (1), pp. 7–26.

Theroux, P. (1993) Going to see the dragon. *Harper's Magazine* (October), pp. 33–56.

Thrift, N. (1993) For a new regional geography 3. *PIHG* 17 (1), pp. 92–100.

Toye, J. (1993) *Dilemmas of Development: Reflections on the Counter-revolution in Development Economics.* Oxford: Blackwell.

Tozer, E. (1994) On the trail of E. H. Wilson. *Horticulture,* (November), pp. 50–61.

Tuan, Y. F. (1977) *Space and Place.* London: Arnold.

Unwin, T. (1989) Urban–rural interaction in developing countries: A theoretical perspective. In R. B. Potter and T. Unwin (Eds.) *The Geography of Urban–rural Interaction in Developing Countries.* London: Routledge, pp. 11–32.

Vandergeest, P. and Buttel, F. (1988) Marx, Weber and development sociology. *World Development* 16 (6), pp. 683–695.

Walker, R. (1988) The geographical organization of production systems. *Environment and Planning D: Society and Space* 6 (3), pp. 377–408.

—— (1989) A requiem for corporate geography: New directions in industrial organization, the production of place and the uneven development [sic]. *Geografiska Annaler* 71 B (1), pp. 43–68.

Wang, C. F. (Ed.) (1990) *Jiangsu sheng ditu ce (Atlas of Jiangsu Province)*. Guangdong: Guangdong Map Publisher.

Wang, F. (1993) Woguo 'sanpu' zi 'sipu' jian shizhen renkou zhenzhang goucheng fanxi (Structural analysis of China's urban population growth between the third and fourth census). *Renkou yanjiu (Population Research)* 17 (4), pp. 11–18.

Wang, J. F. (1984) Ming Qing Jiangnan shizhen jiegou ji lishi jiazhi chutan (Jiangnan cities and towns during the Ming and Qing Dynasties: Their structure and historical value). *Huadong shifan daxue xuebao: Zhexue shehui kexue ban (Journal of East China Normal University: Philosophy and Social Sciences Edition)* (1), pp. 74–83.

Wang, X. Y. (1993) The development of China's small towns. In G. Guldin and A. Southall (Eds.) *Urban Anthropology in China*. Leiden: Brill, pp. 151–166.

Wang, Y. C. (1992) Secular trends of rice prices in the Yangzi delta, 1638–1935. In T. G. Rawski and L. M. Li (Eds.) *Chinese History in Economic Perspective*. Berkeley: University of California Press, pp. 35–68.

Watson, A. (1989) Investment issues in the Chinese countryside. *The Australian Journal of Chinese Affairs* (22), pp. 85–126.

—— (1992) The management of the rural economy: The institutional parameters. In A. Watson (Ed.) *Economic Reform and Social Change in China*. New York: Routledge, pp. 171–199.

Watts, M. J. (1989) The agrarian question in Africa: Debating the crisis. *PIHG* 13 (1), pp. 1–41.

—— (1993) Development 1: Power, knowledge, discursive practice. *PIHG* 17 (2), pp. 257–272.

Wei, X. Z. (1991) Guanyu gaojishu chanye jiqi yuanqu fazhan de yanjiu (Research on the development of high technology industrial parks). *JJDL* 11 (1), pp. 6–10.

Wei, [D.] Y. H. (1993) Zhongguo quyu fazhan yanjiu: Zhuyao yiti he jinqi jinzhan (Research on China's regional development: Major topics and recent progress). *JJDL* 13 (4), pp. 1–7.

—— (1999) Wei, D. Y. H. (1999) Regional inequality in China. *PIHG* 23 (1), pp. 49–59.

Whitfield, R. (1965) *Chang Tse-tuan's 'Ch'ing-Ming Shang-He Tu'*. Unpublished Ph.D. dissertation: Princeton University.

Wong, C. [P. W.] (1988) Interpreting rural industrial growth in the post-Mao period. *Modern China* 14 (1), pp. 3–30.

Wong, C. P. W. (Ed.) (1997) *Financing Local Government in the People's Republic of China*. New York: Published for the Asian Development Bank by Oxford University Press.

World Bank (1993a) *China: Urban Land Management in an Emerging Market Economy*. Washington: The World Bank.

—— (1993b) *The East Asian Miracle: Economic Growth and Public Policy*. Oxford: Oxford University Press

Wu, C. J. (1990) Territorial management and regional development. In Geographical Society of China (Ed.) *Recent Development of Geographical Science in China*. Beijing: Science Press, pp. 1–17.

Wu, F. L. (1994) Urban process in the face of China's transition to a socialist market economy. *Annual Meeting of the Association of American Geographers.* San Francisco, 29 March–2 April.

Wu, H. X. [Wu, H. X. Y.] (1994) Rural enterprise contributions to growth and structural change. In C. Findlay, A. Watson and H. X. Wu (Eds.) *Rural Enterprises in China.* New York: St. Martin's, pp. 39–68.

Wu, H. X. Y. (1994) Rural to urban migration in the People's Republic of China. *The China Quarterly 139*, pp. 669–698.

Wuxi tongji nianjian 1992 (Wuxi Statistical Yearbook 1992). Beijing: State Statistical Publishers.

Xinhua ribao (New China Daily) (1992) Sheng zhengfu caiqu ruogan zhengce cuoshi jiakuai Nantong, Lianyungang, Kunshan kaifaqu jianshe (Provincial government adopts several policy measures to speed up construction of the Nantong, Lianyungang, Kunshan development zones). 4 April, p. 1.

Xu, J. P. (1992) Diandong jiang jianzao yige 'Dianshanhu cheng' (Diandong [Dianshanhu] initiated construction of a 'Dianshanhu city'), *KSJJXX*, 28 August, p. 1.

Xu, X. Q., Ouyang, N. J. and Zhou, C. S. (1995) The changing urban system of China: New developments since 1978. *Urban Geography* 16 (6), pp. 493–504.

Xu, Y. M. and Wu, Q. (1990) Shinian lai xiangzhen qiye lilun yanjiu de huigu (Ten year review of research on rural enterprise theory). *JSJJTT* (10), pp. 17–20.

Xu, Y. M. and Zhu, Z. Y. (1992) Guowuyuan pizhun Kunshan zifei jinru guojia xulie (State Council approves Kunshan's self-financed development zone at the national level. *KSJJXX*, 15 September, p. 1.

Yan, X. P. (1995) Chinese urban geography since the late 1970s. *Urban Geography* 16 (6), pp. 469–492.

Yang, C. Y. (1992) Xiangzhen gongye chengzhang yu fazhan zhanlue yanjiu (Research on the growth and development strategy of rural industry). *JJDL* 12 (1), pp. 66–70.

Yang, K. Z. (1992) Eryuan quyu jiegou lilun de tantao (Inquiry into theories of dual regional structures). *DLXB* 47 (6), pp. 499–506.

—— (1993) Zhongguo diqu gongye jiegou bianhua yu quji chengzhang he fengong (Changes in China's regional industrial structure and its effect on regional growth and specialization). *DLXB* 48 (6), pp. 481–490.

Yang, W. Z. (1991) Chanye jiegou, chanye buju, chanye zhengce yitihua wenti (Industrial structure, industrial location, industrial policy: Problems of integration). *JJDL* 11 (1), pp. 1–5.

Yang, Y. W. (1992) Jingji dili: Kongjian jingjixue yu quyu kexue (Economic geography: Spatial economics and regional science). *DLXB* 47 (6), pp. 561–569.

Yeh, A. G. O. and Wu, F. L. (1999) The transformation of the urban planning system in China from a centrally-planned to transitional economy. *Progress in Planning* 51 (3), pp. 167–252.

Yeung, Y. M. and Zhou, Y. X. (1991) Human geography in China: Evolution, rejuvenation, and prospect. *PIHG* 15 (3), pp. 373–394.

Yu, D. P. (1995) Heli duliang diqu chengshihua shuiping de silu (Considerations for the rational measurement of regional urbanization levels). *Renkou yu jingji (Population and Economics)* (5), pp. 39–42, 38.

Yuan, P. (1994) Capital formation in rural enterprises. In C. Findlay, A. Watson, and H.X. Wu (Eds.) *Rural Enterprises in China.* New York: St. Martin's, pp. 93–116.

Zeng, Z. G. and Lu, C. (1989) Jiangsusheng xiangcun jingji liexing chubu fenxi (Preliminary analysis of rural economic types in Jiangsu Province). *DLYJ* 8 (3), pp. 78–84.

Zhang, F. B. (1988) Jingjiang xian duiwai jingji he shehui de diyu lianxi (External socio-economic regional interaction in Jingjiang County). In Y. F. Si (Ed.) *Zhongguo Kexueyuan Nanjing Dili yu Hupo Yanjiusuo jikan (Memoirs of the Chinese Academy of Sciences Nanjing Institute of Geography and Limnology)*, vol. 5. Nanjing: People's Press, pp. 131–139.

Zhang, G. X. (1993) Jiji wentuo de tuijin chengxiang jiehe buxingzheng quhua gaige (Vigorously and appropriately promote urban rural integration and reform of administrative divisions). *Chengshi wenti (Urban Problems)* (5), pp. 36–38.

Zhang, L. and Zhao, S. X. B. (1998) Re-examining China's 'urban' concept and level of urbanization. *China Quarterly* 154, pp. 330–381.

Zhang, L. J. (1989) *Chengxiang yitihua zhilu (The Path Towards Urban–rural Symbiosis)*. Beijing: Rural Reading Materials Press.

Zhang, P. R. (1993) Diandong gong ming wei Dianshanhu zhen (Diandong changes name to Dianshanhu Town). *KSJJXX*, 20 April, p. 1.

Zhang, S. C. (1991) Fazhan zhongxin zhen de jidian kanfa (Several views on developing central towns). *Jiangsu minzheng (Jiangsu Civil Administration)* (24), p. 41.

—— (1996) *Kunshan fazhan guiji jishi (A Record of Kunshan's Course of Development)*. Nanjing: Jiangsu People's Press.

Zhang, Y. L. (1989) Woguo chengxiang guanxi de lishi kaocha (Historical overview of urban–rural relations in China). *Zhongguo nongcun jingji (Chinese Rural Economy)* (10), pp. 3–8 (second part of a study which appeared in two issues).

Zhang, Z. (1994) Development of rural township enterprises in China: Prospects and problems. *Biennial Conference of the Australian Asian Studies Association*. Perth, 13–16 July.

Zhao, J. X. and Xu, C. X. (1992) Woguo quyu jingji zengzhang zhengce de lilun tantao (Theoretical inquiry into China's policy of regional economic growth). *JJDL* 12 (3), pp. 20–22.

Zhongguo fenxian nongcun jingji tongji gaiyao 1980–1987 (China County Rural Economic Statistical Summary 1980–1987). Beijing: State Statistical Publishers.

Zhongguo fenxian nongcun jingji tongji gaiyao 1990 (China County Rural Economic Statistical Summary 1990). Beijing: State Statistical Publishers.

Zhongguo nongcun tongji nianjian (China Rural Statistical Yearbook) (Several years). Beijing: State Statistical Publishers.

Zhongguo tongji nianjian (China Statistical Yearbook) (Several years). Beijing: State Statistical Publishers.

Zhongguo xingzhenqu huajiance (A Brief Summary of China's Administrative Regions) (Several years). Beijing: China Map Publishers.

Zhou, S. L. and Chen, J. G. (1992) *Zhongguo gongye de fazhan yu gaige (China's Industrial Development and Reform)*. Beijing: Economic Management Press.

Zhou, X. D. (1994) Kunshan tudi churangyun zuo youfang (Kunshan has leased land in the right way). *Renmin ribao, haiwaiban (People's Daily, overseas edition)* 27 June, p. 2.

Zhou, Y. X. (1991) The metropolitan interlocking region in China: A preliminary hypothesis. In N. Ginsburg, B. Koppel and T. G. McGee (Eds.) *The Extended Metropolis: Settlement Transition in Asia*. Honolulu: University of Hawaii Press, pp. 89–111.

Zhou, Y. X. and Yang, Q. (1995) Geographical analysis of the industrial economic return of Chinese cities. *Urban Geography* 16 (6), pp. 505–520.

Zhouzhuang zhenzhi (Zhouzhuang Township Gazetteer) (1992). Shanghai: Sanlian Publishers.

Zhu, J. M. (1993) Zhongguo dacheng shiqu renkou zhenzhang de feizhongxinhua yanjiu (A study of the non-centralization of population growth in China's large urban areas). *Renkou yanjiu (Population Research)* 17, pp. 26–34.

Zweig, D. (1987) From village to city: Reforming urban rural relations in China. *International Regional Science Review* 11 (1), pp. 43–58.

Zweig, D. (1999) *Distortions in the Opening: 'Segmented Deregulation' and Weak Property as Explanations for China's 'Zone Fever' of 1992–1993.* Hong Kong: Hong Kong Institute of Asia-Pacific Studies, The Chinese University of Hong Kong, USC Seminar Series No. 14.

Index

administrative divisions 98–100, 167, 184–5, 196, 200, 203, 206–9
agglomeration 40, 155, 180, 186, 191–2; dynamics of 46–8; economies of 32–3; *see also* rural agglomeration
agriculture 61–3, 66–71, 73, 85, 177; agricultural sidelines 62, 67–9, 183; commercialization of 61–3; and industry 38–9

bureaucratic capitalism 115, 119, 186; and commercial advantages 123

Chinese statistics 19, 92, 94, 197, 202–5
collectivization 63–6, 183
command economy 15, 109, 115, 121–2, 125, 189; *see also* planned economy
community government 40, 46–8, 98–106; and enterprises 137; *see also* local government *and* township and village government
Cultural Revolution 64–6, 118; and returned youths 65, 118, 128–9; *see also* Shanghai

desakota 44–7, 55–6, 187, 199
development 14–17, 187–93; in China 16; Chinese theories of 35–42; and globalization 17, 192; and local factors 28, 32, 40, 45–8, 114, 131, 191; Marxist theories of 14–15, 27, 35; post-Marxist theories of 15, 27; and post-modernism 26–7, 193; in the socialist third world 15; theory in crisis 26
development zones *see* special economic zones

Dianshanhu Town 109, 141–5, 155, 167, 174, 195

Economic Cooperation Commission 102, 105, 118, 120–4, 145; and exchange of quotas 123, 130
Economic System Reform Commission 103, 105, 118, 126
extended metropolitan regions 44, 93, 187; *see also* mega-urbanization

Great Leap Forward 63–5
guanxi 115, 120–2

household responsibility system 1, 66–7, 110

industrial location 31, 46–8, 111–13, 117, 160–76, 188–93; in China 39; and the city 33; and development theory 31; and the enterprise dimension 33, 40; and local capital 161–5; and new industrial geography 32; ownership and 165, 189
industrial zones *see* special economic zones
industry 74–5, 80, 82–5; and agriculture 38–9
institutional parameters *see* institutional structures
institutional structures 16, 30–1, 33, 39–40, 44–8, 97–106, 115, 119–120, 123–5, 176, 182–5, 189–93; and changes in agriculture 149–50; community based 145; paradox of 125; and rural agglomeration 185; *see also* networks

Jiangsu Province 3, 4, 7, 18, 65–7, 72, 78–85, 206–8; *Subei* 54, 58, 77, 80, 83; *Sunan* 7, 54, 171–5

Kunshan 4, 7–8, 18, 59–61, 70, 86–90, 98–125, 208–9; government 98–106

labour and employment 74–7, 94, 167–8, 189
local government 46–8, 106–11, 117; bifurcation of 100; corporatization of 100–5; *see also* community government *and* township and village government
locality and place 12, 45–8, 85, 182–4, 188–90, 193, 198; locale 13, 30, 183; locality 30, 32, 184; place 35, 183; region 13
lower Yangzi delta 3–7, 58–62, 78–85, 183–4; historical geography of 58–60; history of 60–6; rural industry in 7; water management in 60–1; *see also Suxichang*
Lujia Town 119, 153

market socialism 2, 101–4, 177, 182
market towns 62–3, 77, 177, 208
mega-urbanization 45–8, 78, 85, 93, 97, 124, 131–2, 177, 181, 187–93; mega-urban region 44, 85, 93, 194, 196 (*see also* extended metropolitan regions); *see also* urbanization

Nanjing 3, 35, 58, 60, 68, 80, 83, 85, 204, 206
networks 18, 47–8, 121, 171, 176–7, 197; transactional 47–8, 62, 78, 122, 177 (*see also* transactional environment); transportation 132–41, 194

open door policy 1, 47, 119

Penglang Town xxi-xxii, 174
palace economies 117, 128; *see also* bureaucratic capitalism
parochialism and balkanization 125; *see also* bureaucratic capitalism
planned economy 36–7, 41, 115, 122, 125; *see also* command economy
planning 36; *see also* regional coordination
population 70, 73, 204; migration 95; rural 95

procurement and marketing 77, 121–3, 168–74
production responsibility system in agriculture *see* household responsibility system

Qingming Shanghe Tu (Qingming Festival by the River) 10–13, 18, 22

readjustment (*tiao zheng*) 157, 177, 186, 190
regional coordination 90, 193–7
rural agglomeration 181, 184, 186–93
rural enterprises 5, 42, 72, 92, 113–4; technology and management 175; *see also* township and village enterprises
rural industrialization 5, 39, 41, 64–6, 74, 78–86, 124; patterns of 78–86; *see also* rural urbanization
Rural Industry Bureau 105, 108–9, 120; National Rural Industry Administration 66
rural–urban distinctions 42–5, 78, 190–1, 194, 199
rural–urban integration 42, 194
rural–urban linkages 25, 28–9, 37, 41, 61–3
rural urbanization 42–4; *see also* rural industrialization

Shanghai 3, 4, 7, 58, 61, 63, 78–85, 118, 122, 167, 171–3, 175, 204, 207–9; Pudong 118–19, 129, 144, 155, 207; returned youths 128–9 (*see also* Cultural Revolution); vice-mayor's visit to Kunshan 153; window into 119
socialist market economy *see* market socialism
special economic zones 40, 47, 98–9, 111, 115, 150–5, 167, 184, 188–9, 195; and agricultural land 154–5
state owned enterprises 5, 64–5, 83, 111, 113, 191
Suxichang 78, 80, 83, 85, 113, 185; *see also* lower Yangzi delta
Suzhou 3, 4, 18, 59–61, 63, 78–85, 204, 209

Third Plenary of the Eleventh Central Committee of the Chinese Communist Party 1, 66
Tongxin Village 146–50, 153–6, 186

township and village enterprises 72, 74–5, 77, 106–11, 113, 117; in Dianshanhu Town 142–5; and local finances 106–8, 111, 161–5, 189; location of 111–14, 127; sectoral structure of 113–4, 127–8; *see also* rural enterprises

township and village government 66–7, 105–6; and enterprises 106–111 (*see also* township and village enterprises); industrial corporations 108–9; and local banks 163, 189; *see also* community government *and* local government

transactional environment 29, 39, 44–8, 85, 125, 160, 176–7, 182, 188, 190, 197; and transactional linkages 119–20, 196 (*see also* networks); and transactional space 141, 156

Transportation Bureau 103, 136–7, 141

urban penumbra 63

urbanization 38, 41, 88–9, 95, 187–93, 195, 199; and agriculture and industry 38–9; in economic development 37, 42; and industrialization 33; large cities versus small towns 36–8; *see also* mega-urbanization

Wuxi 185, 207

Printed in the United States
by Baker & Taylor Publisher Services

Printed in the United States
by Baker & Taylor Publisher Services